Living LANGUAGE

EXPLORING ADVANCED LEVEL *English Language*

George Keith & John Shuttleworth

Hodder & Stoughton

A MEMBER OF THE HODDER HEADLINE GROUP

Acknowledgements

The publishers would like to thank the following for their kind permission to reproduce copyright material:

p9 *Murder Must Advertise* © Dorothy L. Sayers, Coronet, 1993; p39 'Car' © Alan Frost in *Poetry of Motion* (ed. Alan Bold), Mainstream Publishing Co., 1984; p143 'Child on Top of a Greenhouse' by Theodore Roethke in *The Collected Poems of Theodore Roethke*, Faber & Faber Ltd, 1985; pp152–3 'Strange Fruit' in *North* by Seamus Heaney, Faber & Faber Ltd, 1996; pp152–67, 169–70, 172–5, and 188–90 text reproduced by kind permission of the Northern Examinations and Assessment Board; pp210 and 211 *Life on Earth* © David Attenborough, Collins 1979; p214 *The Cambridge Encyclopaedia of the English Language* © David Crystal, CUP, 1995; p218 'Words of a Jamaican Laas Moment Them' © James Berry.

Every effort has been made to trace copyright holders of material reproduced in this book. Any rights not acknowledged will be acknowledged in subsequent printings if notice is given to the publisher.

Order queries: please contact Bookpoint Ltd, 39 Milton Park, Abingdon, Oxon OX14 4TD. Telephone: (44) 01235 400414, Fax: (44) 01235 400454. Lines are open from 9.00–6.00, Monday to Saturday, with a 24 hour message answering service. Email address: orders@bookpoint.co.uk

British Library Cataloguing in Publication Data
A catalogue entry for this title is available from The British Library

ISBN 0 340 673435

First published 1997
Impression number   10   9   8   7
Year   2003   2002   2001   2000   1999

Copyright © 1997 George Keith and John Shuttleworth

Typeset by Fakenham Photosetting Limited, Fakenham, Norfolk
Printed in Great Britain for Hodder & Stoughton Educational,
a division of Hodder Headline Plc, 338 Euston Road, London NW1 3BH
by J W Arrowsmith Ltd, Bristol.

Contents

The purpose of this book

From 1998, A-level English Language (and Language and Literature) courses will have been re-structured to make it possible for schools and colleges to offer modular as well as linear versions. The application of theoretical concepts and the use of systematic frameworks in stylistics and the analysis of data remain essential assessment objectives. The chief purpose of this book is to teach students how to think linguistically about any kinds of texts and data whether encountered in everyday life or in future examinations. The most direct route to the concepts and frameworks envisaged in assessment objectives is to provide students with a language for thinking and communicating about language.

Throughout this book you will be introduced to ideas and information about linguistics and the English language. The main purpose of the book, however, is to help you develop expertise in applying knowledge about language to your own and other people's uses of the spoken and written word. It is essentially a practical book, moving from ideas and information to activities and investigations, and back again to ideas and information.

Three aspects of learning about language will be covered:

(i) critical reading and exploration of texts and language data;
(ii) developing your own power and control over written and spoken uses of English;
(iii) achieving an informed point of view about major issues to do with the nature and functions of language in human life.

Introduction

Humans invented language by adapting their breathing and their ability to bite, taste and swallow food, in order to produce speech sounds. The American linguist, Charlton Laird, describes language very succinctly as 'educated breath'.

In a fascinating series of BBC TV programmes called *The Making of Mankind*, zoologists, psychologists and anthropologists considered the significance of the arrival of language in the long story of human evolution. Here are some of the things they had to say:

Humans in their modern form, *homo sapiens sapiens*, arose at least 40,000 years ago, and it is reasonable to assume that a refined and precise form of language was on their lips.

(Richard Leakey)

In order to produce speech you have to be able to stop your tongue at 50 different positions in your mouth ... Think of what happens to your tongue when you are trying to do a tricky manipulative task, such as threading a needle: the tongue pops out and moves in sympathy. And young children almost always protrude their tongue when they're writing.

  I see language as a continuum stretching from the written word to the utterance of a single word between two people who know each other so well that it carries as much meaning as a paragraph.

(Roger Fouts)

... tool-making and language skills are similar, if not identical skills.

(Ralph Holloway)

Perhaps the most pervasive element of language is that, through communicating with others, not just about practical affairs, but about feelings, desires and fears, a 'shared consciousness' is created. Language is without doubt an enormously powerful force holding together the intense social network that characterises human existence.

(Richard Leakey)

Using their own physical resources in much the same way as they used flints and wood as tools, humans appear to have invented language out of sheer necessity brought about by their living together. Bound together by speech ('It's good to talk'), early peoples developed cultures some of which in turn invented the writing systems that have come down to us today.

Anthropologists and archaeologists spend much of their time examining fragments of human bone and ceramic artefacts in order to reconstruct the circumstances of their origin and use. We can do a little linguistic anthropology ourselves by looking at some modern fragments and reconstructing their original origins, contexts, intended audiences and purposes.

ACTIVITY

Look at these seven fragments of language, identify them and list all the kinds of knowledge you have that enables you to construct accurately their origins, contexts, audiences and purposes.

1 Dear Sir

2 Once upon ...
3 This way up.
4 ... stirring continually ...
5 250gm
6 ... she said, smiling.
7 Potatoes 89p a bag.

You are not likely to have had much difficulty identifying these fragments, and if you looked at thousands more, so long as they were in a language you knew, you would identify them equally well. The main reason for this is the shared consciousness, or pervasive network, that Richard Leakey talks about. It means that you already possess a great deal of implicit knowledge about language together with lifelong experience simply by virtue of the fact that you are a member of the human race.

1 Thinking about Language: Habits, Attitudes and Perspectives

This first chapter is designed to introduce you to language study. It will give you an overview of the theoretical areas, the methods of enquiry and the kind of descriptive vocabulary required by A-level English language syllabuses and modern introductory courses in linguistics.

Language habits

Language is a human invention; without it, social life could hardly exist in the forms we know it today. One important characteristic of this amazing invention is the way in which a native language is taken for granted by its users. Even on a bad day, **words** come quickly to mind. You hardly ever consciously stop to think about the **structure** of a sentence you are about to utter; greetings arise automatically; turns of phrase lie ready in waiting; words sometimes speak themselves, embarrassingly unintended.

ACTIVITY

1 Write down as many common sayings as you can that describe the fluency of everyday language. For example:
It just came out!
I didn't mean it.
Get your brain in gear before you open your mouth, next time!

2 a Think of occasions when this automatic fluency can be an advantage.
  b In what circumstances is it a disadvantage?
  c Are there occasions when fluency is distrusted?

3 a Think of occasions when you have been tongue-tied, lost for words, speechless, gobsmacked.
  b What sorts of things cause this to happen?
  c What sorts of strategies do people use to get conversation going again?

The 'taken-for-grantedness' of a language is very convenient for human communication, although it is never really noticed until, as with communication in general, it breaks down. One great advantage to a linguistic observer of the English language is a trained habit of noticing not just the errors and the breakdowns, but all the ways in which language works as well as it does.

Every so often it is necessary to try and get outside your own language in order to observe it as a universal kind of human behaviour in which symbols are used to make meanings.

Make a list of the common features of all
spoken and written languages that their users
take for granted.

Compare your list of common features with the following:

- the alphabet symbols
- word order
- sound-symbol correspondence
- where words begin and end
- units of meaning beyond individual words
- punctuation symbols
- reading direction (eg right-to-left).

These are all familiar aspects of language knowledge quite apart from
knowing the word meanings.

Yet despite these common features, translation from one language to
another is never completely straightforward. The translation of poetry and
personal, informal styles of language is particularly difficult. This is because
of the subtle influences a national language has on the ways in which
people think, and nowhere is this more apparent than in idiomatic uses of
language. English contains thousands of **idioms**, familiar to almost
everyone and frequently untranslatable.

Idioms are common expressions in which the meanings of the individual
words give little or no idea of the overall meaning of the idiom. Some
examples are:

gone bananas   in the pink
daft as a brush   this is a fine how's your father
all at sixes and sevens   use your loaf
kick the bucket   we don't want to go down
on the one hand ... on   that road
    the other hand   making eyes

A number of A-level English projects have been successfully devoted to an
investigation of the difficulties English idioms present to adult learners of
the language. Often the misunderstandings are comic: after apologising for
'playing up' his English teacher, a Turkish student, for example, only made
matters worse by offering to 'play down' the teacher. By supposing that
'playing down' was the opposite of the idiom 'playing up', the student only
added unintended insult to injury.

Idioms are very contagious among native speakers and are learned in huge
numbers without anyone ever explaining their meaning. Just occasionally
you might stop and wonder how a popular phrase ever originated: where
did 'going off' someone come from? What about 'She's three sheets in the
wind' or 'keep your hair on'?

1 Collect ten everyday phrases that do not mean what they appear to mean (eg 'boil your head'; 'over the hill') and write a definition for a friend who is learning English.

2 Make a note over the next week of all the idioms that crop up in everyday speech. Look at TV advertisements and newspaper reports, and keep an ear open for DJ patter on the radio.

Idioms are features of a language that might be called collective habits. They are part of folk culture.

Another, related, term is **idiolect**, which refers to all the language habits that give every individual a personal style of language use especially noticeable in ways of speaking. Idiolects are as personal, distinctive and unique as faces, fingerprints, voiceprints and giveaway gestures.

Complete the following idiolect questionnaire. Like all questionnaires, it should not be taken too seriously. You could fill it in about yourself, though personal idiolectal features often go unnoticed until somebody else points them out. Fill it in for somebody you know well, while he or she fills one in for you.

1 Does the pitch of the voice tend to be high/mid-range/low?
2 What words would you use to describe the general impression of the voice?
3 How would you assess the relative warmth or coolness of the voice?
4 Does the voice tend to be hard or soft?
5 Does the voice tend to be loud or quiet?
6 Does speech tend to be fast or slow?
7 Do you detect any particular intonation or **accent**? Describe it.
8 Does the speaker use 'ums and ers' frequently/sometimes/seldom?
9 Are there any words or phrases that the speaker uses frequently? Which?
10 Does the speaker make eye contact most of the time/sometimes/rarely?
11 Does the speaker use hand gestures frequently/sometimes/rarely? What sort?

12 Does the speaker use other body language? If so, what?
13 How frequently does the speaker
  ask questions?
  give orders?
  exclaim (eg swear, curse, laugh, cry out)?
  interrupt?
14 Is the speaker's usual style intimate/informal/semi-formal/formal/very formal?
15 Is the speaker very humorous/sometimes humorous/rarely humorous/never humorous?
16 How good a listener do you think she/he is?
17 Does he/she ever use non-standard **grammar** (eg 'We was...')?
18 Do his/her sentences tend to be long/average/short?
19 Does she/he tend to use long or unfamiliar words often/occasionally/never?
20 Does the speaker have a predominant tone in the way he or she speaks (eg excitable/patronising/facetious/off hand/apologetic/other)?

Gender, age, temperament, regional dialect, occupation, social class, education, all contribute to a person's idiolect or language profile. Some elements are acquired early in life, others develop later in all kinds of voluntary and involuntary ways. Many are deeply engrained in the way a person thinks or speaks, though none are entirely impervious to change. A new job, learning an A-level subject, new friends, marriage, moving to another part of the world, can all have an effect on idiolect.

The influence of an idiolect on personal styles of writing will be of particular relevance to A-level students. This is because much of coursework and examination success depends upon the ability to recognise the need to modify idiolectal habits that may be inappropriate to the kind of writing required. This is both a linguistic and a social issue that will be considered much more fully in the section on writing.

Habits, then, are neither good nor bad in themselves; they are observable data of individual language behaviour. They can certainly act as limitations, especially in new circumstances, but they also serve as psychological supports, making everyday human communication a relatively easy matter.

The following activity will involve you in a little **etymology** and a little **semantics**. Etymology describes the origins and development of words. Semantics is concerned with the meanings of words and how meanings are made.

ACTIVITY

1 Using a large dictionary, find out the origin of the word 'habit'. Next find all the words belonging to the 'habit' family (eg habitat; habitation). How many words derive from 'habit'?

2 Now think about the various meanings of words in the 'habit' family, such as live in (inhabit), a place (habitation), clothes (a nun's habit), a nervous habit (ums and ers). Apply some of these meanings to the ways in which we use language, for example: 'Don't be upset. He just says it out of habit'. 'They *dress it up* in fine words'. (French 'habit' = 'dress'.)

3 Compare your semantic exploration with the one suggested on the right.

habits (good and bad) – what do you consider to be 'good' and 'bad' language habits?

habitat (place) – what is your favourite language habitat?

Can words be said to keep company or live together (co-habitation)?

inhabit – does your language inhabit you or do you inhabit it?

habit (meaning 'garments') – is it possible for words to veil, clothe or disguise meaning?

habit forming – think of some new words and catch-phrases that appear to have become habit forming.

habitual - do you have some words and phrases that you use habitually? Most likely you will have, but you will need a friend to help you spot them. What are your friend's typical sayings, words and catch-phrases?

Attitudes towards language

The fact that a language can be taken for granted by its users is by and large a comfortable and reassuring one. However, the moment you start to talk about language, and not just use it, you have begun to step outside the system you normally never think twice about.

Look at the following statements that have been made about language. All express a point of view.

Language is a loaded weapon.   *(Dwight Bolinger)*

Man is a language animal.   *(George Steiner)*

Without language you wouldn't be able to tell lies.   *(Ten-year-old)*

Language is the dress of thought.
(Dr Samuel Johnson)

Language is called the garment of thought: however it should rather be, language is the body of thought.
(Thomas Carlyle)

You taught me language; and my profit on't
Is, that I know how to curse: the red plague rid you
For learning me your language.
(Caliban in Shakespeare's The Tempest*)*

It is language that transforms the biological organism into the human person in history.
(William Walsh, Professor of Education)

The English have no respect for their language, and will not teach their children to speak it … It is impossible for an Englishman to open his mouth, without making some other Englishman despise him.
(Professor Henry Higgins in George Bernard Shaw's Pygmalion*)*

All these points of view are considered and worth debating. A professor of Education celebrates the transforming power of language, by implication a good thing, while an American linguist warns that that same power can be lethal. A ten-year-old seems wiser than her years, and whatever kind of language animal Caliban has become, he can only curse. Thomas Carlyle disagrees with Dr Johnson, while George Bernard Shaw seems utterly exasperated by the attitudes of the English to their native language. Shaw draws attention to people's attitudes toward language, the topic for this section of the chapter.

Personal attitudes toward one's own use of language (such as the presence of a regional accent; fluency in conversation; the ability to write well) are extremely important but consider, for now, attitudes toward other people's uses of language. Almost always, when expressed in public, these attitudes reveal varying degrees of hostility, censure, distaste and alienation.

There is a popular saying, that if something is enjoyable in life, it will be immoral, illegal or fattening. If people encounter something they do not like in another's use of language, it will usually be called sloppy, incorrect or ugly – the equivalent of immoral, illegal and fattening. The possibility of ignorance being a cause provokes varying degrees of sympathy: they don't know any better; blame the parents; they ought to know better; what can you expect?; blame television; blame the teachers; blame the Americans; blame Radio 1; they just don't read/listen/care; English has been going downhill for a long time; blame modern life.

Here is an extract from the *Daily Mirror*, 29 June 1989. It highlights the sorts of things that upset people or, to put it another way, make good newspaper copy.

YOU CAN'T WRITE PROPER

And you ain't talking nice neither, says Charles

ANGRY Prince Charles yesterday branded his own staff dunces – for not writing and speaking properly.

And he said it was because English was taught so badly.

He declared: "All the people I have in my office, they can't speak English properly, they can't write English properly.

"All the letters sent from my office I have to correct myself. And that is because English is taught so bloody badly. That is the problem.

"If we want people who write good English and write plays for the future, there is no way they can do it with the present system.

"I think the whole way schools are operating is not right. They don't educate character at all."

Immediately, furious teachers hit back by claiming it was Gordonstoun-educated CHARLES who needed lessons in the Queen's English.

Nigel de Gruchy, deputy chief of the National Association of Schoolmasters and Union of Women Teachers, said: "His grammar is appalling and I don't think he speaks at all well considering his education.

"I know people who've been to State schools who speak better than him.

"If he has to swear, he's proving public schools are as bad as State ones.

"It's a case of the pot calling the kettle black."

Mr de Gruchy added that he thought poor pay was the root of Charles's staff problem.

He said: "He probably doesn't pay enough to attract the right quality of staff to write his letters."

Fred Jarvis, leader of the National Union of Teachers, added: "He's gone over the top.

"To talk about educating character into pupils is a stupid phrase.

"Prince Charles doesn't know anything about the State school system.

"He never went to one, and does not send his sons to them either."

Last night, Education Secretary Kenneth Baker jumped to Charles's defence.

He said: "Prince Charles echoes the concerns of many parents."

The Queen's English Society also sided with Charles.

Secretary Ivan Thompson said: "Over the last 50 years there has been a decline in literacy."

Buckingham Palace said: "The Prince was illustrating the importance he attaches to the correct use of English."

ACTIVITY

1 Identify the main issues of controversy in the extract on page 6.
2 So-called language abuses frequently provoke letters to the press and to the BBC. Make a list of Top Ten language sins, starting with the ones that most irritate you, for example:
   I ain't got none (double negative)
   must of (must have)
   us books (our books)
   I like fish and chip's (inappropriate apostrophe)
   Do remember to keep clearly in mind what it is that is being criticised. Avoid generalisations such as 'bad English' or 'not speaking properly'. Be specific.

3 When you have completed your list, look to see how many of your Top Ten language sins are matters of spelling, punctuation, grammar, pronunciation or choice of vocabulary. Is there one area where more misdemeanours are committed than elsewhere?
4 Ask yourself why particular language offences should provoke strong attitudes in some people and not in others. Can some offences be worse than others?
5 To find out more about non-standard forms of English and about their history and modern attitudes, read David Crystal's *Who Cares About English Usage?* (Penguin, 1984).

Criticism of spelling, punctuation, grammar and choice of vocabulary is almost always slightly painful and embarrassing. For some adults it is their strongest memory of schooldays. The spirit in which it is given makes all the difference. Have you ever felt patronised, put down, scoffed, mystified, or alternatively helped, encouraged, complimented on any of these things?

Dialect and accent

The terms 'dialect' and 'accent' are frequently confused. Dialect refers to any consistent set of variations in the way in which a language is used by a specific group of people. The variations will occur in:

■ the vocabulary
■ the grammar
■ the pronunciation.

The most familiar dialectal variations in English are the regional ones which have been established for many centuries and which are immediately discernible in pronunciation. Regional accent is the characteristic way in which people of that region *pronounce* the English language, and the most immediately noticeable signs are the pronunciation of a particular vowel or consonant and the intonation patterns.

Examples of dialectal vocabulary can be seen in the different names given up and down the country to small loaves of bread: barm cakes; bread buns; baps; cobs. Examples of dialectal variation in grammar are the frequent use of the question form 'Have you not?' in parts of Lancashire, and the use of 'Look you' in parts of Wales. Noticeable too are variant uses of forms of the verb 'to be' for example: 'I be'; 'I is'. Examples of dialectal variation in pronunciation are different vowel pronunciations in a word like 'right', such as 'raait', 'roight', 'reet', 'rate', 'richt' and 'reight'.

Intonation is frequently linked to a distinctive grammatical feature. In Blackburn, for example, there is a particularly warm and friendly intonation given to the question, 'Have you not?', whereas in Cardiff, there is a distinctive note of seriousness and concern in the intonation of 'Look you' at the ends of sentences (though 'Look you' appears to be far less prevalent in Wales nowadays than 'Have you not?' in Lancashire).

In the examples given, you can see how vocabulary, grammar and pronunciation are interrelated.

Stereotyping and social class

The regional dialects, including the accents, are an inheritance from a time when regional separateness and dialectal differences were much more pronounced than they are today. In the intervening time two factors have considerably affected our view of dialects and accents. One factor is the generation of stereotypical versions. ('Look you' has become part of the traditional Welsh stereotype, whereas 'Have you not?' is nothing like as familiar a stereotypical Lancashire saying as, for example, 'Ee by gum', which very few Lancashire people actually say.) The other, much more significant factor is the rise of social-class accents reflecting economic and educational developments of the last 300 years or so.

Stereotypes depend upon social communication and the media by which this takes place. Thus, without having any personal knowledge of a particular region or group of people, we can carry in our minds 'sound-bites' of typical speech. So far as accent is concerned, the development of radio, film and television has created a number of stereotypical foreign and regional accents in which English is spoken chiefly for the purpose of entertainment. Perhaps the most extreme, and self-parodying, example is the hugely successful TV series, *'Allo 'Allo* in which British actors spoke their French parts in exaggerated versions of French pronunciation of English. The local gendarme is in fact a British agent who speaks French with an almost impossible English accent. The situation is absurd.

ACTIVITY

The motive for stereotyping can range from malice to good-natured humour, but there is always a danger. Novelists have attempted to represent accent, for example, by phonetic spelling, in order to give a more vivid life to the character on the page.

1 Look at the following examples from Dickens's *Pickwick Papers* (1837) and a detective story by Dorothy L. Sayers written in the 1930s. What is gained by the attempt to convey actual speech? Do you detect social-class attitudes or implications in the writing?

Text A
'How old is that horse, my friend?' inquired Mr Pickwick, rubbing his nose with the shilling he had reserved for the fare.
'Forty-two,' replied the driver, eyeing him askant.
'What!' ejaculated Mr Pickwick, laying his hand upon his note-book. The driver reiterated his former statement. Mr Pickwick looked very hard at the man's face; but his features were immovable, so he noted down the fact forthwith.
'And how long do you keep him out at a

time?' inquired Mr Pickwick, searching for further information.

'Two or three veeks,' replied the man.

'Weeks!' said Mr Pickwick in astonishment – and out came the note-book again.

'He lives at Pentonwil when he's at home,' observed the driver, coolly, 'but we seldom takes him home, on account of his veakness.'

'On account of his weakness!' reiterated the perplexed Mr Pickwick.

'He always falls down when he's took out o' the cab,' continued the driver, 'but when he's in it, we bears him up werry tight, and takes him in werry short, so as he can't werry well fall down; and we've got a pair o' precious large wheels on, so ven he does move, they run after him, and he must go on – he can't help it.'

(Charles Dickens, *The Pickwick Papers*)

Text B

He wouldn't 'ardly fancy 'is dinner after a thing like this. Thank you, sir. Well now, doctor, wot kind of weapon do you take this to 'ave been?'

'It was a long, narrow weapon – something like an Italian stiletto, I imagine,' said the doctor, 'about six inches long. It was thrust in with great force under the fifth rib, and I should say it had pierced the heart centrally. As you see, there has been practically no bleeding. Such a wound would cause instant death. Was she lying just as she is now when you first saw her, Mr Brotherton?'

'On her back, just as she is,' replied the husband.

'Well, that seems clear enough,' said the policeman. 'This 'ere Marinetti, or wotever 'is name is, 'as a grudge against the poor young lady –'

'I believe he was an admirer,' put in the doctor.

'Quite so,' agreed the constable. 'Of course, these foreigners are like that – even the decentest of 'em. Stabbin' and such-like seems to come nateral to them, as you might say. Well, this 'ere Marinetti climbs in 'ere, see the poor young lady standin' 'ere by the table all alone, gettin' the dinner ready; 'e comes in be'ind, catches 'er round the waist, stabs 'er – easy job, you see; no corsets nor nothink – she shrieks out, 'e pulls 'is stiletty out of 'er an' makes tracks. Well, now we've got to find 'im, and by your leave, sir, I'll be gettin' along. We'll 'ave 'im by the 'eels before long, sir, don't you worry. I'll 'ave to put a man in charge 'ere, sir, to keep folks out, but that needn't worry you. Good mornin', gentlemen.'

'May we move the poor girl now?' asked the doctor.

'Certainly. Like me to 'elp you, sir?'

'No. Don't lose any time. We can manage.' Dr Hartman turned to Peter as the constable clattered downstairs. 'Will you help me, Lord Peter?'

(Dorothy L. Sayers, *Murder Must Advertise*)

2 Write a short scene from a detective story or traveller's tale catching something of a local accent without making the speaker seem comic.

Cutting across the ancient sound boundaries of regional accent are more recent notions of social class and political and economic power in which a new dialect has been nurtured. The term Standard English is used to define the vocabulary and grammar of the new dialect, and Received Pronunciation (also referred to as RP) to define its accent. Standard English is a dialect very much oriented toward the written rather than the spoken word and embodies a clearly defined set of norms and conventions governing the use of English spelling. It tends toward formality (though not necessarily pomposity) and avoids all regional characteristics in the interest of universal usage. Many scholars argue that, human variety being what it is, there are variations within standard English and RP. Most of us, if we have been educated to GCSE and beyond, will speak widely varying mixtures of regional pronunciation, RP and personal idiosyncrasies. The Department of Education has explicitly stated in the National Curriculum that Standard English can be spoken acceptably in a regional accent.

ACTIVITY

1 Explore your own attitudes toward different English accents. Do you have a favourite? A least favourite? Do you find a particular accent posh/sexy/friendly/authoritative? Which?

2 Here are some attitudes collected for an A-level project on accent variations. Whether you agree with them or not, ask yourself three things:

■ What is the phonological (ie audible sounds) basis for these views?
■ What do the views tell you about the people who hold them?
■ Do such views do more harm than good? or not matter very much?

a Lancashire people speak in a warm way; the Yorkshire accent is more blunt.
b The Scotch (sic) accent is good for selling things.
c Cockneys sound very cheerful when they talk.
d Cockneys sound very disrespectful to everything.
e I think Glaswegian is very aggressive.
f Brummies sound miserable all the time, don't they?
g The Welsh are very musical.
h I find people in the north east very friendly in the way they speak.
i They have a very thick, country accent in Norfolk.
j I think they speak with a brogue in Cornwall.
k I hate the way they talk in some parts of Leeds; it's always 'wa'er', 'le'er', 'ma'er', for 'water', 'letter', 'matter'.
l They didn't talk properly where I was brought up (Moss Side, Manchester).
m They didn't talk proper down our way (Wapping).
n We used to be told that the BBC accent was the best, but that's not so anymore is it? Even the BBC doesn't think so.
o Upper-class accents are all lah-di-da. Working-class accents are more down to earth.
p Our GP has a strong working-class accent. My mum doesn't like it.
q Accents are disappearing, aren't they?

Perspectives on language

The final section of this chapter outlines major perspectives on language which have something to contribute to A-level English language syllabuses. Each perspective opens up a vast range of knowledge and experience central not only to the English language but to all the languages of the world.

The geographical perspective: the other languages of Britain

Languages learned in infancy are pure accidents of birth. More than half the world's population needs to learn at least two languages very early in life in order to get by in everyday family and social situations. Some readers of this book will be bilingual but many will be monolingual, British nationals who may have studied one or more 'second languages' for GCSE and who may have continued with these languages for A level.

Since 1945 there has been such an immigration of peoples and languages that it makes sense to describe Britain as a multilingual country. Multilingualism is not however a modern phenomenon; it is a consequence of migrations that seem to have been going on since the dawn of time.

In 1985 the Linguistic Minorities Project published a report entitled *The Other Languages of England.* This report described the origins and development of many language communities now into their second and third generation of existence: Bengali, Punjabi, Gujerati, Hong Kong Chinese, West Indian, Portuguese, Spanish, Greek, Turkish Cypriot, Polish, Ukrainian, East African, Asian, Vietnamese Chinese. One interesting aspect of the report was a consideration of the extent of bilingualism in the everyday lives of many students in Peterborough and Bradford.

ACTIVITY

Look at the following table and discuss some of the implications of bilingualism or multilingualism.

Language used by bilingual pupils with family members and schoolfriends

	Peterborough				Bradford			
	Total number asked	% minority language	% English	% both equally	Total number asked	% minority language	% English	% both equally
To my father I usually speak:	129	51	17	32	203	71	16	13
To my mother I usually speak:	32	62	13	25	209	78	11	11
To my brother(s) I usually speak:	112	16	50	34	200	19	60	21
To my sister(s) I usually speak:	107	17	49	34	189	25	54	21
To my grandfather(s) I usually speak:	83	74	16	10	127	87	6	6
To my grandmother(s) I usually speak:	95	78	13	9	130	78	6	16
My father usually speaks to me in:	128	62	16	22	203	76	14	9
My mother usually speaks to me in:	133	70	14	16	206	87	8	5
My grandfather(s) usually speak to me in:	83	82	14	4	131	87	8	5
My grandmother(s) usually speak to me in:	95	82	11	7	132	88	9	3
In school breaks, my friends and I usually speak in:	131	3	81	16	202	9	84	6

Of course in Britain today there are much older linguistic sub-divisions than the number of minority languages. There are the well-known Welsh, Scots and Irish national languages, for example. Cornish, an ancient Celtic language, has not survived so effectively; its last speaker died in 1777. Yet its influence remains, most notably in place names such as Mevagissey, Penzance and Polperro. It also survives in family names such as Tremain and Trevelyan.

However, in recent years there have been attempts to revive the Cornish language. The *Western Morning News* prints weekly articles in both Cornish and English, including this example from 16 January 1995. Do you detect any clues at all for translation purposes?

An Goloven Gernewek

Mes martesen dasvewnans an aswonvos Kernewek a dheth dhe'n pryk gans Henry Jenner ha'n tavas Kernewek dasserghys, fundyans an Cowethasow Kernow Goth ha'n Orseth, sewyes gans Mebyon Kernow ha lyes bags moy, bysy'n jeth hedhyu.

Yn sur, nyns yu possybyl dewys daw dek poynt a vry, mes dhe'n lyha hem yu dalleth.

The Cornish Column

But perhaps the revival of Cornish consciousness reached a high point with Henry Jenner and the renaissance of the Cornish language, the founding of the Old Cornwall Societies, the Gorseth, followed by Mebyon Kernow and so many others, to this day. It isn't possible to select just ten points, but it's a start.

The problems of diversity

Whilst it is true that the number of languages in the world has reduced dramatically in the twentieth century, there are still over 3000 languages in use. Marriage, entertainment, holiday travel, sport, hobbies, penfriends, literature and the arts are all pleasurable ways of learning other people's languages. However, in wider political and economic contexts, language differences create problems that have no easy solutions.

ACTIVITY

1 Read the following comments made in *The European* newspaper about languages in the European Union.

Text A

ONE of Europe's greatest glories is its diversity of languages. National governments and the European Union must ensure that these tongues continue to flourish. But this enthusiasm cannot be readily extended to the use of so many national languages by European institutions, where present practice owes more to pride than common-sense.

The Union must now confront the need to change a policy which was designed for a Community of six members and was barely workable for 12, but will be an expensive administrative nightmare for 16. Small working groups of the Commission and Council of Ministers have agreed to limit the number of interpreters. The European Parliament will be harder to reform. It would be invidious if candidates were unable to stand because they could speak only their mother tongue. As a first step, national governments should pay the direct cost of their translators and interpreters in the Parliament.

But this will not be enough. The Union will eventually have to agree on one working language. Europe's leaders, rather than fight for their own mother tongues, should agree to let the dominant language develop naturally. Historical accident and widespread accessibility – not linguistic imperialism – suggest that this will be English.

(10 February 1994)

Text B

Bigger club creates linguistic nightmare

THE enlargement of the EU club from 12 to 16 may bring with it a linguistic, administrative and budgetary nightmare, writes Rory Watson. The addition of Finnish, Norwegian and Swedish to the nine existing official languages will bring more linguists and take the EU even nearer a modern-day Tower of Babel. The Commission, the largest employer, has 1,100 full-time translators and will need up to 60 more for each additional language. The European Parliament has 400 translators and would need around 40 per new language. The Commission already has 400 full-time interpreters, but employs about 300 freelances a day to handle its daily diet of up to 40 meetings. With 12 official languages, there will be 132 possible combinations. EU officials say privately that the system cannot continue. Efforts are being made to restrict the number of working languages.

(10 February 1994)

Text C

Nine languages are a waste of money

HAVING worked for many years as an interpreter for a number of European and international organisations, I entirely fail to understand why the EU needs nine official languages and, additionally, a few more quite soon. To my mind, this is the greatest waste of money one can imagine. The level of error is considerable, since all speeches, decrees and laws have to be translated into all nine languages. It entails enormous expense and difficulty. Who, for example, can translate from Greek into Danish, etc?

Why is it that the EU needs so many languages when the entire UN 'family' can get by with four and Gatt with three?
Roger Battisse
Strasbourg

(17 June 1994)

2 Discuss your own views on the present situation so far as languages are concerned in the European Union.

3 What reasons might there be for the decline this century in the number of languages in the world?

Language 'invasion'

Languages, created out of human need, become factors of political power, ethnic intolerance and cultural suspicion. Some French politicians, for example, have expressed serious concern about the effect of the English language on modern-day French, which is especially ironic when you consider the powerful influence the French language has exerted on English since the Norman conquest of 1066.

The following newspaper items illustrate this concern. If you are unable to read French, find somebody to help you translate.

« NEXT », c'est le nom que Renault a choisi pour sa nouvelle voiture.
(Photo Gamma.)

Chez les commerçants, dans les rues des villes, les annonces, enseignes et informations rédigées en Anglais se multiplient.
(Photos Olivier Corsan et Paul Delort/Le Figaro.)

FRANCE

PRIME MINISTER Edouard Balladur took over as leader of the crusade to protect the French language from what is seen as an Anglo-Saxon cultural invasion.

Last month the government unveiled a Bill banning the use of foreign words in public announcements, employment contracts and advertising, and on radio and television, except for foreign-language programmes.

As he inaugurated the Higher Council of the French Language, made up of 29 'wise men' and one woman, Balladur said 'the mark of France's genius' was at stake because of the overuse of English in the country.

Intellectuals say that English is adulterating French into 'Franglais', corrupting the way young people speak and monopolising science and technology. Setting the example, Balladur said that he would issue guidelines to state employees on French usage, 'especially in international relations'.

According to an opinion poll published on 8 March by the culture ministry, 65 per cent of French people believe a strong political will can help defend their language.

(*The European*, 10 February 1994)

L'alignement sur l'anglais

La compétition industrielle et commerciale entre les nations rend leurs langues rivales. Une déstabilisation du français est à craindre sous la pression de l'anglo-américain qui s'exerce dans tous les domaines de la vie économique, mais aussi culturelle. Les technologies de communication ont rapproché les frontières, et le français se trouve de ce fait dans une situation précaire, comparable à celle du Québec il y a trente ans, avant la réaction exemplaire et décisive des Québécois pour la survie de leur langue.

(*Le Figaro*, 8 February 1996)

Language invasions, takeovers, borrowings, whatever you wish to call them have occurred throughout history and have always generated mixed reactions. In British schools in the 1950s, the influence of American English on the young was blamed for all manner of social ills. More recently, the influence of Australian English, via TV soap operas, has come under scrutiny in Britain.

The following extract is taken from a newspaper article by an English novelist and literary scholar, Malcolm Bradbury. What is your own view on this issue?

WHY ARE YOUNG BRITONS TALKING MORE LIKE AUSTRALIANS?

THE QUEEN'S English is in trouble again, a bit like the monarchy itself. For nearly half a century now, the British have been worrying about what's been happening to their spoken language.

The great post-war worry was that it was becoming Americanised – as radio presenters, disc jockeys and celebrities took to a form of speech that was positioned somewhere over the Atlantic.

In the Eighties, the world shifted. Now the concern was with Estuary English, a glottalised, loose form of speech that drifted into London from downriver and out of the Essex marshes. It was soon being widely spoken even by the younger Royals. Mysterious forms of discourse – a supreme example was Janet Street-Porter, thought by many linguists to speak no known human tongue – began to swamp not just the airwaves but clubs, pubs, classrooms and dinner parties.

Now a new phenomenon has been noted. According to a new survey by academic Barbara Bradford, young Britons are widely taking up a form of speech that closely resembles Australian. Soap operas like Neighbours and Home And Away are thought to be a major influence. So is the impact of speech patterns from Liverpool and Northern Ireland, also spread by the media.

The influence is chiefly on speech

rhythms. Sentences end on a rising intonation, sounding more like a question than a statement. 'I borrowed your ghetto-blaster. Yeah?'

Specialists give different explanations. It could be that young people are unwilling to offer confident information, or state views with precision and clarity. It could be that they want a way of speech that is as classless as possible. Or it could be that in modern backpacking youth culture, this is where the language of the peer group comes together.

I'm just back from Australia myself – a freewheeling society that has always been proud of its lack

of class and formality, its easy outdoor energy. The country was settled by convicts and explorers, lawbreakers as well as society-makers, and it shows. It remains a very youthful country – a backpackers' paradise with a lively, surfy, physical culture, now open to a mix-and-match influence from many different parts of the world.

But this vitality is coupled with a lack of confidence the Australians themselves have christened 'cultural cringe'.

(Malcolm Bradbury, the *Daily Mail*,
20 March 1996)

The geographical perspective: regional variation - dialect

Variety is in the very nature of language (see Chapter 13) and geography is a significant factor in variation. Not only is there variation between different languages, but also within the same language. Variations within languages are usually referred to as dialects, and the dialectal variations with which you will be most familiar are those in different geographical regions.

While there is clear evidence that the old dialects of Britain, especially rural ones, are declining in use, there is also evidence of new ones appearing. Estuary English is one example, others have developed out of **code**-switching in which bilingual speakers eventually mix elements from both languages. Blendings of Hindi and English, for example, have come to be called Hindlish or Hinglish. In Hindi-speaking parts of India, a 'city police-station' is known as a 'city-kotwali'. In Huddersfield, a dialectal mixture of Panjabi and English is known as Panglish. 'Hai na' in Panjabi means 'isn't it', hence 'It's a nice day, hana?'

The following activity will give you an opportunity to think about the regional dialect with which you are most familiar and to compare it with another dialect of which you have some knowledge, perhaps through a relative or friend. Remember that regional dialects differ most noticeably in accent, but sometimes in vocabulary and grammar.

ACTIVITY

1 Draw an outline map of Britain on an A4 sheet of paper. Give yourself plenty of room.
2 Identify and draw the area of the regional dialect you know best. Consult a more detailed map before you do this and show as accurately as possible where you think the regional dialect boundary should be drawn. Where, for example, do people begin to talk differently? You may need to consult with other people in your own area. Be as local or as regional as you wish.
3 List on your map one or two of each of the following that seem typical of the dialect you have chosen:

- ways of pronouncing individual words
- particular rhythms or intonations over a number of words
- words peculiar to the dialect
- common words that have a different meaning
- grammatical features that would be thought non-standard elsewhere.

4 Now identify any other regional dialects of which you have some knowledge. You may not be quite so accurate at drawing the boundaries, but don't let that put you off.
5 Try to list some typical features of this dialect. Remember to listen to the real thing, rather than just the stereotypes. So-called 'Geordies', for example, make a clear distinction between Tyneside and Wearside regional variations.

The historical perspective

The English language has a long history from its earliest period, Old English (to *c.* 1100), through Middle English (to *c.* 1450) and Early Modern English down to today, but that history is only part of a much longer history stretching back thousands of years across Europe into southern Asia. It is a long history of geographically and culturally related families of languages mingling with one another as people migrated from one part of the world to another and as trading networks spread wider and wider. All languages that have survived show signs of continuing change in every aspect: in pronunciation, the acquisition of new words, changes in the meanings of existing words, grammatical constructions and in styles of talking and writing.

ACTIVITY

Below are two conversations written in texts separated by about 400 years. The later one is separated from our own time by about 500 years.

Text A
A pupil is talking to a teacher
Pupil: We cildra bidda e eala lareow þaet þu taece us sprecan rihte, forþam ungelaerede we sindon, and gewaemmodlice we sprecan.
Master: Hwaet wille ge sprecan?
Pupil: Hwaet rece we hwaet we sprecan, buton hit riht spraec sy and behefe naes idei oþþe fracod?
Master: Wille ge beon beswungwn on leornunge?
Pupil: Leofre is us beon beswungen for lare þaenne hit ne cunnan; ac we witan þe bilewitne wesan, and nellan onbelaedan swincbla us, buton þu bi togenydd fram us.

(Aelfric, Abbot of Eynsham, c. 1000 AD)

The easiest way to understand this text in the original is to say it aloud. This is not as difficult as it first looks. Assume the spelling to be mainly phonetic and remember two things: the runic symbol 'þ' is pronounced 'th'; the æ symbol is a short 'a' as in 'cat'. As you say the words, listen for echoes of versions that have come down to the present day.
Here is a modern translation.

P: We children beg you, teacher, to teach us to speak correctly, because we are ignorant and speak corruptly.
M: What do you want to say?
P: What do we care what we say, as long as it is correct and proper speech, not trivial and worthless?

M: Are you willing to be beaten in your course of learning?
P: We would rather be beaten for the sake of learning than not know anything; but we know that you are kind and will not give us beatings unless we force you to.

1 List some notable spelling, pronunciation and vocabulary changes between Aelfric's version and the translation.

Text B
An uncle (Pandarus) is visiting his niece (Criseyde) who is reading a book with some friends.
Quod Pandarus, 'Madame, God yow see
With al youre fayre book and compaignie!'
Ey, uncle myn, welcome iwys,' quod she;
And up she roos, and by the hond in hye
She took hym faste, and seyde, 'This
      nyght thrie,
To goode mot it turne, of yow I mette
And with that word she down on bench
      hym sette.

'Ye, nece, yee shal faren wel the bet,
If God wol, al this yeer,' quod Pandarus:
'But I am sorry that I have yow let
To herken of youre book ye preysen thus.
For goddes love, what seith it? telle it us!
Is it of love? O, som good ye me leere!'.
'Uncle,' quod she, 'youre maistresse is nat
      heere'.

(Geoffrey Chaucer, Troilus and Criseyde, 1385)

Again, say this aloud and listen for modern echoes. Here is a modernised version.

Pandarus said, 'Madam, God bless you, your friends, and that fine book you're reading!'
'Welcome, uncle,' said Criseyde.
She got up, quickly took him by the hand, and said, 'I dreamt of you three times last night. I hope it's a good sign!'
Then she sat down on the bench.
'Yes, niece,' said Pandarus, 'if it's God's will, you'll have better luck all this year. But I am sorry I have stopped you reading the book which you like so much. What does it say, for God's sake? Tell me! Is it about love? Maybe you can teach me something useful!'

Criseyde said, 'Uncle, your mistress isn't here now'.

2　List the spelling, pronunciation and vocabulary differences between the two versions of Text B.

3　Many words in Chaucer's text are of French origin. Why should this be so? To answer this question you will need to look up the origins of some of the words. Use a dictionary that gives etymologies (ie word origins).

4　What proportion of the words in Aelfric's text are Germanic/Old English compared with the Chaucer text?

Language changes are observable not only over long periods of historical time. They occur year by year. One estimate calculated that new words are created at the rate of 300 a week, though most are too specialised for general knowledge. It is also estimated that there are six million words waiting to get into the *Oxford English Dictionary*! Whether many of them will is another matter.

Language changes of any kind can arouse considerable dismay, indignation and resistance, especially in an older generation. There is a deep-seated attitude, possibly in all of us, that resents change, whether it be in fashion, technology, in a familiar landscape or in linguistic matters such as pronunciation, usage, or the names things are called. An historical perspective on language will observe the changes and seek to explain causes and effects.

ACTIVITY

Read the following passage from Rod Menghem's *The Descent of Language* (1993) in which the author considers recent changes.

Much more disturbing than telephone culture, which now seems completely natural to us, is the language environment that has accompanied the growth of information processing machines. What the computer effects, particularly when it is employed in various types of learning process, is a constant translation of knowledge into measurable terms. 'Technobabble' and 'computerspeak' cannot be simply dismissed or quietly put in their place by humans who think they know better ... What are the practical effects of translating the concerns of a natural language into the equivalent terms of a computer language? In contemporary written English, the number of words in an average sentence is about 20, while in standard programming jargon the average would be half a dozen. The average number of grammatical rules according to which the sentences of a computer language are constructed is little more than 100, as compared to the thousands that are available in contemporary usage. A fundamental reduction of scope and expressive power ... is increasingly likely with the growth in computer literacy. For many students nowadays, being introduced to a subject of study may well be correlated with a means of processing data that discourages, rather than encourages, an individual ability to give shape to their own knowledge.

(Rod Menghem, The Descent of Language, 1993)

1　Think about the effects of IT on the ways in which we use English today. If it helps, draw up a list of pros and cons. Do you see yourself as one of the 'many students' referred to at the end of the extract?

2　Think of two or three IT terms that have become familiar now but which may need to be translated by the IT archaeologist of the future.

The Aelfric and Chaucer texts demonstrate how the language, still recognisably English after nearly 1000 years of history, used to be. The Menghem extract appropriately draws our attention to how English may be used in the not too distant future.

A historical perspective on language contributes much to an understanding of how English has come to be the way it is. The historical perspective is sometimes referred to as a diachronic view of language, that is, words and their meanings, for example, are considered as they have evolved through time. In the hurly burly of everyday existence, language is used according to 'the way we are now', without any conscious reference to historical changes. This view of language is known as the synchronic view. In modern arguments and attitudes, there exists a tension between these two points of view, though a modern student of English needs to be able to appreciate and investigate both. Changes in meanings, pronunciations and language style, together with the creation of new words and phrases, reflect, however slightly, changes in society from one generation to another. This brings us to another influential perspective on language, the sociological.

The sociological perspective

The society in which we live and the language, or languages, we use are intimately bound up with each other. The ways in which language is used reflect what its users believe and value, but it is equally true that language shapes people's beliefs and values. Language is considered by sociologists as the prime socialising agent because of its power to influence thoughts and actions, especially those of the young. We slip into ideas because the language is so easy to slip into. Novels and soap operas are completely fictional but so believable and entertaining that they win us over very easily. Later in this book, you will consider persuasion as a distinct mode of writing (compared with information or instruction, for example). There is however a sense in which all language is persuasive in that it persuades minds to attend to it. Entertainment does this very well, but information and instruction also need to gain attention even though there is no intention to persuade in the manner of advertisers and politicians.

A word used to describe this close connection between society and language is 'sociolinguistic', which neatly blends the two elements. The big sociolinguistic issues in Britain today are:

- language and social class (does the way you talk matter?)
- language and gender (do women talk more co-operatively?)
- language and education (why so much emphasis now on grammar?)
- language and power (how influential are the media, IT and government on what we read, watch, say and think?).

All social groups, whether interest groups, occupational groups or age groups, tend to develop distinctive characteristics of language use. This phenomenon, combined with the wider issues listed above, creates a rich language environment in which sociolinguistic awareness is very important. Everybody has an attitude toward language, especially other people's uses of it. Some uses we distrust, ignore, revile, oppose, reject; others we absorb, admire, imitate, encourage.

One interesting linguistic topic that can seem quite a straightforward matter is the names we give to things. Fierce debates, however, have taken place about the re-naming of a village hall, for example, or about the name for a new model of car or, worse still, a new baby! Behind names lie all kinds of assumptions, expectations and connotations.

ACTIVITY

In the newspaper article below, David Edgar is drawing attention to a changeover by British Rail from the word 'passenger' to 'customer'. To some observers it may seem unimportant, to others, a welcome change. Yet others may not even have noticed. David Edgar clearly does not approve and explains why. Read the article and discuss your own view about the new emphasis on the word 'customer'.

The c-word that puts all of us on a lower level

IN the Seventies, the left sought to change the world by rewriting the language. In the Eighties, the right struck back. For the left, the idea was to challenge pejorative descriptions of *groups* (gays, women, blacks, the disabled). For the right, the notion was to change the way in which individuals thought about their relationship with public institutions.

From the schoolroom and the surgery to the railway station and even the playhouse, the nation found itself translated. No longer patient or passenger, playgoer, pupil or parent – suddenly, we were all customers.

It is in these terms that we find ourselves described in countless polytechnic mission statements and hospital business plans; it is as such that we are apologised to by British Rail for the non-availability of buffets and the cancellation of trains; it is thus that the Conservative Party treasurer chooses to refer to what in happier times he might have called his 'members'. And when Labour-controlled Birmingham education authority advertises for senior bureaucrats, it promises them a turnover of more than £300m, more than 500 'service delivery points' and, yes, 'around 400,000 customers'.

What's the problem? Shouldn't we *want* to be treated as customers – positive, active, knowing the score, clear on our rights – rather than as dormant and submissive 'pupils', 'patients' or 'passengers'? The terms of engagement between pupil and school, patient and doctor, party member and party, are defined by the institution. As customers, *we* call the shots and make the terms. We don't just *have* rights, we *are* right. What's wrong with that?

What's wrong with it is what's wrong with the market as the sole or even principal medium for our public dealings. It individualises us, it divides us and it ultimately dehumanises our relationships in the public world.

First, customerisation effectively *limits* the power of the consumer. Individual customer preference has certainly influenced producers on environmental questions, but so have organised consumer boycotts and Green voters. Pupils, patients and party members protest and petition; customers complain. This disenfranchises those inadequately trained in the complaining arts and also subtly alters the feasible *grounds* of complaint, from collective concerns to the shortcomings of an individual transaction.

Second, the customer role *discriminates*. It is interesting that the p-words all refer to what people have in common in their relationship with the institution or service. Whatever they pay, all patients are treated and all pupils are taught; wherever they sit, all playgoers see the same play, and all passengers are carried by the same train, which arrives at its destination at the same time. The implications of the c-word are different. They imply a concern with differentials, with those elements of interaction which relate to price.

Thus, in the hospital or surgery, the customer is concerned with the privacy of the room and the length of the queue rather than the quality of the treatment. On the railway, the customer is bothered more about the perks of the chosen service (whether 'first', 'standard' or, now, 'silver' class) than the mundane matter of whether the train gets in at the advertised time. Certainly the corporate sponsor in the playhouse or the sports hall often appears more exercised about the exclusivity of the entertainment suite than with the play or the game. And the point of the old school tie is that not everybody wears one.

Third, the customer relationship *homogenises* the relationships we have with the outside world, denying their specific (and essential) character. The fact is, a mental patient's relationship with a hospital is not the same as my relationship with Waterstone's.

This is not just because of the different expectations we have of these relationships. When I've bought my hi-fi, I may, if I wish, take a hammer to it. When I've bought my theatre ticket, this does not entitle me to heckle the performance. Buying a place on a course does not confer permission to disrupt it, nor does it guarantee that the purchaser will pass.

In the late Seventies, the Thatcherites pointed to the way in which socialism politicised and, thereby, homogenised our dealings with the world; their most enticing promise was to sweep away the monolithic sameness of socialism and to create in its stead a marketplace of infinite variety.

What we have ended up with is a new homogenisation, the cramming of all our public relationships into the useful but essentially two-dimensional geometry of the customer relationship. As a sole and final arbiter, the market limits and restricts us in our ways of being. *And* it's unequal. To coin a phrase, there must be an alternative to that.

(David Edgar, the *Independent*, 23 April 1991)

At the beginning of this book you looked at some fragments of language and made a number of deductions about their origins, purpose and context. This was in fact an exercise in sociolinguistics in which you filled in, as it were, the social details of each fragment. It is always best to pin down social aspects of language to specific data, otherwise discussion gets lost in generalities about class, gender, politics or whatever. The word 'customer', for example, gave David Edgar the opportunity to explore an idea and state a point of view. The fragments you looked at were both the data and the evidence on which you based your deductions.

ACTIVITY

Below are some samples of language (complete this time) which belong to very distinct social contexts and/or which contain social attitudes and assumptions about people and even about language itself. Look at them and ask yourself:

a Who is addressing whom?
b What is the social context?
c What purposes are being served?
d What form does the language take?
e Is it spoken or written communication? (There's a world of sociolinguistic difference here.)
f Are there any implied meanings?

These questions will help you investigate the data. The first three have been done for you as examples.

1 You have the right to remain silent.

   a spoken by police to arrested person
   b an apparent criminal act
   c to assert an arrested person's right according to a criminal code that lays down what should be said on such occasions (ie going by the book)
   d it is a statement that begins with the second person pronoun; it is a formula that must be reproduced exactly
   e definitely spoken but not impromptu; police required to speak it and prefer to be witnessed speaking it
   f one implied meaning is that the police have the right to arrest someone; another is that the law protects the rights of people not yet proven guilty; despite the fact that it is spoken by an arresting officer, it is meant to reassure; failure to say it would amount to wrongful arrest

2 I promise to pay the bearer on demand the sum of £10. (signed) G. E. A. Kentfield, Chief Cashier, Bank of England.

   a the Bank of England is addressing the possessor of a £10 note, through the person of its Chief Cashier
   b cash transaction backed up by a vast banking system
   c to make cash transactions convenient but also to guarantee, by what is written on it, the value of a piece of paper
   d notice the first person pronoun, reinforced

by a signature; promises are known as speech acts or performatives because the word itself is the action (see also 'promissory note')
   e very definitely writing of the most formal kind; a piece of language you would not wish to lose
   f the essential meaning here is explicitly stated as a promise, but implied is a great deal of national trust and confidence that the promise will be honoured; notice though how carefully shop assistants check for authenticity

3 *Child:* want teddy
   Adult: say please
   Child: please
   Adult: there's a good boy

   a child addressing adult who responds
   b likely to be domestic context
   c child expresses want; adult wants to teach politeness
   d child makes a statement that implies a request; adult gives an instruction; child co-operates; adult exclaims praise
   e quite clearly a spoken context
   f implication is that politeness matters and that adults expect it, especially in speech

(*Note:* you have to assume here that the intonation pattern in the child's voice meant 'I want . . .' and not 'Do you want . . .?'. The context normally makes these things clear, but if the adult had misinterpreted the child's intonation, the lesson in politeness would have been quite unwarranted. If language enables social processes and events to be achieved, misunderstandings can easily defeat social intentions.)

4 *Mother:* For someone who is at a university, she has a very common way of speaking.
   Son: You shouldn't judge people by the way they speak, mother.

5 The North Sea will sooner be found wanting in water, than a woman at a loss for a word. (Jutland proverb)

6 Please leave your message after the long tone.

7 Under the Data Protection Act 1984 you are entitled, on payment of a fee, to a copy of the personal information we hold on computer about you.

The psychological perspective

As with the sociological perspective, psychology and language are so interconnected that the term '**psycholinguistics**' has arisen to describe this field of knowledge and activity.

Psycholinguistics is concerned with how language works in the mind and is especially interested in language disorders, educational processes, language learning, and aspects of persuasion and creative imagination. The acquisition of a first language by infants, and what goes on in conversations are also of special interest to psycholinguists, although these topics draw equally upon sociolinguistics. Practical issues to do with effective reading and writing are also matters of psychology and language but are dealt with more fully elsewhere in the book.

It will be sufficient introduction to look at two topics here: (i) how young children make nouns do the work of verbs they have not yet learned; and (ii) the psychology of misspelling.

'Inventing' verbs　　　It has been observed by researchers in the United States and several European countries that young children 'invent' verbs out of nouns they already possess, and do it very effectively. Later, they do not need to be corrected; they automatically discontinue the strategy when it is no longer needed.

ACTIVITY

Look at the following examples.

Utterance	Likely meaning
The man is keying the door	The man is opening the door with a key
I want to button it	I want to turn it off by pressing the button
I'm souping	I'm eating soup
They're teaing	They're having tea
Pillow me!	Throw a pillow at me!
I'm darking the letters	I'm scribbling over the letters to make them dark
She's rounding it	She's making the skipping rope into a half circle
Can you higher that?	Can you make that higher?

1 From your observations of the data above, write a short paragraph on why verbs are so important.

Now look at the data below (from Eve Clark, *Strategies for Communicating*, 1980). The utterances were made by a two year-old boy. The 'ə' symbol indicates a vowel sound inserted between the words as in 'make-a-that'.

Utterance	Context
I do it again	Said as *S* knocks over blocks
You doing that	Said as adult builds blocks into a tower
You do do it, OK?	Asking adult to unroll some tape, after trying unsuccessfully to do it himself
You do [ə] that!	Indicating which toy the adult should take out of a box

Uh oh. I did	Said as *S* turned off tape recorder by pushing a knob
The clown do!	Asking adult to make the toy clown do what clowns do
Make name!	Telling adult to write his name
I make a little doggie	Said as *S* cuts a dog shape out of Play-Doh
Make it go in there	Asking adult to get a crayon back into its box
Make [ə] that	Said as *S* pointed to the hand moving on a clock; seemed to be a request for the adult to move the hand on
It go there	Talking about a block lying on the floor
Red went boom	Talking about a red block that fell on the floor
They go in the car	Talking about two storybook characters
'N turn [ə] go up	Said as *S* turned a puzzle piece the right way up
'N go like that	Said as *S* dropped puzzle pieces on the floor

2 Write a paragraph on what you have observed about young children learning to use a familiar English verb.

Do not make the mistake of assuming that the children in these data samples are at a primitive stage of development. They are at an early stage, yes, but their uses of language are intelligent and effective. They have a purpose for using language and a competence to communicate what they mean. For example, they know how to fasten the present tense participle '-ing' to the nouns in order to make them work as verbs. Nobody taught them to do that; they worked it out. Notice also, the use of a comparative **form** at the end of the first sample of data, 'higher'.

In the second sample of data, the following aspects of grammatical competence are apparent in the use of verbs:

■ use of phrasal verbs: 'go in', 'go up'
■ use of irregular past tense: do/did, go/went
■ combined verb forms: 'make it go', 'turn go up' (unusual, but it works).

Note also 'go like' to describe manner and the emphasis in 'you do do it'.

The remarkable thing about young children's uses of the language is not deficiency or incorrectness but the efficiency and the logic of the language strategies they use in making meanings out of limited resources. The limitation is merely a factor of age and inexperience, not of ability.

Look now at a drawing and some writing done by Kelly Jo, aged three years and ten months. The writing says: 'I like Superman. When the girlfriend comes, Superman flies up.' What do you notice about this child's early attempt to draw a picture and write English? What does it tell you about ways in which young children think?

Look, for example, where Superman's eyes have been located. Notice though, that belly buttons have been very accurately sited. Even though Lois Lane is wearing a dress, her belly button is clearly visible!

One letter of the English alphabet that Kelly Jo does know is the initial letter of her own name. She was also wearing a badge that said 'I am 4' which was not strictly true, but she wanted to be four. The combination of these two important symbols in her life appear to have been used to stand for the pronoun 'I', a not unreasonable strategy.

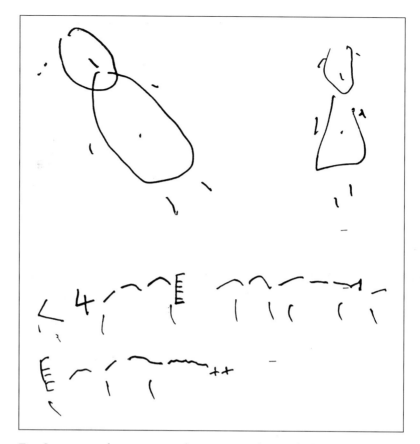

For Superman she appears to have invented a symbol that looks like a comb standing on its end. She then uses it consistently to stand for Superman when he reappears as the subject of her next sentence. Notice also the two crosses at the end, which, she explained, were not kisses but simply marked the end. Interestingly enough, in his early days as a printer, Caxton used the same symbol to indicate the end of a sentence.

The eleven vertical marks underneath the writing were put in later when she was asked where her words began and where they ended. She seems to recognise 'Superman' as one word and 'girlfriend' as two.

A casual observer might dismiss this text as scribbling, yet behind it a great deal of thinking has been going on, and one of the prime concerns of psycholinguistics is the relationship between language and thought, not only in young children but in adults too.

Misspelling

English spelling is a topic that can be investigated in a historical perspective (for example, the initial 'k' sound in words like 'knife' was always pronounced until about the fifteenth century when it gradually fell into disuse; the letter 'k' has however been retained in spelling). It can also be investigated as a sociological issue (for example, incorrect spelling is regarded by some employers and politicians as a stigma out of all proportion to other aspects of language use). There are, too, psychological aspects to spelling. Quite apart from the distress chronic misspelling can cause, there is a very obvious mismatch between the spoken form of a word and its written form. In the Italian language there is a much closer correspondence between how a word is pronounced and how it is written.

English uses 44 speech sounds (consisting of a mixture of vowels and consonants) but its alphabet has only 26 letters. That is a problem in itself, but when you add to it all the sound and spelling adjustments that have been made to the large number of words borrowed from other languages, especially French, the problem becomes much bigger. Not only does English pronounce all five vowel letters in a variety of ways, it also combines the letters to represent sounds that are not easily predictable for new learners. The combinations (called vowel digraphs) are set out below:

aa	ae	ai	ao	au
ea	ee	ei	eo	eu
ia	ie	ii	io	iu
oa	oe	oi	oo	ou
ua	ue	ui	uo	uu

ACTIVITY

1 Look through the vowel digraphs above and select some combinations you think are quite common in English, and others you think are rare.
2 The 'ea' combination occurs very frequently. Make three lists of English words containing this vowel digraph in (i) the *initial* position (ie at the beginning of a word), (ii) in the *median* position (ie somewhere in the middle) and (iii) in the *final* position. Don't worry if one list is much longer than the other two; this is a high statistical probability.
3 When you have made a start on your lists, observe the number of different pronunciations there are (eg 'She was reading in Reading in the early hours'). Only add to your lists words in which 'ea' is pronounced differently. You should find about nine or ten, but remember that people from different regions may well pronounce a word like 'early' quite differently from you.

The philosophical perspective

'Philosophical' may sound a rather grand, or nebulous, term, but philosophy and language have always been closely linked; indeed, one is impossible without the other. The whole history of western philosophy can be described as a long debate about the meanings of certain **abstract** nouns: goodness, faith, existence, mind, society, evil, happiness, suffering, freedom, equality, democracy, honesty.

ACTIVITY

A modern linguistic philosopher might well say, 'Leave the abstract nouns alone for a while and concentrate on how people use adjectival forms of these words.' Look, for example, at the adjective 'true'. Here are some uses:

a true story
make it good and true (a woodworker's advice)
a true likeness
true (spoken as a sign of agreement)
spoken like a true friend

will you always be true to me?
true grit
it flew straight and true

1 Decide how 'true' is being used in each example above.
2 Write a definition of the word 'truth'. Then compare your definition with one in a dictionary.
3 Now choose another familiar abstract noun and see how many different adjectival meanings it can have.

The study of the meanings of words and how meanings are made is called semantics. In the activity above, you have been doing semantics, which is the branch of linguistics most obviously related to philosophy.

Another topic in semantics that raises philosophical questions is **metaphor**. Metaphors express ideas and describe things using words normally associated with quite different ideas and things. If a speaker addressing a trade union meeting says, 'We are not getting a fair share of the cake', everybody knows that he is talking about wages, not confectionary. Metaphors can be very persuasive; they can add humour, passion, contempt, down-to-earthness and many other kinds of emotions to an idea. They appeal to the imagination.

ACTIVITY

Metaphors do not have to be elaborate or literary creations. There are many in everyday idioms and sayings. Take health, for example:

I'm feeling a bit low	You're going down with 'flu
I need a pick-me-up	on top of the world
under the weather	He's on a high today
down in the mouth	It will give you a lift
down and out	I've reached rock bottom
feeling low down	up and about in no time
on the crest of a wave	down in the dumps
laid low	

1 What is the everyday metaphor at work here?
2 Why do you think there is such a consistency of idea in all these phrases? Think of other metaphors to do with health and see if they are connected or different: eg pull yourself together; on the mend; in the pink; gone downhill.

3 Think of another familiar area of human experience, such as fortune (good and bad), love, youth and age. Make a similar list of metaphors and look at any connections between them.

Technically speaking, figurative phrases that use the words 'as' or 'like' are called **similes** because they explicitly say that one thing seems like another, which alerts you to the fact that a comparison is being made. The things being compared are kept separate, for example:

as happy as a sandboy
as quick as a flash
she ran like the wind.

Metaphors dispense with the explicit connecting word and are all the more effective for doing so, for example:

she is drowning in work and worry
he drives them too hard
you foot the bill.

The literary perspective

'Beauty is truth, truth beauty' – that is all
Ye know on earth, and all ye need to know

In these last two lines from John Keats' 'Ode on a Grecian Urn', two mighty abstract nouns, both with a long history of philosophy behind them, are joined together by that deceptively simple verb 'is'. They are repeated in inverse form, and then rounded off with a rather down-to-earth statement which sounds wise because of the use, twice, of an archaic pronoun, 'ye'. Most people would agree that this is a literary text: it sounds right, and by instinct or craft, or both, it is formally structured. Though they do not rhyme at the end, there is a poetic rhythm to both lines, achieved yet controlled by the equal number of syllables in each line. They round off a poem of five verses in a neat, pointed way. If you read the lines aloud, they seem to hover between everyday speech and a faintly 'religious' declaration. If 'ye' were replaced by 'you' for example, and 'on earth' by 'in life', it could conceivably occur in a conversation. What literature does, however, is transform everyday language into art.

Whilst acknowledging its poetic and literary character, some readers may disagree violently with the view expressed. Read in the light of the Holocaust, Hiroshima, the Vietnam war, torture and unjust imprisonments all over the world, the thought expressed seems wimpish at best, dangerously untrue at worst. As a philosopher would say, it all depends on what you mean by 'beauty' or by 'truth'.

ACTIVITY

1 Choose two abstract nouns that you think could be linked by the verb form 'is'. Then write two lines in a similar epigrammatic way. Aim for a pleasing sound and rhythm too. Think of your finished product as a motto or a text to pin on the wall. You can be as tough or as tender as you like. Remember, only allow yourself ten syllables in a line, for example:
Love is patience, patience love, – that's what most

People look for in a relationship.

Money is power, power money, – that's
The only thing that matters; that's what counts.

2 What do rhythmic effects and conscious shaping of the language contribute to what is actually being said? Your answer to this question will partly explain why we value literature.

But literature is not just a matter of using metaphor and abstractions. Quite the contrary, as you will see in Chapter 8. Look at the speech below from Shakespeare's *Henry V*. It occurs after the battle of Agincourt, and is spoken by the Duke of Burgundy who beseeches the English and French kings to make peace.

Great Kings of France and England! That I have labored
With all my wits, my pains, and strong endeavors
To bring your most imperial majesties

Unto this bar and royal interview,
Your mightiness on both parts best can witness.
Since, then, my office hath so far prevailed
That, face to face and royal eye to eye,
You have congreeted, let it not disgrace me
If I demand before this royal view,
What rub or what impediment there is
Why that the naked, poor, and mangled Peace,
Dear nurse of arts, plenties, and joyful births,
Should not, in this best garden of the world,
Our fertile France, put up her lovely visage.
Alas, she hath from France too long been chased,
And all her husbandry doth lie on heaps,
Corrupting in it own fertility.
Her vine, the merry cheerer of the heart,
Unprunèd dies; her hedges even-pleached,
Like prisoners wildly overgrown with hair,
Put forth disordered twigs; her fallow leas
The darnel, hemlock, and rank fumitory
Doth root upon, while that the coulter rusts
That should deracinate such savagery.
The even mead, that erst brought sweetly forth
The freckled cowslip, burnet, and green clover,
Wanting the scythe, all uncorrected, rank,
Conceives by idleness, and nothing teems
But hateful docks, rough thistles, kecksies, burrs,
Losing both beauty and utility.
And all our vineyards, fallows, meads, and hedges,
Defective in their natures, grow to wildness.
Even so our houses and ourselves and children
Have lost, or do not learn for want of time,
The sciences that should become our country;
But grow like savages, as soldiers will,
That nothing do but meditate on blood,
To swearing and stern looks, diffused attire,
And everything that seems unnatural.
Which to reduce into our former favor
You are assembled; and my speech entreats
That I may know the let why gentle Peace
Should not expel these inconveniences
And bless us with her former qualities.

(Henry V, Act V, Scene 2)

Notice how much vivid, concrete detail there is here. One section sounds
almost like a botanical catalogue. Yet how rhythmical and moving the
effect is. It is likely that you will not recognise some of the common
Elizabethan names for some weeds but that hardly seems to matter. The
overall effect is a rich mixture of the concrete and the abstract, each
illuminating the other. Above all, notice the rhythmic flow. It will help to
read it aloud, and you should try to listen to this speech on an audio or a
video recording.

ACTIVITY

Below are three texts about motor cars.

1 Read and compare them.

Text A

126BIS, 1988   £650

Just rolled, many new parts,
clutch,   distributor,   three
new tyres, exhaust, buyer
removes, Halfords receipts
showing. 01386 553907. P

(Exchange and Mart)

Text B

Text C

Car

I am an agent of death
Beware me
Though I respond to your impatient feet
And grind my teeth
At your ham-fisted gear-change
Think me not a faithful slave
Do not mistake patience for servitude
Beware me –
        I am an agent of *death*

I am a Jezebel of steel
Desire me
For I respond to your pulsating drives
And flash my torso
Through your urban armadas
Think of me as seductive
Purring as you lapse into fantasy
Desire me –
        I am a Jezebel of *steel*

I am a symbol of wealth
Worship me
For I respond to your pagan desires
And turn men's heads
Through your screaming manoeuvres
Think of me as impressive

Catching women's eyes for your vanity
Worship me –
        I am a symbol of *wealth*

I am a rusting heap of scrap
Abuse me
For I respond to your depressing needs
And serve my driver
Through your tedious routines
Think of me as expensive
Breaking down but vital to your functions
Abuse me –
        I am a rusting heap of *scrap*

I am an agent of death
Beware me
Though I respond to your various feet
And show my worth
At your arrogant demands
Think me not a faultless thing
Do not mistake safety for synthesis
Beware me –
        I am an agent of *death*

(Alan Frost, *The Poetry of Motion*, ed. Alan Bold)

2 On the evidence of the language used in the three texts, explain, with detailed references, some differences (if you agree that there are differences) between texts usually referred to as 'literary' and 'non-literary'. Which represent the extremes? Which lies between 'literary' and 'non-literary' and why? The poem is much longer than the other two. Is this significant? What effect does the picture have?

The linguistic perspective

Linguistics is very much concerned with all the areas of experience and knowledge of language mentioned previously. It is also concerned with language as a special kind of system that works on its own and in conjunction with other signing and signal systems used by human beings to communicate within their particular society. A distinctive feature of the linguistic perspective is that it makes connections between the wider issues of the previous sections and the much smaller, nitty-gritty elements of a language system, such as the sounds it uses, the use of pronouns, verbs and adverbs, and the 'rules' or conventions that govern conversational styles and the construction of written texts.

The wider issues may be grouped under four headings:

(i)   Language and society (eg language and power; language and gender; language and social class)
(ii) Language acquisition (eg how babies begin to talk; communicative competence; lifelong learning of language skills)
(iii) Language change (eg the origins and development of the English language; reasons for changes in a language)
(iv) Language varieties (eg differences between speech and writing; genres; variation between dialects)

Each of these categories leaks slightly into the others, but that is as it should be given the number of interactions that take place between each of them in everyday life. The acquisition of any aspect of language, for example, will be influenced by social norms, will be affected by changes over time, and will be learned in relation to other varieties of form and **function**.

The fifth category of linguistic knowledge is language as system. This can be broken down into:

- phonology (ie the sound system of the English language)
- **lexis** (ie the wordstock of the English language including all borrowings – the Anglo-Saxons had a nice term for this: the 'wordhoard')
- grammar (the rules, structures and patterns for combining words)
- semantics (how meanings are constructed and communicated, eg the literal and the metaphorical; explicit and implied meanings)
- **discourse** (how texts, spoken or written, are initiated, woven together and concluded; features of **register** and style; text types).

By the end of an A-level course in English language you should be able to approach any texts and data from all of these perspectives and ask yourself, 'What is there here of significance?'

On page 33 is a diagram showing the different linguistic perspectives from which any data or text may be investigated. You will find it helpful to copy this out on a large sheet of paper (A3 size) and fill in each section with your observations. This not only ensures that you investigate systematically, it also provides you with an at-a-glance overview when you have finished, and to which you can add later. Not every perspective will be equally revealing or relevant. Language and society and language variety questions always need to be explored. You can never be sure when language change issues are going to arise in any data or text, while language acquisition is a self-evidently specialised area. All aspects of language as system are applicable to all the data and texts you will encounter, though phonology will obviously yield more in spoken texts. Do bear in mind though, so far as phonology is concerned, that in a written text such as the Shakespeare speech from *Henry V*, the writing is intended for speaking and many effects of poetry need to be heard, if only in the mind's ear.

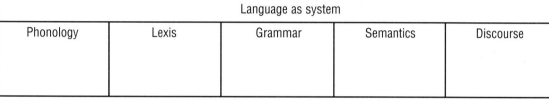

| Language and society | Language acquisition | Language change | Language varieties |

Texts and data

Language as system				
Phonology	Lexis	Grammar	Semantics	Discourse

2 Differences between Speech and Writing

Whatever the IT revolution achieves in the next millennium, it is unlikely to supplant the power of the written word. By written word we do not just mean 'written on paper with a ballpen' but also electronic forms such as e-mail.

Writing has existed for thousands of years and is likely to go on existing for thousands more. The historical journey from cave walls and scratches on slate to word processing is a remarkable one; who knows what the future has in store? Remember though that your own mind is still the original and best word processor; machines can do little without it. Writing, invented long after talk, can be described as the technological means whereby speech, a mere 'mouthful of air', can be recorded and communicated in more permanent form. Walter Ong calls it 'a technologising of the word' (*Orality and Literacy*, 1979).

Writing now exercises an enormous power over our social lives. A prime aim of education is the teaching of reading and writing. Think for a moment about the importance of writing in getting qualifications, proving ownership, getting married, making a legal contract, entertaining people, giving a statement, booking somebody for overparking, buying a house, doing the football pools. Nevertheless, speaking and listening have more than held their own in western culture and neither appears to be dying out.

In this and the next two chapters of the book you will explore different aspects of spoken English. You will not be trained in what used to be called 'elocution', that is, speaking more impressively or more beautifully, but in how to observe interactions between speakers and listeners in everyday, social situations, and how to describe what is going on. The motivation behind all this observing and describing is reaching a better understanding of human thought and behaviour through the medium of possibly humankind's greatest invention, language.

The word 'language' is a particularly **abstract** kind of noun. It can mean something and nothing, anything and everything. The days have gone when the word was used as a verb. The Elizabethans talked of 'languaging' people which meant teaching them a language. A person who knew languages or spoke particularly effectively could have been described as 'well languaged'. Notice, though, how language is thought of here in a passive sense, that is to say, language is something you have done unto you.

In more recent years, and especially in education, it has become more common to talk about language in terms of its actions or behaviours –

speaking, listening, reading and writing. These **words** are all derived from verbs and signify actions rather than abstractions. There's nothing wrong with abstractions as such, but by looking at language in terms of its four modes, which is the term given to speaking, listening, reading and writing, it is made more concrete, more observable, more familiar. The National Curriculum for English, which came into force during the secondary schooling of many, though not all, readers of this book, adopted the four modes, calling them Profile Components.

Speaking and listening

In this section you will investigate two interacting language modes: speaking and listening, Profile Components not only of English in schools but of living language in the world. The approach is essentially that of the natural historian rather than the armchair philosopher: investigate the habitat, identify some creatures getting on with their lives and observe what it is that they do and how they do it.

There is, however, for students of language, an extra dimension to 'listening' and that is the need to listen in a more practised and knowledgeable way to the **structures** of speech and to what is going on beneath the surface.

ACTIVITY

1 Think of two recent days in your life (eg a school/college weekday and a day last weekend). Think carefully through each day from waking until sleeping again and note under four headings (speaking, listening, reading, writing) all your language activities that day. By all means add headings for thinking, dreaming, etc if you wish, since language is used there too.

   Looking at two separate days is better than constructing a typical day in your life because typical days, as such, never actually happen.
2 Compare the two days in your language life. Which mode are you most often engaged in? Which least? More significantly, perhaps, how do the modes interact with each other in your life? Can you talk and listen at the same time? When do you write what you have read?
3 Compare your days with someone else's.
4 Now answer the following questions on the basis of your autobiographical data.
   a Is it possible to make a distinction between formal and informal listening?
   b How 'good' are you as a formal listener

(eg in the classroom), and as an informal listener (eg to a friend's problems)?
   c What is the use of writing during formal listening?
   d When you read 'silently', do you hear voices? (There is no implication here that you might be going mad; it is a straight question even though the voices can only be in your imagination.)
   e Are you ever prompted to write as you read? When? Why?
   f Do your lips move (if ever so slightly) when you read?
   g Do you ever read your writing aloud? When? How often?
   h Are you embarrassed by reading aloud or speaking in class? Why do you think this is?
   i Do you have difficulty getting a word in edgeways?
   j Do you get annoyed when interrupted? Do you interrupt?
   k Do you talk to yourself? Please treat this question seriously!

ACTIVITY

1 Look back on one or two occasions in your life when speaking and listening played a very significant part even if everything went terribly wrong (eg an argument, or a declaration of love). Think of happy, unhappy, difficult and easy times.

2 Now identify some of the things uniquely achieved by speaking and listening and/or some of the problems of spoken communication. Be specific and share your experience with a friend, partner, fellow student. You might begin with, 'The trouble with talk is . . .' or 'The great thing about talk is . . .'.

3 There is likely to be the germ of a good short story in this activity, or a piece of instructional/advisory writing for the shy, or a short radio script on a day in the life of a brilliant listener. If you know the work of Alan Bennett (eg *Talking Heads*), you could try a monologue in his style. A possible title could be, 'Nobody ever listens'.

ACTIVITY

Choose a particular social context or situation and observe carefully the forms and functions of speaking and listening. You can also observe when and where there is recourse to the written word (eg in a lesson; at a meeting). You do not need a tape for this activity; a notebook will be sufficient to record your observations.

You could visit a market stall, a courtroom, a classroom, a play rehearsal, an office, a switchboard, the customers' enquiries desk of a department store, a hospital, a teachers' staffroom(!), the sixth-form common room, a cafe, a sports event, an infants' playground, a day centre for the elderly, a citizens' advice bureau, a public library (is it all 'Silence Please'?).

Observe and note reasons for talking, levels of formality, duration, strength of feeling, relationships, power, turn-taking. In other words: who talked to whom? When? About what? How? Why? What was the listening response?

There is a germ in this activity for a piece of fascinating informative writing on ways in which people talk to each other. It doesn't have to be snoopy and supercilious; it could be a witty, curious, objective, fly-on-the-wall piece of journalism. It could also be the start of an investigative project.

Looking at transcripts

The preliminary activities above have been necessary in order to see speaking and listening in the context of language use as a whole but also to begin the process of observing talk in its own right. As a student of language, you will need to overcome the thousands of years of power, privilege and prestige that writing has enjoyed over the spoken word, whatever the native language, save the small number of languages in the world today that have survived without a writing system.

Of course writing is indispensable, but speech is older, more intimate, more immediate, closer to the ways in which we think and the preferred means of communication of most people in all walks of life. The two are complementary; they do different things in different ways, but equally well. So often however, their equality goes unacknowledged in the popular view. Speech is regarded as inferior to writing, full of errors and imperfections of **accent** and dialect, ungrammatical, inelegant and sometimes offensive.

George Bernard Shaw remarked that an Englishman has only got to open his mouth once for another to be offended.

The situation is not helped by the fact that the very section you are reading is written rather than spoken. It would be an interesting, if inconvenient, experiment if this section of the book were recorded on tape. But if convenience has won the day, don't let it trick you into underestimating the equal powers and qualities of the spoken word. You will need to take especial care with transcripts, a wonderfully convenient way of studying (and examining!) aspects of spoken language. They put the spoken word into writing, tidily and accurately, but in so doing, they leave out much else in the living, literally breathing language. Transcripts are about as true to the life of a conversation as a black and white photograph is to an Impressionist painting by Renoir or Monet.

A transcript is a written version of speech, of a conversation for example, which may use either conventional English spelling plus occasional phonetic spelling (eg 'cos, innit, p'raps), or it may use a set of sound symbols known as the International Phonetic Alphabet (IPA). Most dictionaries refer to IPA in their pronunciation guide.

Most of the time you will encounter conventionally spelt transcripts but do not expect conventional punctuation. Punctuation is a signal system for readers, highway code signs in written texts if you like; it accurately marks off written grammatical units. In speech, grammatical units are signalled in phonological ways, and even the pauses occur in different places for different reasons. In a transcript it is the grammatical units of speech, rather than the grammatical units of writing, which are recorded. 'Phonology' refers to any spoken or audible aspect of a particular language. The term 'phonetic' refers to any human, vocal sound made anywhere in the world whether in a known language or not. Your concern is with the set of sounds that make up the English phonological system and how they communicate meanings.

The following transcript comes from an A-level project completed by an eighteen-year-old student. It is one of a number of informal conversations recorded on a canal holiday and transcribed later.

The transcript has been set out in the way you would find it on an examination paper, with an introductory statement about the context. It consists of one continuous utterance only. The ( ) sign indicates short pauses in the speech while (2) indicates a two-second pause. Note that a capital letter has been used for the pronoun 'I'. It is also permissible to use initial capital letters for any proper names that occur in transcripts.

A girl, aged seventeen, is talking to two friends about a minor mishap steering a cabin cruiser close to a jetty. They are all on family holidays on a canal.

```
     so I er well you know ( ) I sort of swung it round too hard and and
2    oh no before that I hadnt pulled back the throttle ( ) well I
     thought I had ( ) so I was going too fast (2) look theres one
4    just like ours only without this awning thing ( ) I think this
     is the trouble you know you cant see out properly ( ) anyway it
6    bumped and he went mad and he said get off the boat ( ) there
     wasnt any damage ( ) I got it in neutral and it cut out I said I
```

8   was sorry and I picked up all the things (2) but hes just not
    er well Im not his favourite person just at the moment

This is typical of spontaneous thought making its way into immediate speech. It is very fluent compared with other speakers who, in similar situations, might be more at a loss for words. Always remember, when reading a transcript, to ask yourself how you would have performed in a similar situation. Don't speculate on motives; look at what happens in the language. Here are some linguistic features you may have noticed:

- the use of 'so' twice as both an attention getter and a device for ordering one's own thoughts
- the use of 'er' twice as a filler, that is it fills in a pause for thought or uncertainty or both; whatever the reason, it is psychologically useful and so can be called a psycho-linguistic feature of speech
- the use of 'well' twice as a useful adverb for all sorts of reasons, such as emphasising what is coming next; giving yourself time to sort out the next thing you are going to say
- the use of an **exclamation** 'oh', a common feature of speech but much less frequent in writing
- the interruption of logical time sequence by backtracking, 'oh no before that . . .'
- the use of pronouns 'I' and 'you'
- the sudden change of subject (or agenda) in 'look there's another one . . .'
- the use of the adverb 'anyway' to return to the main topic
- the recounting of one conversation inside another one – a frequent feature of this kind of talk
- the pronoun shift at the end of the transcript from 'he' to 'I', reflecting a shift in focus in the speaker's mind
- the use of the ( ) sign by the transcriber to indicate a pause of no more than two seconds
- the use of the (2) sign to indicate a pause of two seconds
- the capitalisation of the pronoun 'I'
- the absence of apostrophes, commas, full stops
- the numbering of every second line to make references easier
- the use of the pronoun 'it' without any need to explain what 'it' is because the listeners already know
- the use of 'and' (repeated once) to maintain continuity
- the use of **elisions**, typical of speech, such as 'I'm, 'can't', 'there's'
- the choice of words that are usually regarded as less formal, such as 'sort of', 'awning thing', 'went mad', 'I got it', 'just at the moment', 'bumped'.

These kinds of detailed observations point to data that is evidence of what real people do in real situations, and show that the route taken by thoughts and feelings toward the spoken word differ considerably from the routes taken toward written forms.

It is also important to note any issues to do with purpose and context. The speech recorded here is part narrative (telling what happened) and part explanation (why it happened). You may want to say that there is an element of excusing, or self-justification, here, but avoid getting on your high horse. Remember, it could be you in a similar situation, talking to your friends. Notice also the sense of deflation at the end and the interesting use of a negative, perhaps to soften 'his' disapproval, 'I'm not his favourite person at the moment', which sounds very much like an understatement.

It is reasonable to assume that the context is supportive gossip. Don't think of gossip as a malicious waste of time; it can be, but most often it is very necessary human behaviour. Call it 'informal talk' if you prefer.

On the evidence of this particular transcript, you can only guess about accent, volume, pace, intonation – all important features of language, but requiring a different kind of transcription if they are to be represented. Similarly you can only made educated guesses about the body language that might have accompanied this speaker's utterances. There is, nevertheless, a great deal that can be observed accurately and knowledgeably.

A transcript is a written record of actual speech and gives insight into the thoughts and circumstances that generated the speech. To apply to it attitudes, habits of mind and perspectives appropriate to writing is to wholly misunderstand not only the purpose of transcripts but the nature and functions of speech itself.

Before looking at conversations in the next chapter, read the following remarks on the previous transcript, all of which have appeared in one form or another on examination papers, making it extremely difficult for the examiner to credit the candidates concerned with any real understanding:

- the speaker doesn't speak in proper sentences
- you shouldn't begin with 'so'
- the speaker hasn't thought it out carefully
- the speaker uses colloquialisms
- the speaker keeps using 'and'
- there are no full stops (!)
- the speaker keeps saying 'er'
- the speaker must be working class because she doesn't use standard English (?)
- it (the transcript ?) uses **slang**.

All these criticisms stem from a prescriptive view of language that flies in the face of nature and common sense. What is meant by proper sentences? Apart from the fact that it is much better to speak of speech units as 'utterances' rather than sentences, where in this transcript is there anything that doesn't effectively convey its meaning grammatically and intelligently? Do you like being criticised for doing such things as beginning with 'so', especially when there is a good reason in speech for doing so? Surely, by definition, colloquialisms are expected features of speech?

One of the functions of talk, especially among friends or sympathetic listeners, is to find out what you think and to reorganise ideas as you go along. What is so fascinating as well as amazing is that it works out so often. When did you last say exactly what you had planned beforehand?

The speaker doesn't in fact 'keep' doing things. There are, for example two uses of 'er'. Not bad, considering the situation. Excessive use of fillers can become tiresome in anybody's speech, but isn't that a question of nervousness rather than incorrectness?

Finally, beware using the pronoun 'it' plus a verb when talking about transcripts. Transcripts don't intend or do anything; they just are.

ACTIVITY

The exercises below are intended as follow-up activities. It is possible to take notes of conversations, but it will be easier, and your transcript will be more accurate, if you have a cassette recorder handy to record phone-ins, DJ chat and discussion programmes, for example. Ideally, it should be capable of making live recordings of people talking. The listening quality need only be tolerable, as long as it is distinct enough for you to be able to copy down what has been said. As you work through these activities and those in the following chapter, you should aim to have recorded and transcribed at least three bits of live talk.

1 Tape record some spontaneous speech, live or from radio/TV. Listen to one speaker and transcribe a fragment that interests you. See how it compares with the features of speech observed so far.
2 Video a discussion programme on TV, and play it back without the sound. Watch a small fragment three or four times making careful note of the body language. Guess what is being said. Again, concentrate on one speaker. Next, listen to see how accurately you have guessed. And then transcribe the fragment.
3 Transcribe an interesting fragment of unscripted radio or TV talk and invent your own system for indicating emphasis on individual words and where there is a gradual rise or fall in pitch.
4 There follows a transcript of part of an interview with Henry Cockburn who played football for Manchester United in the 1940s and 1950s. He is recalling what he was doing when he first heard about the 1958 air crash at Munich in which many Manchester United players were killed. He is obviously moved just by recollecting the events 30 years later. Trace the ways in which his ideas

and emotions express themselves from the evidence of his use of language. Notice, for example, hesitations, repetitions and sudden changes of thought such as 'I had my little car'.

I was – I was in Peterborough at that time – I was playing for Peterborough United – and I had a job as well – that was the first – professional player they'd signed you see – ur – I mean ur – it made headlines down in Peterborough but – the Empire News had it on – on the placards you know – well – I worked for the ur Evening Evening ur Peterborough Advertiser – down there at the Evening Chron – Evening News its called – no – aye – Evening something in Peterborough and I used to make the contents – close out – you know for the – and I used to take them round – I had my little car – great after I'd finished training – and then it came down – the sub editor phoned it down to me – and I was just making things out like – local girl gets married – ur so on and then – man – found stealing and so on and then this phone ring and – anyway there was something happening here – get ur get this down and he used to – tell me what to put down I used to write it – Manchester United – plane crash – many feared dead – and I thought oh dear me – and then it struck me – you know – and then that's how I received it and I had to make these bills out and take them round – and it came through the teletype every so often – who was dead and oh it was-a-shocking.

5 Here is another narrative, this time an imagined one by a ten-year-old boy. The contributions of the adult listening to the story are given in brackets.

A donkey and a giraffe ... came out (uh-huh) And ... the ... giraffe said, 'Hi! Would you like to play with me?' And ... the donkey said, 'No! I'm mad' (uh-huh) And ... she said, 'What happened?' ... and ... the donkey said, 'Well, I made a box to keep my things in.' (uh-huh) 'And I found a penny. And I put it in the blo-box but now I can't find the penny' (uh-huh) ... and ... and ... the giraffe said, 'Well, maybe it's at school! Remember? You took it to school!' And the donkey said, 'How do you know? I think you're the one that took the penny.' (uh-huh) And the gi-giraffe said ... um ... , 'No I didn't.' And ... oh ... she said, 'How do you know?' He said, 'Well ... you know, I remember you took it' (uh-huh) And ... then she thought about it for a while and she s-said ... , 'Well, friends don't steal! I'm sorry I was mad at you! Now let's go play.'

a Track the different things the boy does with language as he tells the story. For example:

'A donkey and a giraffe' identifies the characters; giraffe initiates a conversation with a question/invitation to play; negative response plus personal remark, 'I'm mad'; question, followed by hesitations; note use of 'Well' to begin utterance. And so on.

b What do you learn about young children telling stories from this transcript?

So far you have explored utterances by individuals. Your observations should have given you some insights into the following important concepts:

- thinking aloud (what evidence is there for this in talk?)
- **deictics**, that is making sure the listener knows what, where and to whom the speech is referring (eg 'There was this woman ...'); the unambiguous use of words like 'it', 'this' and 'that'; pronoun references
- pauses, repetitions and the use of fillers
- affective features such as the expression of emotion, doubt, confidence
- establishment of interpersonal relationship (or not, as the case may be)
- the key role of intonation in stating, implying, reinforcing meaning
- four types of utterance (statements, questions, commands, exclamations).

You should also be beginning to ask yourself some statistical questions like:

- How long is an average single utterance?
- How frequent are pauses and fillers?
- How frequent are questions compared with commands, for example?
- How many words a minute do people speak on average?
- What effect do factors like topic, context, situation, relationship and purpose have on statistics like these?

Remember, you can only get statistical impressions, or informed guesses, but these can be useful. Getting a wider view of talk helps to put individual transcripts into perspective. It will make you aware of their limitations, typicality, if any, and how they are usually a mixture of features you have encountered before and features distinctive to a particular kind of talk in a given situation.

Describing and assessing differences between speech and writing

There follows a general mapping out of major differences between speech and writing in the light of the transcripts you have just explored. However, the concepts underlying these differences are so important to your own development as a student of language that you should first of all write down your own version of the differences before reading the one below. Don't think of this as a test; a regular review of what you know about a linguistic topic is a good way of learning more and not merely a stocktaking of what you already know.

Imagine that you are contributing a double-page spread to a particular issue of a colour supplement. The general title is 'You and Your Language' and is aimed at making its readers more aware of speech and writing in their lives.

Use any text strategies you like: parallel lists; speech bubbles/thought bubbles; pictorial effects. Make it as comprehensive and as interesting as you can, and think of the double-page spread as something that could be blown up to poster size.

Produce a first draft from your own ideas and then read the suggestions below, set out under different headings. Add anything you wish, or make changes, to your first draft and then complete your final version.

Differences may be categorised under the linguistic headings introduced in Chapter 1, though there is no need to use the heading 'Varieties' since we are already considering the most significant variation in language use.

Language and society

One distinction drawn by Michael Halliday is between what he calls the 'interpersonal' nature of speech and the 'ideational' nature of writing. He is drawing attention to the close proximity of speakers and their listeners and to the range of other communicative signal systems human beings use in face-to-face, interpersonal contexts; for example, the 400 or so face muscles, all of which combine to communicate an extraordinary range of facial expressions, hand gestures, perceived status, accent, intonation, pronunciation, gender and age. Writing, on the other hand, is disembodied; it exists in the minds of writers and readers who can communicate across thousands of miles and thousands of years. Writing has much more permanence whereas the possibility of recording speech for posterity has only existed for about 100 years. The handy, portable cassette recorder is only about 35 years old.

Accepting the general usefulness of Halliday's distinction, it would nevertheless be too simplistic to see speech as just a physical activity (however important the physicality is) and writing as a purely intellectual activity. A comparison could be made of the different physical/technological aspects of both speech and writing. Unlike speech, writing needs an external technology in order to come into existence. Old English, for example, only came into existence in writing when the early Latin missionaries copied down in manuscript the spoken forms. They did this by adapting an existing piece of technology, namely the Latin alphabet, with the addition of some symbols borrowed from Runic technology and a little bit of invention. Note, too, the essential part played in all this by such inventions as paper, writing implements and inks, and by education and training enabling people (the scribes) to do the job.

Differences between speech and writing can also be observed in cultural terms. Think about four modes of language use: entertainment, information, instruction/advice and persuasion. For each it is possible to draw up parallel lists of different cultural practices and traditions, for example:

	Writing		Speech
Entertainment	novels	theatre	pub tales
	magazines	poetry	gossip
	comics	song	stand-up comedians
Information	letters	TV news	hearsay
	newspapers	radio talks	conferences
			sports commentaries
Persuasion	pamphlets	party	preaching
	posters	political	public debate
	adverts	broadcasts	
Instruction/ advice	manuals	legal	sports coaching
	labels	consultation	counselling

The above are just a few examples of different socio-cultural contexts and purposes for speech and writing. Why do you think some have been placed in between?

Some other very important differences between speech and writing may be discerned in the ways in which speakers and writers perceive their audiences. Getting the **register** or **style** of a piece of writing right depends very much on how well the writer understands the expectations of an audience that is absent and therefore unable to give the kind of feedback speakers expect. It is very welcome sometimes not to be interrupted but the price for that in writing is a high degree of unsupported loneliness and continuous output on the writer's part. You can gauge a listener's response almost instantly, and make adjustments accordingly; readers' responses to texts are much more a long-distance affair.

Language acquisition

In Chapter 5 you will have an opportunity to consider the role of speaking and listening in the language development of young children, but it will not come amiss here to give some thought to differences in the way that speech is acquired compared with reading and writing. How far is it true to say that speech is learned in everyday, pre-school contexts whereas reading and writing (literacy) are explicitly taught by education systems? Look at spelling, for instance, and compare what you have to do to learn English spelling with learning the native pronunciation of words.

Another important question is: what happens to the relative importance of speaking and listening and reading and writing as a child progresses through school? Can you learn to listen for example, or does it just happen?

Language change

Another way of observing differences between speech and writing is to look at the ways in which both have changed over time. It is generally agreed that language changes first occur in the spoken word. Why should this be so? There is also general agreement, though more argument in recent years, that legal writing is the slowest of all to change. Why might this be so? You will need to look at examples.

The 'common tongue' or 'the speech of ordinary men' has been cited by poets, philosophers and novelists as a naturally revolutionary, progressive phenomenon whereas writing has been described as naturally conservative, the preserver of yesterday's thoughts in yesterday's language. How far is it true that the speech of today's 'young generation' is much closer to tomorrow's English than any writing could be? More importantly, how would you collect data by which to investigate the idea? What sort of data would do?

The above points are wider issues concerning differences between speech and writing. You can also take a more detailed look at the systematic aspects of language: lexis, phronology, **grammar**, semantics, **discourse** and **pragmatics**.

Lexis

The term 'colloquialisms' is often used to criticise the use in writing of words and phrases that are more likely to be used in speech. Some examples are:

sort of thing   fancy man
bit of skirt   a nice hows-your-father

and thousands more.

Sometimes the term 'colloquialisms' is applied to speech in a tautologous way, for example, 'there are a lot of colloquialisms in this speech', and this should be avoided.

Differences of lexical choice are very clearly evident between speech and writing, speech tending toward less formal choices, writing tending toward the more formal. Note, though, a slightly grey area in which very informal writing (such as chatty letters) merges with slightly formal speech, as on the telephone. Comparing these two would make a good project.

Phonology

There is much common sense in the view that speech is all phonology and writing all graphology. An interesting focus for exploration however is the difference between intonation and punctuation. They work differently; do they achieve similar or different ends? There is also the question, raised earlier (page 35) about the 'voice' or 'voices' you hear as you read a text or transcript.

Grammar

There are a number of differences between the surface grammatical features of speech and those of writing. Clearly it is the same grammar underlying both, otherwise making and comprehending meanings in both would be very problematical. Nevertheless, the surface grammar of speech is less tidy, less explicit and often communicates very clearly in extremely compressed or implicit ways.

Failure to understand that these surface differences occur for very good reasons leads some people to regard grammar as sub-standard in speech or 'incorrect'. It is rather like telling a gardener who has tended a wild flower meadow that she should have uprooted everything and planted 'garden' flowers in geometrical beds.

Semantics

One extremely significant difference in the ways in which speech and writing construct and communicate meanings is the remarkable degree of implicitness that is possible in speech compared with the degree of explicitness required in writing. This affects both lexical and grammatical choices. So much meaning in speech is implicit in the context, the relationships and even the purpose. Body language too communicates meanings. Making the change from talking about something to putting it in writing is largely a matter of enabling the written word to communicate effectively on your behalf to a reader in your absence.

Discourse

A good, uncomplicated definition of discourse is any continuous stretch of speech or writing longer than a single utterance or sentence. Once a conversation or a piece of writing gets underway there is a sense of continuous movement, despite the fact that ideas and expression may come to a halt or start to fly all over the place. Planning may appear more obvious in writing (as in paragraphs, for example), but spoken discourse too is planned. However, the opportunity to think aloud (to speak in order to find out what you think), while acceptable in speech, is much less acceptable in writing, especially in final draft form.

Examine some of the ways in which continuity is maintained in speech compared with writing. The word 'and', for example, can be used in a variety of effective ways in educated speech, whereas its repetition in writing would seem imprecise and tedious.

Another way of investigating differences between spoken and written discourse is to compare opening strategies for getting attention and closing strategies for taking leave of both audience and topic. Where would you locate the following last words – in speech or in writing? Note also the different degrees of formality, an important discourse feature in both speech and writing.

enough of this idle chatter
Here endeth the lesson
and they lived happily ever after
You may go now
Yours faithfully
Keep this in a safe place
Cheers
Ite missa est
Now switch off the tape and turn to page twenty

Pragmatics

A distinctive feature of conversation is the presence of at least one other person. Sharing, participating, co-operating are things we normally expect in talk. Our general dislike of excessive dominance, reticence, obtuseness and 'deaf ears' indicates how much we expect norms of agreeable collaboration to be observed. An important aspect of pragmatics is understanding the unwritten rules for language interactions. It is always a good idea to look at everyday idioms and phrases for down-to-earth confirmation of linguistic ideas. Look how the following express pragmatic expectations from conversations:

There's got to be give and take.
A full and frank exchange of views.

We didn't see eye to eye but . . .
Let's talk it through.
You haven't listened to a word I have said.
Do you get my meaning?
Now listen to what I have to say.
I can't get a word in edgeways.
Speak now or forever hold your peace.
No, I tell a lie!
Are you listening to what you are saying?
Do you really mean that?
Listen, I'm talking to you.
Hang on! Will you say that again please?
Are we ready to move on?

This list is only the tip of the iceberg and a similar one could be compiled to illustrate pragmatic aspects of more formal kinds of talk. It will not be difficult to identify the contexts of the following examples:

Madame Speaker . . .
. . . my learned counsel . . .
Get undressed please.
. . . anything you say will be written down and may be used . . .
Name, please.
Who giveth this woman . . . ?
Have you anything to declare?

When writing is considered, the pragmatics are much less obvious but no less important for communication. You will occasionally find a direct form of address such as 'gentle reader' in eighteenth- and nineteenth-century novels; you might even come across a file of documents marked, 'For Your Eyes Only'. Generally, however, getting a rapport or an understanding with readers is a more indirect business than it is in speech. For an initial exploration of pragmatic aspects of writing, look at such things as guarantees, hire purchase documents, the new income tax return forms and accompanying booklets, responses to readers' letters in newspapers and magazines. Anywhere, in fact, where the writer has to tread carefully in order not to be misunderstood.

The most popular way of making writing speak more directly is of course to introduce colloquialisms, to use the first- and second-person pronouns, and to think about the listenability of the text. These matters however take us into consideration of the connections between speech and writing, discussed more fully in later chapters.

Speech and writing: some connections

So far, this chapter has concentrated on investigating speech, and to do this it has been necessary to emphasise some important differences in social contexts and psychological awareness between speech and writing. Far from being an inferior form, or a poor relation of writing, speech is the source of the written word, and this final section looks at some of the connections between speech and writing. Not only do we need to consider more obvious connections such as the writing of dialogue in playscripts and novels, the taking down of statements in evidence and the transcriptions in Hansard of parliamentary debates, we need also to look at more subtle influences of speech and writing such as tone of voice, rhetorical strategies and the ways in which writers establish relationships with readers.

Talk is every human being's prime mode of language learning: it is a physical, interpersonal activity; it is close to the ways in which we think; it expresses our personalities as well as our geographical origins; it is used as an indicator of social class and it is a means whereby both intensely private and widely public communications take place.

As a starting point to thinking about connections between speech and writing, consider again some differences from the common sense point of view.

Here is a list of differences between speech and writing as perceived by a class of ten-year-olds in a Cheshire primary school:

with writing you have to make an effort to destroy it;
with speech you have to make an effort to save it

in writing you have to rub out your mistakes;
in speech you just say it again, properly

signing your name is not the same as saying it

writing is a lot slower than speech

writing gives you a headache: speaking gives you a sore throat

you don't need anything to talk but you do to write

people believe it more if it's in writing

it's easier to tell something; writing is hard

you can contact people a long way away with writing;
with speech, they have to be able to hear you

with speech, you can run out of breath;
with writing, you can run out of ink

There is a lot of intuitive wisdom here; no doubt you could compile a list equally as interesting.

The children were also asked to say what sorts of things you can do with the power of speech. At first they were fairly basic in their responses: 'you can telephone, read aloud, sing hymns, talk in class'. But once somebody said, 'you can tell people off', a great flood of ideas came forth, including 'tell jokes', 'swear', 'be rude', 'ask questions', 'frighten people', 'give orders', 'tell lies', 'say nice things', 'hurt people', 'talk to yourself', 'make a speech', 'shout warnings', 'act in a play' and 'read the news on TV'.

ACTIVITY

1 Identify three uses of language that are most usually achieved through speech, such as telling a joke or commentating on a sport.
2 Now think of similar contexts in which writing has to be used instead, such as writing a comedy or writing a newspaper report.
3 What factors does the writer have to take into account that are different from a speaker/listener context?

Some differences you may have noticed in the previous activity can be set out in the following way:

Speaking/Listening	Reading/Writing
shared and known context	have to create context
immediacy	distance and time lag
intonation	punctuation
moving text	static text
body language	entirely in the head
pointing and seeing	imagining
less formal	more formal

ACTIVITY

Look again at the account of the boating incident on pages 37–8 and, based on the transcript, write a letter of apology to the angry owner.

Stick closely to the content of the transcript. Change the order of it by all means but add as little as possible. Concentrate on changing the mode of address to one more suited to a reader who is not present, unlike the audience of friends in the original transcript.

Consider now some of the ways in which speech has considerable influence on different varieties of writing. Even though there are very important differences between them, speech is never far away from writing. Novels, playscripts, even poetry use forms of dialogue, while some philosophical and religious writings are called 'dialogues'. Religious texts, along with many legal texts, would normally be regarded as very formal kinds of writing yet they are frequently designed or required to be read aloud.

When trying to describe a writer's effect on readers, the term 'tone of voice' is used to describe that effect, and experienced writers sometimes tell beginners how important it is that they find their own voice and not write in somebody else's. You may have noticed yourself saying 'It doesn't sound right' rather than 'It doesn't look right' about writing of your own that you are not sure about.

ACTIVITY

There follows a series of texts, all of which have been expressly constructed for written communication yet they use aspects of the spoken word very prominently. Their sources are:

Text A: an advertisement from a 1930s edition of *Good Housekeeping*;

Text B: an informative text from a 1950s comic, *Girl*;

Text C: a Nissan job advertisement that appeared in the early 1990s;

Text D: part of a public information leaflet on Self Assessment, published by the Inland Revenue in 1996.

1 What particular aspect of speech is featured in each text?
2 What is achieved, in each case, by the construction of imaginary conversations? Is there a scenario?
3 Think of, and collect, other examples of this approach to written communication.
4 How do you react to these texts? Are there, for example, any off-putting effects?

Text A

Text B

Text C

IF YE DIVENT TARK WOR LANG-WIDGE, WH'EES GANNA NAR WOT THE CRACK IS?

<u>TRANSLATION:</u>

IF YOU DON'T TALK OUR LANGUAGE, WHO IS GOING TO KNOW ABOUT THE POSITIVE THINGS HAPPENING HERE AT NISSAN?

PRESS/PR PROFESSIONAL

North East   c£25k + benefits + full relocation

We're told that some people can't understand us here in the North East.

Surely not. A passion for football and peas pudding, the most breathtaking coastline in Britain, beautiful countryside and our unique welcome ... what's so difficult to understand about that?

Don't forget too, our talent for making Europe's finest cars – we were Britain's largest exporter of cars in 1993 and have won 3 Queen's Awards for Export Achievement.

To fully appreciate the success of Nissan in the North East, you really need to know the fine traditions of quality and excellence which exist here – especially as the person responsible for determining the best ways of letting the rest of the world know.

So first you'll need to learn the language of both our shop floor and directors (and just about everyone in between). You'll need to gain the confidence of reporters in the local, national and trade press; in radio and on TV; and you'll need the ability to highlight the most positive aspects of our organisation externally and through our own internal publications and communications.

You'll need to be able to arrange press conferences on industry and business matters confidently and efficiently, which means a high degree of organisational and communication ability.

And you'll also know how to handle (or at least hide) the pressure. Because, make no mistake, this is a high profile and extremely critical position which only someone with previous experience in a similar large, blue-chip environment is likely to understand, let alone succeed in.

In return for the positive impact you'll create in the press and in terms of valuable PR, you can expect an attractive salary and benefits package as you'd associate with one of the world's most prestigious and exciting vehicle manufacturers.

So h'away, write or telephone for an application form, quoting reference PR/CON, (returning it by 31st July) to: Ian Fawdon, Personnel Controller, Nissan Motor Manufacturing (Ltd), Washington Road, Tyne & Wear SR5 3NS. 0191 415 2076.

Nissan is an equal opportunity employer.

NISSAN

Text D

Inland Revenue

Self Assessment

Your Statement of Account

*Payments on Account of
Income Tax and Class 4
National Insurance contributions
for the Tax Year 1996-97*

*The Tax Return we sent you in April 1996
enclosed a short leaflet about Self Assessment
and how you can get more information.*

SA351   22851 8.96 Niceday Stationery & Print Limited   CCO896   W2P2367

How is the total figure of payments on account split between 31 January 1997 and 31 July 1997?

For most people, the split closely resembles the system they are used to where

- tax on business/professional profits is usually split between January and July and
- tax on rents and investment income received gross is due in January.

If your relevant 1995-96 assessments were issued before 1 June 1996, this same split will apply to your 1996-97 payments on account.

(For relevant 1995-96 assessments issued on or after 1 June 1996, the payments on account are an equal split of the total tax (and NIC) shown at the bottom of column D in the working sheet in this leaflet.)

A small number of people have certain pensions and employment earnings on which tax is usually paid in two or four instalments each year. The figure of tax for 1995-96 will be split equally between their two payments on account for 1996-97.

Can you claim to reduce your payments on account for 1996-97?

You can claim to reduce your payments on account for 1996-97 if you think they add up to more than your total tax (and NIC) bill will be for 1996-97 (net of tax deducted at source or tax credits on dividends).

First, you need to be satisfied that you know the correct figure of payments for 1996-97, based on the working sheet overleaf. Then you should

- estimate your expected total tax (and NIC) liability for 1996-97

  write the figure here £ [X]

- estimate the amount of tax you expect to pay under PAYE, on SC60's, on investment income or through tax credits on company dividends

  write the figure here £ [Y]

- subtract **Y** from **X**

  write the figure here £ [Z]

*If **Z** is less than the total payments shown on your working sheet you can claim to reduce your payments on account for 1996-97.*

You will be charged interest if your final liability for 1996-97 is more than the reduced payments on account you make.

How to make a claim to reduce payments on account for 1996-97

Enclosed with this leaflet (or available from any Tax Office) is a form SA303. This should be used if you wish to claim to reduce your payments on account. The form gives guidance on how to complete it. When completed, send it back to your Tax Office. You should change the figure on the payslip to match the amount you are claiming you should pay.

What should you do now?

You need to make sure you pay the first instalment on account by 31 January 1997. If you don't or pay too little you will be charged interest.

If you are sending your payment on account through the post, please enclose in one envelope your cheque and the payslip from your statement.

When will the second payment on account for 1996-97 be due?

The second payment on account will be due by 31 July 1997. We will send you a reminder.

How do these payments on account affect the 1996-97 self assessment tax (and NIC) bill?

You will receive a Tax Return for 1996-97 in April 1997.

You should complete this and send it back to your Tax Office by 30 September 1997 if you want us to calculate your tax bill for you. (If you want to do the calculation yourself you have until 31 January 1998 to send it back.)

Your total tax (and NIC) will be based on your completed Tax Return for 1996-97. Your total bill will be reduced by the payments on account you have already made. Any remaining tax (and NIC) will be due by 31 January 1998. For example,

A calculation based on the Tax Return for 1996-97 shows

Tax due	£1,600
Class 4 NIC	£200
Total due	£1,800
Less payments on account	£1,800
Payment due 31 January 1998	nil

How to get help or more information

If you have any questions about your payments on account for 1996-97 or on any other aspect of self assessment, please contact your Tax Office or tax adviser. When phoning your Tax Office please quote your tax reference as shown on your statement of account.

When the Tax Office is closed, you can phone our Helpline on 0645 000444 for general advice. The Helpline is open in the evenings and at weekends. Calls to the Helpline are charged at the local rate.

3 Aspects of Conversation

Y ou are going to look now at transcripts recording conversations between two or more people. Phrases such as 'the meeting of minds', 'interpersonal communication', 'turn taking', 'interaction', 'exchanges', '**pragmatics**' and 'agenda setting' are some of the concepts that you will meet in discussion of the transcripts. They are all to do with the largely intuitive negotiations that go on in quite ordinary conversations. The idea (in chapter 2) of looking first at single utterances was chiefly a strategy for getting started on the description and analysis of talk. All the examples in the previous chapter were taken from longer stretches of conversation involving two or more people, so that each of the speakers was aware of a listener and would be in the process of making constant adjustments and changes of nuance for the benefit of a listener. We do this all the time, unless totally insensitive.

It is easy to take casual, informal conversations for granted, and imagine that there are no rules and regulations for behaviour beyond passing the time of day. Nothing could be further from the truth. The 'rules' in conversation are not prescriptions about how people *should* behave; they are observable regularities in the ways in which people intuitively behave. Quite apart from the necessity of listening and politeness in turn-taking, there are the opening and closing procedures that usually mark the beginnings and ends of conversations (but always bear in mind that a transcript may come from elsewhere in the conversation).

ACTIVITY

1 Over a single day, observe and note down:
a the many ways in which people open a conversation, including specific greetings, body language, questions, **commands**, etc.
b the strategies people use to end conversation (assuming the conversation has not been terminated by interruption).

2 Compare opening and closure strategies with another student's observations. Are there any familiar strategies? Are there some unusual ones? Do any patterns emerge?

Now read the following transcript. Notice the use of italics to indicate emphasis.

A mother and daughter are in conversation at home. They are arguing about the break-up of the daughter's relationship with Peter.

Daughter: and we weren't arguing (.) we shouting and screaming (.) I don't think we were

Mother: I wasn't trying to say you were (.) but he's still moved out (.) didn't *he*

Daughter: *what would you rather have* (.) what would you rather have Peter walking out (.) or me and him shouting and screaming and throwing things at each other

Mother: I'd prefer neither (.) *thank you*

Daughter: I said which one would you prefer

Mother: I wouldn't prefer either of them (.) I'm giving you my answer

Daughter: yeah mum (.) that's a really good answer (.) which one

Mother: *neither*

Do not assume that this transcript records the whole of the conversation. Most likely the transcripts you will work on will be fragments from ongoing conversations. You have, as it were, been given a slice of language life to consider. Here are some observations that you could make.

(i) The daughter's first remark begins with the word 'and' suggesting that she is continuing a train of thought.

(ii) The grammatical **form** 'we shouting and screaming' is non-standard as it appears on the page but is characteristic of the kind of short cuts speakers make when thinking aloud and arguing at the same time; it may have been spoken in a rising tone indicating a question and with a mini pause between 'we' and 'shouting'.

(iii) The daughter appears to be repeating an accusation which she then answers.

(iv) The mother's first utterance also contains a non-standard grammatical **structure**, 'he's still moved out (.) didn't he'. Conventional usage would expect either 'he still moved out didn't he' or 'he's still moved out, hasn't he' to ensure agreement between the verb and its subject. However, how well can you guarantee your own grammatical precision in an emotionally charged argument? Thoughts are often grammatically untidy, however educated or uneducated the thinker.

This particular non-standard form could also be an instance of speech not being able to move as quickly as thought; if it is an error, it is caused by a rapid shift of thought rather than by ignorance of standard forms.

(v) The daughter then asks a question emphatically, repeats it and gives alternative answers; the transcript records her actual pauses though you are likely to have 'read' a pause between the words 'have' and 'Peter'. One of the differences between speech and writing is that writers always put spaces between words (they are expected to) whereas speakers, more often than not, don't pause between individual words. If you do not believe this, listen attentively next time somebody speaks to you. The interesting thing is that listeners have no difficulty understanding the continuum of words and would indeed find rather ponderous, a speaker who *did* pause between every word. It can create the impression that the speaker thinks the listener is deaf, foreign, daft or infantile.

(vi)   The mother replies and gives an emphatic 'thank you' which is not difficult to 'hear' in the imagination; notice how it seems a rather exaggerated politeness. Do you think she is being sarcastic?

(vii)   The daughter demands an answer but the demand is expressed in the form of a statement (I said) plus question (which one...).

(viii) The mother repeats her answer in a slightly different form, asserting also that she is giving the daughter an answer.

(ix)   The daughter's use of the affirmative is spelt phonetically, 'yeah', but don't jump to conclusions about her **accent** and social class for 'yeah' often occurs in educated speech.

(x)   Most readers of the daughter's last remark, if they listen with an inner ear, will detect a vein of sarcasm or exasperation here; by calling the mother's answer 'really good' she actually means the very opposite.

(xi)   The mother's reply is one word spoken emphatically.

The above is one way of tracking some linguistic features of this conversation. Apart from its intrinsic interest as a domestic argument it illustrates all sorts of features you could expect in other kinds of everyday conversation. Despite the fact that it is an argument, the speakers are co-operative: they listen to each other; they take turns; they are polite (the daughter even uses an intimate form of address, 'mum'); they express their points of view in clear, standard spoken English ('me and him' notwithstanding).

ACTIVITY

1   Count the number of words spoken by each participant in the transcript of the argument. Divide the numbers you get by the number of times each speaker speaks, and that will give you what is referred to as the mean length of utterance (MLU). Who speaks most? Is there any significance in this?

2   Utterances usually express a command or request, ask a question, make a statement or exclaim a feeling. Look through the transcript again and list which of these are spoken by the daughter and by the mother. There may be more than one in each utterance.

3   Which confers more power in conversations: speaking most or speaking particular kinds of utterances (eg asking questions)?

4   Who do you think is 'in charge' here? Daughter or mother?

5   Look through the transcript and note all the pronouns. These are the means whereby we address the listener and refer to ourselves and others. What effect does the use of a term of address like 'mum' have?

6   Make a note of the ratio of positive to negative remarks in this conversation. Who uses most negatives? Is there any significance in this?

7   Conversations are said to have a topic or an agenda. Who called the agenda of this fragment? Or are there two agendas?

All everyday conversations have interesting undercurrents and implications that can be discovered by linguistic analysis. The important thing is to recognise which details throw interesting light on the ways humans behave when they talk to each other for whatever reason.

As a conclusion to your investigations of this transcript, look at the following collection of comments made about it by examination candidates. The remarks in brackets indicate the sort of reactions examiners have.

'the two women are obviously working class' (*So what, even if it's true?*)
'they don't use correct grammar' (*Where? What do you mean?*)
'they don't speak in proper sentences' (*Do you? Anyway, what exactly is proper in this context?*)
'typical of women's speech as there is a tag question, "didn't he"' (*On such microscopic evidence you dare to say what is typical!*)
'they don't use standard English' (*Presumably you mean standard spoken English, which is in fact used in at least 95% of this conversation*)
'they speak in dialect' (*Rubbish! How can you know? The only evidence you cite is 'weren't', 'didn't', 'I'd', 'that's', and these are all elisions characteristic of educated speech*)
'you can tell they speak with an accent' (*How do you know? Which one? Welsh? Bedfordshire? Panglish? Anyway, everybody speaks with an accent*)

What is clear from all these remarks is that the candidates have not investigated the language data in the transcript but projected onto it a stereotypical mother and daughter that even the scriptwriter of a soap opera would find hollow and unconvincing. By all means comment on their relationship as evidenced by the data but don't unconsciously construct a life history-cum-character study for them as though you had been reading a playscript instead of a transcript.

ACTIVITY

Work on the following transcript, applying the ideas and methods introduced earlier.

Taken, again, from an A-level project, this transcript records the conversation of a fairground stallholder and a group of boys. He is trying to persuade them to try their luck at a game in which snooker balls have to be accurately aimed at targets. It is actually impossible to win the game.

(SH = stall holder)

SH: you havin' a go boys see what you can nick can I show you this one before you go no money show you this one mate no money we don't charge owt to listen before you go speak to me

Boy A: I might as well how much is it

SH: it's it's a dead easy game mate it's 50p mate you get three shots all you've got to do mate is knock over the golf tee to win get a prize if you lose mate (.) that's it are you havin a go

Boy A: yeh

SH: mate's not havin' a go on as well

Boy B: no

Boy C: got no cash

Boy B: got no dosh

Boy A: can you put it anywhere

SH: anywhere in that D mate

Boy B: chalk yer chalk your thingy mate

SH: yeh chalk the cue first that's it that's the best idea where yer from boys

Boy A: Middlesbrough

SH: Middlesbrough so you just here for the day

Boy A: no we've been playing | football tournament

SH: | you've been playing playing football Lytham St Annes

Boys A,
  B, C: yeh

SH: I see who yer playing today

Boy B: Rad(.) Radcliffe

SH: Radcliffe

Boy C: two Scottish teams

SH: two Scottish teams I see you sure you're not gonna have a try see what you can do

Boy C: I've no money

(*Boy A plays the game*)

Boy A: it's impossible

SH: tell you what I'm gonna do I'm gonna take away that ball make it easy for yer

Boy B: ha ha

SH: oooh missed the idea is to hit the balls listen

I'll tell you what you were rubbish that time if
you have the last go with yer mates if all of
you have a go right three shots for 50p the
one who knocks it down the most out of three
of you I'll give a little cuddly toy too for trying
you wanna do that boys

Boy B: yeh
SH: competition between | the three of yer but all
                            | three of yer
Boy B: | 50p
SH: have to play
Boy A: do I have to still play
SH: you have to play again o.k. so the one who's
        the best gets a cuddly toy
Boy A: did you get that
SH: things I do for some people
Boy B: hold on just giving the change
SH: I see
Boy B: me an my little bank account

Boy C: I'm gonna win
Boy A: I want 50p
Boy B: is it only 50p
SH: it's only 50p
Boy B: erm
Boy C: I'll get ready then
SH: that's for you if I give that I owe
        you | nine pounds
Boy B: | my change
Boy C: well let's pash it
Boy B: nine pounds
Boy C: before one that
SH: I'll have to take it out this who do I owe nine
        pounds fifty to
Boy B: me
SH: here two five six six pounds seven pounds
        fifty eight pounds fifty there's nine pounds fifty

ACTIVITY

The following transcripts record a wide variety
of conversations. Choose one that interests you,
read it and then go through it systematically
observing as many aspects of language use as
you can discover. A good way of sharpening
your observation and analysis of what goes on
in conversations would be to work through all
these transcripts over a period of time.

1 Here is another part of the interview with
   the footballer, Henry Cockburn (see page
   40). This time you have contributions from
   the interviewer, Alex Shorrocks, as well.
   They are discussing how Cockburn came to
   play for Manchester United.
       Notice the use of 'okay' to reassure and to
   get started. Look at the interviewer's
   utterances. What does each one do? There is
   obviously more to interviewing than just
   asking questions. How important, for
   example, are the interviewer's three 'yeahs'?
       Find some examples from Henry
   Cockburn's speech to demonstrate that
   people do not think in straight lines. Note
   also the use of 'anyway'. Don't assume these
   are faults in language use.

AS: okay how you first came to sign for United
     because all the books say is ur – born in
     Ashton-Under-Lyne and then ur joined goslings
HC: that's true

AS: is there anything to add to that
HC: no – I joined gosling you know and ur – at that
     time – there was another player playing as well
     as me that's Jack Crompton
AS: how how what was the age range of the people
     playing in that
HC: oh ur let's see – I should say the average age
     was about twenty-three
AS: yeah yeah – but you'd have been a bit younger
     than that wouldn't you
HC: oh yes I was only about oh whatever –
     nineteenish – you know – yes
AS: yeah and what about the actual incident of
     signing who sort of spotted you
HC: at that particular time – ur – there's one
     occasion – I was ur I had the 'flu
AS: yeah
HC: and one ur – a man had been round a couple of
     times a scout for Blackpool – and ur he wanted
     me to sign for Blackpool – and he came round
     to sign me – one particular – Saturday – Cyril
     Edge he was called Mister Edge – and his son
     played for the second team Lancashire second
     team fast bowler – and ur – I was in bed with
     the 'flu and I ur he said oh well I'll come again
     if he's not very well – in between that – ur Bert
     Whalley who got killed in the era – in the ur
AS: Munich
HC: Munich air crash
AS: yeah
HC: ur came along and asked me would I sign for
     Manchester United – amateur forms which I – I

was quite willing then because it's quite near you see

AS: yeah

HC: so that was ur – that was – I says OK yes – that was it you know

2 In a study of language in her working life, a nurse in an American casualty department recorded this conversation between herself, a doctor and a patient. What motivates the doctor's words? What is different about the nurse's awareness of the patient's needs?

Doctor: you have diabetes ( ) your pancreas metabolism is impaired in ability to manufacture insulin and therefore your digestive processes cannot utilise your intake of glucose

Mr C: (to nurse) what did he say ( ) other than that I have diabetes

Nurse: diabetes results when an organ in your body called the pancreas isn't able to manufacture insulin ( ) without insulin in adequate amounts your body cannot handle all the sugar you eat daily ( ) the doctor plans to supply your body with the insulin it needs so that the sugar you eat will be used up and not wasted

Mr C: so why didn't he say that in the first place

3 Here is another conversation in a medical context. It is a fragment of the ongoing chat among switchboard operators at Bristol Royal Infirmary. Notice how the women each keep two conversations going, the personal one between them and their individual telephone conversations.

Op 1: Good afternoon, Bristol Royal Infirmary. Can I help you?

Op 2: Good afternoon, Bristol Royal Infirmary ... Thank you ...

Op 4: Good afternoon, Bristol Royal Infirmary.

Op 2: ... King Oliver's Cheeseburgers Blues, er, spare ribs ...

Op 3: Yes, but I don't like spare ribs.

Op 1: Good afternoon, Bristol Royal Infirmary. Can I help you? You want Mr Smith's secretary? Hold the line.

Op 4: What did you have last time?

Op 1: I think I had the ribs, spare ribs, I'm not sure, but I didn't like them much.

Op 2: Mississippi Steam Boat Special ... switchboard ... Yeah, what number?

Op 3: Oh, I had ice cream, and everyone was giving me their ice creams.

Op 2: Umm ... and Sally's favourite, her desserts, there's chocolate fudge cake.

Op 1: I didn't like ... I didn't like the pianist. Good afternoon, Bristol Royal Infirmary ... (*emergency phone rings. Op 1 lifts it and listens*)

Op 4: Thank you. Good afternoon, Bristol Royal Infirmary.

Op 1: Cardiac arrest, casualty! Cardiac arrest, casualty!

4 Finally, a transcript of political debate in the House of Commons. The whole of the debate is of course recorded in Hansard but this fragment has been taken from a transcript of a videotape recorded for an A-level project. The exchanges recorded here took place at Prime Minister's Question Time. The Leader of the Opposition, Tony Blair, is challenging the Prime Minister, John Major, about his allegedly changing view on a referendum on Europe.

This is a formal, larger scale kind of talk – almost a performance. Notice that the two politicians are not so obviously speaking to each other but 'addressing' a wider audience, not only in the House but also TV viewers and radio listeners who tune in to broadcasts from Westminster. There's a good deal of politeness; do you also detect wit and possibly sarcasm? Notice the convention of addressing each other through 'Madam Speaker'. What is the purpose of this device? What pronouns are used and what effect do they have?

Blair: Madam Speaker can I say how much I support what he's just said on Northern Ireland (.) now does he recall that last year he said unequivocally that he was against a referendum on Europe a view he repeated again this year yet last night (.) he said that he didn't rule one out (.) now what has changed.

Major: let me say to the right honourable gentleman that I continue to welcome his support on Northern Ireland I think it is a strength to the peace process that it carries the support of honourable members in all parts of the house (.) on the subject of a referendum let me make clear the point I made yesterday (.) there are many people who see the referendum simply as a tactical device (.) I strongly suspect that is true of many honourable members opposite (.) but I do not see it in that fashion (.) I think we do have to consider the constitutional implications of British democracy of er referendums generally (.) there are advantages there are disadvantages (.) what I have said and what my right honourable friend the foreign secretary have said is that we are not prepared to rule one out.

Blair: Madam Speaker isn't it clear that what has changed is not his belief about a referendum but his ability to unite his party without one (.) and isn't that his problem (.) and that of the country (.) isn't that [*Speaker intervenes to restore order*] I see madam speaker that the yobbos are out in force today (.) isn't that his problem (.) isn't that his problem though (.) that whether it's the referendum or v.a.t. or indeed post office privatisation or the rebel whips (.) isn't the problem that the decisions of his government are now taken by a cabinet of crisis managers driven by each day's headlines making or unmaking policy

according to the tyranny of the factions when what his country is crying out for is a government that will serve the national interest.

Major: Perhaps er if the honourable gentleman feels that way about referendums he can explain why he's committed to one as far as Scotland and Wales are concerned (.) perhaps (.) perhaps it's to heal divisions amongst his right honourable (.) and honourable friends (.) as far as the question of country and party is concerned this is er (.) this is a sound-bite the right honourable gentleman has been trailing around from studio to studio over the last day or so (.) let me make it er entirely clear to the right honourable gentleman we will put the country first as we always do (.) in all issues (.) and it is precisely because we have put the country first that we haven't shrunk from difficult decisions that this country is now in a position for the longest and most sustained recovery for all its people that we have seen for very many years.

An alphabet of conversational features

A revision summary for this chapter has been arranged in alphabetical order to avoid giving undue prominence to any single feature. Conversations exhibit a very wide range of **styles**, nuances and linguistic strategies. If you approach analysis with a checklist of 'main features', you need to be careful to identify which ones are most appropriate to the conversation you are investigating. It is an interesting linguistic fact that alphabetical ordering confers neither more nor less importance on each item.

You may find it helpful to turn this revision summary into a practical activity by going through all the transcripts in this chapter to identify an example or two of each item. Some of the terms here are familiar from other contexts, some are more specialised. Remember that it is the concept behind the terminology that matters. If, for example, you have spotted an adverb or calculated a mean length of utterance, you need to decide if this is significant and if it is, explain its effect.

One final piece of advice: avoid saying 'He or she uses an adverb (for example) to persuade the listener that . . .'. The effect of an adverb (such as 'undoubtedly') may well indeed be persuasive but the expression above makes it sound as though a speaker consciously intended it. There is no need to prove intention at every stage. Many effects of language are achieved unintentionally, even accidentally, and are often derived from habits of expression rather than deliberate intention.

Address – the level of formality, intimacy, deference, equality and authority with which people address each other. It usually marks such things as status, role, age, gender, social class, ethnic difference, inclusion or exclusion, for example: 'mum'; 'sir'; 'my good woman' (admittedly old fashioned); 'hey you, mate'; 'pal' (which can be menacing despite its normal meaning); 'Madam Speaker'; 'you lot'; 'Customers for Huddersfield should change at . . .'.

Agenda – the topic, subject of conversation; 'the thing we're on about' or 'what we're on about is . . .'; 'what are you on about?' Agendas are interesting because in every conversation somebody, consciously or unconsciously, has to initiate one and participants have to perceive it and follow it. This does not have to be a formal process, nor will an agenda be fixed and unchanging. Many researchers have drawn attention to the subtle, implied ways in which an agenda is 'negotiated' by participants in a conversation. It is often easier to comply with an agenda than to resist it. The right to remain silent, in recent times questioned by governments wishing to take a hard line on law and order, is nevertheless the strongest legal form of agenda resistance. Any kind of silence is a potential disrupter of conversations. Redirecting, terminating or rejecting an agenda (rather than remaining silent) requires strategy and sometimes 'bottle':

'I think we are barking up the wrong tree'
'I don't wish to discuss this'
'I wondered why you were being so nice!'

Adjacency pairs – believe it or not, people tend to be co-operative in conversations. Adjacency pairs is a term to describe the way in which conversations can be segmented into pairs of exchanges that are connected in some way even though spoken by different speakers. A question, for example, expects an answer. A statement invites a response (such as agreement, modification, disagreement). A command or request expects compliance. **Exclamations** are odd because they are non-interactive. If someone calls out 'Help', it is action not language that is required. If the exclamation is 'ouch', it is likely to elicit a question, 'What's the matter' which in turn starts off an adjacency pair, completed by, for example, 'I've cut my finger'.

The idea of adjacency pairs is interesting because it is a way of understanding two kinds of ebb and flow in a conversation. There is the ebb and flow of cohesion, that is the connection between things said and the way in which things move from one to another through a text, spoken or written. A question/answer format sets up a series of adjacency pairs in a rather rigid framework. If, on the other hand, the person usually answering, turns the tables and asks a question, there is a blip in the adjacency pairs which affects another kind of ebb and flow in conversations, namely the ebb and flow of power. Power doesn't have to be thought of as taking advantage in a menacing, underhand or overbearing way. It is an effect in the grammatical choices, especially in the use of questions and commands. Responding to a question with a question causes a break in any pattern of adjacency pairs, as does replying to a command with a question. Interestingly, exclamations do not seem to assume or confer power.

Some researchers have observed that whilst adjacency pairs are a normal feature of much everyday conversation, they tend to be rounded off by a third element in conversations of unequal power distribution, such as those of doctor/patient, teacher/pupil or parent/child. For example:

Doctor: Are you sleeping well?
Patient: No, not at all.
Doctor: Hmm. That could be the problem.

Teacher: What is the capital of France?
Pupil: Paris, Miss.
Teacher: Good.

Parent: You've been playing in the mud again.
Child: I haven't.
Parent: Don't answer back. And don't tell lies.

Adverbials – these are easy to spot, quite frequent and have a way of affecting everything that follows. Common ones in conversation are 'well', 'so', 'now then', 'right', 'actually', 'really', 'quite', 'rather', 'only', 'just'. They are all little persuaders in one way or another and you are not likely to have any difficulty imagining a tone of voice for each one of them.

Backtracking – interrupting what you are saying in order to introduce information that ought to have come earlier in a logical/chronological sequence. The interesting thing about it is what it tells us about the way in which speakers monitor themselves in order to keep the listener fully informed. Given the spontaneity of much of what we say, backtracking is a clever strategy for instant correction or clarification.

Co-operative signals – the very act of not remaining silent is itself a sign of co-operation, but there are other explicit verbal signals, such as 'yes', 'yeah', 'okay', 'I see', 'carry on', 'I'm listening', 'then what', 'mmm'. Short responses by listeners should not be overlooked, for example: 'Get away!'; 'Fancy that!'; 'Tell me more'; 'Well, I never!'; 'Gosh!'.

Disagreement – in the top 20 words most frequently used in English conversations you will find the word 'yes' at number 12. The word 'no' doesn't appear at all. A frequent strategy however for introducing disagreement is the phrase 'Yes, but . . .'. It is interesting that the word 'but' appears at number 15 in the statistical frequency table. The word 'but' is sometimes referred to as an 'adversative' because it introduces contrast ('however' works in a similar way).

You will observe in conversation a wide spectrum of disagreement strategies ranging from the unequivocal 'no' to mild suggestion. Notice too the ways in which any negatives are used, particularly in responses, such as 'not exactly' or 'I wouldn't say that'.

Humour – something that is fascinating to study in linguistic terms but difficult to classify. Its presence, intentionally or not, can completely undermine a conversation or any kind of talking. Don't overlook it or underestimate its significance.

Implicatures – these are implied meanings, which happen all the time in conversation. It is usually the context that ensures that the implied meaning is understood. If you were in a hurry and a friend called out, 'Look, there's a bus', you would understand it to mean 'Quick, let's catch it' and would not reply, 'Oh yes, so there is. What a lovely colour!' Everyone knows that 'What's yours?' means 'I'm paying', and that 'Don't you find it hot in here?' means 'I wonder if the windows can be opened'. Much humour is created by ignoring the conventional implication. Observers can easily mistake insults between friends to be offensive rather than affectionate. But perhaps friendly insults are an implicit way of discharging a touch of enmity. Why do good friends enjoy insulting each other?

The frequency with which implicatures occur and the predictability with which they are correctly understood is further evidence of the deep-seated co-operativeness in human conversation. One certain way to be annoying is to not pick up implied meanings that are clearly intended. Sadly, people with mental and social handicaps have difficulty with implied meanings as do second language learners unfamiliar with everyday idioms.

Monitoring talk – something that goes on all the time. It is a way of checking your own communicativeness ('Do you see what I mean?' or 'I'll say that again'), commenting on somebody else's speech ('You didn't say that earlier') and reviewing the conversation at any given point ('We're getting nowhere' or 'We've been over this before').

People who speak at any length, but spontaneously, may be observed at some point to insert a monitoring remark such as 'I think I've already mentioned . . .' or 'I'm going to move on now.'

Simultaneous speech – tolerable and even stimulating if infrequent, progressively less tolerable as it becomes more frequent. It is a normal part of conversation and often causes pleasure and satisfaction when two people say the same thing at once. Usually it occurs in the form of overlap. Do not assume it is a deficiency in language use, for whilst it appears to be impatience in turn-taking, it can indicate very co-operative and engaged talking between participants. Self-monitoring usually comes into operation to ensure that the talk is co-operative, and in conventional social behaviour there are acceptable styles and rates of interruption. It is very easy when transcribing to misrepresent simultaneous speech since it is a little bit more complicated to set out on the page. If it is tidied up for the reader's convenience, it means that the transcript is less true to the living language. See page 58 for one method of transcribing simultaneous speech.

Tag questions – familiar questions, sometimes rhetorical, that occur at the end of statements (or **declaratives**, another name for statements). Common forms are '. . . isn't it?' '. . . aren't they?' '. . . don't you?' and '. . . wasn't she?' You need to consider what they do to the preceding statement.

For many years tag questions have been regarded by snobs as signs of working-class deference or truculence (take your pick). In the 1970s they were observed as frequent in female speech and indicative of uncertainty and apology. In the late 1980s they were interpreted as co-operative strategies inviting response and giving the listener the last word.

Consequently, if tag questions do appear more frequently in female speech, it is an indication that females are not hesitant, weaker talkers, but confident and co-operative.

Whatever the gender or class issues here, observe the use of tag questions by anybody and note whether a 'yes' or a 'no' is expected. Almost always they are rhetorical questions containing a preferred response.

Uncompleted sentences – frequently observable in real-life conversations. What makes a TV soap-opera script, however good, so different from real life is the absence of simultaneous speech and uncompleted sentences. On the rare occasions on which they do occur in soap-opera scripts or plays, it is for very calculated effect. A good scriptwriter knows how to leave the actors room to breathe life into dialogue.

Again, it is very easy to assume that uncompleted sentences are yet another imperfection in language use to be regretted. To the natural historian of language use, uncompleted sentences are what happen. To regard them as imperfect is to regard trial and error and being spontaneous as imperfect ways of living when in fact they are a necessary condition of living. They indicate all sorts of things: that the mind is alive and quick, that the listener is trusted as an accomplice in the conversation, even that there is genuineness in what the speaker is saying. People who are close to each other – lovers, friends, colleagues, family – do not need to complete everything they say because their listeners are finishing it off in their own minds.

Uncompleted sentences are frequently a sign of very fluent and co-operative talk. Remember the popular saying, 'I'm way ahead of you'. However, like everything else (simultaneous speaking, for example), they can prevent understanding if excessive. They may indicate a highly anxious or emotional state that needs calming or incoherent thinking that needs to be quiet for a while. The truth of the matter is that there is a great deal of mutual regulation in language use that allows for implication, ambiguity, trial and error and idiosyncratic variations of all kinds before exercising control.

4 The Spoken Word: Phonology and Accent

One of the sciences of language is phonetics – the study of sounds produced by the human voice. Articulatory phonetics is concerned with how speech sounds are produced, auditory phonetics with how we hear those sounds. Human voices all over the world collectively produce many sounds and any voice can potentially produce every one of these sounds, though some may require practice if they are very unfamiliar.

Phonology is the study of the set of sounds that work together to form the sound system of a language. This sound system will be a selection from the world-wide repertoire, though it is likely to share quite a number of individual sounds with all other languages. A term used to describe these individual speech sounds is 'phoneme' which means a unit of sound that conveys specific meaning. The **words** 'pat', 'hat', 'mat', 'rat', 'fat', 'cat' and 'sat' differ from each other by only the initial phoneme but that difference constitutes a fundamental difference in the meanings of the words. In the words 'bait', 'bat' and 'but' it is the middle phoneme that alters the meaning, and in 'bell', 'bet' and 'bed' it is the final phoneme. Notice that the words 'eat' and 'oat' seem to follow the pattern but this is only a spelling, not a phonological feature. The pronunciation of these words requires a completely different vowel sound.

ACTIVITY

1 Make a list of ten words which are the same apart from a sound change in the *initial* position.
2 Make a list of ten words in which the sound change is *median* (in the middle), such as 'been', 'bin', 'ban', 'Ben', 'bone'. Do not be misled by spellings that don't match; just listen to how many sounds you can hear.
3 Make a list of ten words in which the sound change is made in the *final* position, for example, 'cod', 'con', 'cop', 'cot', 'cog', 'cob', 'cough' (again, don't be misled by the spelling).

In each list, any two words should make a minimal pair.

The International Phonetic Alphabet (IPA)

British English phonology consists of 44 phonemes, 20 of which are vowel sounds. With only five vowel symbols in the English alphabet, phoneticians use the International Phonetic Alphabet in order to represent sounds more accurately. This is given below along with examples of each sound in English words. The small 'r' symbol indicates vowels that are known as 'r' controlled, that is they blend with an 'r' sound. The slanting lines are traditionally used to indicate a phoneme – a sound unit that has a distinct meaning.

The consonant sounds of English are:

/p/	as in *part*	/f/	as in *food*	/h/	as in *has*
/b/	as in *but*	/v/	as in *voice*	/m/	as in *mat*
/t/	as in *too*	/θ/	as in *thing*	/n/	as in *not*
/d/	as in *did*	/ð/	as in *this*	/ŋ/	as in *long*
/k/	as in *kiss*	/s/	as in *see*	/l/	as in *let*
/g/	as in *get*	/z/	as in *zoo*	/r/	as in *red*
/tʃ/	as in *chin*	/ʃ/	as in *she*	/j/	as in *yes*
/dʒ/	as in *joke*	/ʒ/	as in *measure*	/w/	as in *will*

The vowel sounds of English are:

(long vowels)		(short vowels)		(diphthongs)	
/iː/	as in *each*	/ɪ/	as in *it*	/eɪ/	as in *day*
/ɑː(r)/	as in *car*	/e/	as in *then*	/aɪ/	as in *by*
/ɔː(r)/	as in *more*	/æ/	as in *back*	/ɔɪ/	as in *boy*
/uː/	as in *too*	/ʌ/	as in *much*	/əʊ/	as in *no*
/ɜː(r)/	as in *word*	/ɒ/	as in *not*	/aʊ/	as in *now*
		/ʊ/	as in *put*	/ɪə(r)/	as in *near*
		/ə/	as in *again*	/eə(r)/	as in *there*
				/ʊə(r)/	as in *truer*

ACTIVITY

You do not need to learn IPA by heart but it is quite easy to use. Make a list of any ten English words and write IPA versions for each word alongside their alphabetical spelling. You will need to listen to the word to get it right. Then exchange lists with another student and check the transcription. Are there any words you pronounce differently, leading to a different transcription?

Received Pronunciation

Remember that the only right answer to the previous activity is a transcription of how the word is spoken, so it will be possible for there to be two IPA versions if there are two transcribers relying on their own pronunciations. The notion of Received Pronunciation (RP) exists to define an agreed, non-regional or non-idiosyncratic pronunciation that would, for example, be taught to people learning English as a second language. If you differ in one or two pronunciations of a vowel sound, for example, or by the omission of a consonant, you should be able to agree on what the RP version would be, even though you may not use it yourself.

Received Pronunciation is not another name for phonemes, it just refers to a standard way of pronouncing them. Phonemes themselves can withstand wide variations in pronunciation before they become completely incomprehensible. The varied, individual and regional pronunciations with which people say their phonemes are called **allophones**. Allophones are the realities people speak and hear, while phonemes are a kind of recognition chart that exists in the mind.

Intonation

If human speech consisted of strings of phonemes spoken with equal emphasis, it would sound like the electronic voice of a robot. It has already been observed that the moment you get two people speaking the same language there will be some allophonic variation. More significant still, are variations in intonation. Intonation refers to the rhythm, the tunes, the musicality in people's voices. All these are features of language that put individual sounds into patterns of sound (the ups and downs, if you like) which are usually more noticeable than even whole words. In Britain, Welsh is popularly cited as the most musical of **accents**, yet all regional accents have tunes in them. A voice is like an instrument; it *intones* the language in ways that express emotion, energy and other personal characteristics.

Intonation patterns in English can be broadly grouped into rising tones (as when asking questions), falling tones (as when emphasising a statement) and rising-falling tones (up and down) that communicate a wide variety of meanings and help to create the unique voice pattern, the voice music of every individual. One amusing but reasonably accurate way of representing phonology is to record it in such a way that the line of writing shows the intonation. Here is an example:

Jack: I'll put the kettle on, you lay the table.

Sally: Shall I make some toast?

Jack: If you can manage not to burn it.

Sally: DON'T be sarcastic.

1 In pairs, invent a short dialogue in which a man and a woman are having a heated discussion.
2 Now working on your own, show the intonation using the method above. Indicate changes in volume by using capitals for loud words.
3 Compare your version with your partner.

Issues of dialect and accent

In the chapters on speech and writing and on conversation, speech has been explored in terms of its purposes, contexts, **grammar**, vocabulary and **style**. Occasionally reference has been made to specific phonological concepts such as intonation, stress and fillers, all easily identifiable vocal features of conversations. So far in this chapter we have concentrated on the idea of human voice, a unique characteristic of the species. The remarkable thing is the sheer variety of individuality (**idiolect**) that can be expressed in a sound system of only 44 units spoken by several million people all over the world. Frequently the remarkable persistence of this uniqueness, these millions of uniquenesses, is overlooked in a social preoccupation with dialects and a political preoccupation with standardisation. And whenever the notion of dialect occurs in popular contexts, the topic of accent is sure to follow. Indeed, many people use the terms 'accent' and 'dialect' to mean one and the same thing, which they are not.

Dialect is a term describing consistent variations within a language. Dialects can be social, occupational, cultural, technological and geographical, for example. The variation will show itself in alternative vocabulary, grammatical deviation and in accent. Accent refers to spoken features of a dialect, and that is all it refers to. Accent can refer to variations in the way non-native speakers pronounce English, and it can also refer to variations spoken by individuals. To 'accent' a word or phrase, for example, is to give it emphasis.

Almost invariably, the words 'accent and dialect' occur together in that order. Strictly speaking, if they are to be used together, it should be 'dialect and accent' since the accent is a part of dialect. It makes perfect sense to talk of 'vocabulary and dialect' and 'grammar and dialect' but they do not come to mind as readily in everyday discussion.

For centuries accents have been a 'problem' in English social attitudes. Shared accent is a source of community feeling, familiarity, bonding, togetherness; an unfamiliar accent signals difference, distance, foreignness, strangers, and the possibility of misunderstanding. Foreignness, so far as accent is concerned, need only be a few miles away: 'You're not from round these parts, are you?'

1 Working with one or more partners, write down as many words as you can think of that are used to describe accents, for example: 'broad', 'funny', 'country'. Make sure your list is a long one; at least a dozen items.

2 Sort the words in your list into three groups:
   (i) derogatory expressions
   (ii) expressions of pleasure or admiration
   (iii) neutral terms meant to signify the region only.
   Which is the longest list?

3 Discuss people's attitudes toward other people's accents. What kinds of stereotypes have you noticed? Why do you think accents give rise to prejudice?

Accents and soap operas ·

An important ingredient in naturalistic fiction is a strong sense of locality and community. Novelists, for example, often resort to phonetic spelling to convey a particular feature of pronunciation. But having an ear for the intonation patterns is what matters most, and will show itself in the dialogue. In TV soap operas the writers and the actors are immersed in accent; some actors will have an authentic regional voice, others will speak an exaggerated authentic version, while yet others will speak a mimic version hardly distinguishable from the authentic if they are good mimics. *The Archers* is a well-known radio soap, and the long line of TV soaps includes *Coronation Street*, *Emmerdale*, *Brookside* and *EastEnders*. In addition, accents of Australian English are becoming well known and varieties of American English accents have become familiar through decades of Hollywood films.

In this activity you are going to investigate some aspects of a regional accent (British or abroad) as represented in an episode of a soap opera.

1 Choose your programme and video an episode.

2 Focus on a particular character and listen on playback to the way he/she speaks, noticing any features that you think are characteristic of a region. Use your basic knowledge of English phonology to help you identify just what it is that signifies 'regional accent'. It may be a consonant pronunciation, a vowel pronunciation or it may be a combination of these over a series of words (intonation).

3 Transcribe the examples as accurately as you can. Use IPA symbols to show a distinctive vowel pronunciation; use an apostrophe to indicate a missing sound (such as the glottal stop eg the pronunciation of the word 'butter' as 'bu'er'); underline stressed words or syllables; use an ascending line above the words to indicate a rising tone, a descending line to indicate a falling tone. If there are other features, invent your own symbols but ensure that a reader would be able to understand them.

4 When you have investigated one or two speeches from one character, turn to another who shares the accent and see if you can identify what it is they have in common. If your second subject is a person of different age, gender or status, see if that makes any difference to the accents. Is it more or less pronounced? gentler? harder?

5 Set out the report of your investigation as follows:

   ■ title: 'Some notes on regional accent in (name of soap opera)'
   ■ characters studied: (names)
   ■ character A: (some features transcribed)
   ■ character B: (some features transcribed)

- observations on the regional accent from the evidence above
- reservations, qualifications, additional factors of relevance.

(You will need to listen to the segments you are transcribing three or four times at least. If you have the facility for copying the sound of a video recording onto an audio cassette, this will make replaying very convenient.)

During the course of the last activity you will have become increasingly aware of ways in which scripted talk is very different from spontaneous talk. There are many ways in which good scriptwriters and actors can sustain the illusion of everyday naturalness, but ultimately the talk is not natural. It is too tidy for one thing, and nobody is ever stuck for what to say next. One very important aspect of real-life conversation is the spontaneous, 'real-time' speech planning that goes on in people's minds and which shows in their faces, their non-fluency and in the ebb and flow of tensions during a conversation. In scripted talk interactions are, if you like, directed or stage managed, however well done. Accents are exaggerated for effect, to highlight or emphasise character, and characters are impossibly fluent.

You are likely to have found that other factors of characterisation are related to the degree and kind of regional accent spoken by a particular character in a soap. Even though your examples were spoken by characters and not real people, issues of gender, social status, age and level of education will have been at work in the minds of the writers. These issues, in real-life talk, all contribute to an individual's identity and nowhere is that identity more evident than in the voice.

Voice

This chapter ends with an activity that focuses on the concept of voice rather than accent. Human voices are personal; they express much more than regional origin, socio-economic status, gender, age and education. It is true that personality can be heavily overlain by one or more of these factors, especially in public contexts, but just consider some of the additional factors that can figure strongly in a person's intonation and voice qualities. Habitual factors might include:

a tone of authority
hesitation, diffidence
very precise enunciation
a tendency to laugh and speak at the same time
surliness.

Occasional factors might include:

a thinking-aloud tone
excitement
weariness
telling a lie
wheedling.

All these factors can be 'heard' or detected as signals in the voice. They can be described objectively, measured even, in terms of volume, pitch, pace, breathiness and other phonetic characteristics.

A person's individual voice consists of many factors such as these, as well as accent. In addition, the anatomical and physiological characteristics of breathing and vocal equipment with which that person was born should also be taken into account.

When the term *accent* is used, a person's speech is usually being considered in relation to a group or groups; when the term *voice* is being used, the considerations are usually about individuality. The life history of a person's voice, or a voice profile at any given time will consist of all these factors.

Building a voice profile

ACTIVITY

1 Choose a person you know – a friend or relative – and ask him or her to agree to be interviewed. Do not say that you are investigating the voice characteristics of an English speaker because this will inevitably raise your subject's level of self-consciousness which in turn will affect voice production. Choose a particular topic that you think will interest your subject and stimulate a conversation with some questions handy to keep it going. Don't rely solely on questions; try to get as much spontaneous talk as possible. Tape-record the conversation but be prepared to try again until you get a satisfactory recording. You will need about five minutes of continuous talk to be able to pay close attention to intonation but the five minutes may not occur until the conversation has warmed up.

2 Listen to the recording and make notes on phonological features as you hear them. You will need to listen two or three times. Don't attempt to transcribe everything at this stage. Concentrate on your listening.

   a Identify two or three accent features in your subject's speech that are typical of a region or locality. If your subject's first language originated in another part of the world, make it clear where.

      Listen to the vowels and the intonation. Sometimes a dialect word or phrase may be used but concentrate on the pronunciation.

   b Now identify features in your subject's speech that seem to you characteristic of your subject as a person rather than as a member of a particular community. Don't approach your data in a negative way, such as 'She says that wrong' or 'She is always saying 'erm''. Instead listen in a positive, objective way and describe what you hear. Features to note might include:

- pitch, pace, warmth, hard/softness, volume
- the range of variations (such as a habit of dropping the voice when being confidential)
- the frequency and type of non-speech sounds such as laughter, fillers, sighs, exclamatory sounds
- the breathing
- where the voice appears to be produced (for example, forward or backward of the mouth, throaty, chesty or deeper still)
- any consonants which are pronounced 'unusually'
- any vowels which are pronounced in idiosyncratic ways.

3 Discuss what you have investigated with another student and compare findings. From your combined observations write a brief

account of the many things that contribute to an individual human voice. Do not rely solely on the profile you have constructed; consider too, such influences as local accent, other languages, age, gender, 'social class', physique, occupation, education, 'lifestyle' and temperament.

5 Language Acquisition for Life

The term 'language acquisition' is sometimes used to describe a process or aptitude that distinguishes humans from all other creatures. This is in itself a fascinating area of study but though relevant to A-level English Language studies, it cannot be central to a syllabus because it would require extensive study of animal behaviour and of the psychology of perception and thought processes.

However, one activity that will be useful to your linguistic understanding is to explore the vocabulary we use when talking about the differences and similarities between animal and human communication. Whilst humans communicate a great deal through sight, sounds, smells, touch and gesture, it is important to understand just what makes **words** different from body language.

ACTIVITY

Below are two sets of words: one consisting of terms used to describe animal communication, the other to describe human language. Look up in a dictionary any words you are not entirely sure about.

Animal communication depends upon perception by one or other of the senses, ie animal communication consists of *percepts*. Percepts are signals, apparently innate, such as warnings, mating calls, mother/offspring recognition. Animal communicators have to be in the same perceptual field, that is, they are context bound (even though whales can transmit signals over great distances). Animal communication depends upon directly physical means of production and reception. It is **concrete**.

Human language depends upon *concepts*, ie the signals of human language have symbolic meaning. Concepts are words, abstraction, intellectual. They are quite arbitrary, ie the sounds and the alphabetical letters for the word 'cat' have no logical or biological connection whatever with the actual animal. Human language is not always subject to immediate context. A wide variety of indirect means are used to communicate via human language (writing is the supreme example).

1 Write down some examples of animal communication that illustrate the nature of animal communication. Do the same for human language.
2 Write a brief account explaining differences between animal communication and human language. Illustrate the things we share with other animals (signals and perception) and the things that make a big difference (symbols and concepts).

It is clear that in their strategies for communicating, humans share quite a lot with other animals. The zoologist, Desmond Morris, goes so far as to learning. Your idiolect in its spoken form may not change a great deal after your student years, though it is very observable how much a person's idiolect changes between the start and the end of those years. Inside your head however there is limitless room for language (and languages) of all kinds.

ACTIVITY

Remind yourself of the account of Catherine's language development (pages 76–78) and then think about a later stage of development in your own language experience. It may be as recent as now or a little while ago. It may have to do with learning new terminology, or writing differently, or reading a difficult text. It may be about a stage in speaking/listening development. It need not be especially problematical but look at it from the point of view of what it teaches about a stage in mature language development.

Write about your recollections in the third person and in a positive way that illustrates what people go through as they acquire new language abilities.

If you write about a particular problem such as misspelling, look at difficulties in the language itself and not just at individual failure. Write for a reader interested in human behaviour and make your account as vivid and accessible as the one by Eurfron Gwynne Jones.

Further reading

Some books you should consult for detailed accounts of different aspects of language acquisition are:

Listen To Your Child, D. Crystal (Penguin, 1990)
Early Language, P. A. and J. G. de Villiers (Fontana, 1979)
The Articulate Mammal, J. Aitchison (OUP, 1989)
A Child's Learning of English, P. Fletcher (Blackwell, 1985).

6 Grammar in Action

Many readers are likely to grit their teeth at mention of the word 'grammar'. It is almost a national anxiety, along with misspelling and self-consciousness about regional **accent**. All three provide very good opportunities for gaining a little power, influence or status over those less confident about the effectiveness and value of their own use of language.

This chapter is concerned with grammar as a feature of language that can be investigated in useful and illuminating ways. Put to one side habits and attitudes, and approach grammar in a positive rather than a negative spirit. After all, you are already an intuitive expert in grammar or you wouldn't be capable of studying an A-level course. Always remember that students who regard themselves as very poor spellers will find, on looking through the last 100 words they have written in any essay, that at least 95 per cent have in fact been spelt correctly. This is not an excuse but an observable fact that puts a different light on spelling problems. The same is true of grammar. You may be embarrassed by an occasional use of a non-standard **form** of grammar in your writing when it is pointed out to you: for example, 'we was', 'I like fish and chip's' or 'She must of...' (though it is arguable whether this is a grammatical or a spelling error). The existence of one non-standard form does not cancel out the effectiveness of the remaining 99 per cent of your written standard English.

Grammar is an ingredient that makes a powerful contribution to the meanings of the words we casserole together into sentences, paragraphs, whole essays, stories and examination answers. You cannot see grammar as obviously as you can see the words, hear the phonology and know the word meanings. The two clearest indications that grammar is doing its work inside a sentence, as it were, are punctuation and word endings. The rest lies in the rhythm of the sentence, word order and **function**.

ACTIVITY

1 Find a novel. T
continuous pri
count the num
the number of
an average leng
in the book and
give you sometl
whole book. If
average for the
more reliable.

2 Compare your
students. Are th
What factors co
variations? Thir
author, the peri
the novel, and t
adults/children)

3 Compare the se
short stories. Do
sentences than l

4 Now look at a r
you like. Calcul
length and com
of other student

5 During the cou
you will have no
and some unusu
with the norm.
poster, particula
how much punc
sentence. Do yo
between length a

ACTIVITY

Identify features of punctuation and word ending in the following sentences and describe the grammatical job they are doing.
The first one has been done for you.

1 The students demanded shorter lectures, better food, longer vacations and higher marks for their essays.

(Sentence clearly marked by initial capital letter and full stop; two commas used to separate items in a list; plural 's' used five times; final '-ed' signifies past tense; final '-er' indicates comparative form of four adjectives.)

2 It's a long way to Tipperary; it's a long way to go.

3 Will there be a
  degree?
4 Go directly to j
  £200.
5 Ah!
6 To err is huma
7 'Let's all go for
8 brown's chased
  garden mrs

Focusing o

Getting an idea of sentence length does not add up to much as an end in itself but it is a way of taking a first objective, structural look at sentences and it will lead to noticing other, more important structural features. Long sentences, as such, are not necessarily good ones. They may be grammatically correct in detail but convoluted in overall effect. On the other hand, a long sentence contrasted with a short one may be very effective.

It should not take long for you to be able to notice automatically the norms and variations in sentence length. Sometimes it may be of no significance whatever, but if it does prove significant later on, you will have noticed it.

Once you have got an idea of your own 'sentence breathing rate', you could investigate whether you have habitual ways of starting sentences (look at the first three words). These words have considerable structural significance since they will determine to a large extent the overall shape of the sentence. Once you have written the first two words even, you are committed to a grammatical flight path.

ACTIVITY

Look at the following sentence openings and complete each one in three ways. When you have done this, look at the ways in which the first three words guided your construction.

1 Having tried for ...
2 Although I am ...
3 To open the ...

Reading the grammar of a specific text: 'The Dead Pigeon'

Reading the grammar of a text is an addition to your repertoire of reading strategies. You are not looking for errors but to find out how the ideas in a text are woven together and expressed to the reader. Looking at the grammar as part of a stylistic investigation will tell you, not just about language, but also about humans and the society they live in.

In the following series of activities you will make a grammatical journey through a text written by a ten-year-old. It is a personal narrative, using exactly the same grammatical resources available to an adult, professional writer. The **style** may be immature, but the grammar is perfectly competent, though you may wish to query two items. Later, you will have an opportunity to compare it with the grammar of a text written by an A-level student in answer to an examination question.

The first piece is called 'The Dead Pigeon'. Every word is as Lesley wrote it, though some spellings have been corrected and punctuation added. The title and the sequence of grammatical structures are entirely her intuitive choices.

The Dead Pigeon

Today, at afternoon play, just when we were coming back into school, Mrs B. found a pigeon on the floor, next to the Haygreen Lane side. Some children had gone in but I was there when Gary Destains said,

'Hey up! There's a pigeon on floor.'

We all rushed up but Mrs B. shouted,

'Stop. Come back and let me look what's happened to it, poor thing.' I just thought it was resting a bit but Dobbie said, 'It's dead'.

It was. When Mrs B. picked it up, its neck just flopped over.

'Poor thing,' I said to Dobbie.

She lifted it up with its wings, and they were like big, lovely grey fans. I didn't know wings were so lovely and big, with so many feathers especially.

When we had gone in, we were just sitting in our class and telling Mrs Sanderson and the others about it, when Mrs B. came and held it up with its lovely grey wings. I was sorry for it, poor thing, and Mrs Sanderson was sad. And we all were.

ACTIVITY

1 Count the number of words in 'The Dead Pigeon' and divide that number by the number of sentences.

You will now have a statistic for the average length of Lesley's sentences. Notice though that her longest one is 34 words and her shortest, two words.

2 **a** How do you think this average would compare with that for other ten-year-olds, or younger children?

b How does this average compare with the average length of your own sentences?

c Does the kind of writing make a difference?

d What makes some sentences longer than others?

Sentence openings

There is a tendency in English for the phonological stress and the burden of meaning to fall at the ends of sentences. It is nevertheless instructive to observe the first three words in a sentence because of the influence they have on the overall grammatical structure. An obvious example of this is the way in which verbs tend to appear at the beginning of command sentences, as in recipes ('Take two eggs...').

ACTIVITY

1 Read the text again and write down, in the form of a list, the first three words of each sentence, as follows:

Today, at afternoon ...

Some children had ...

2 What sorts of different ways are there of beginning sentences? Compare the beginnings of any two of Lesley's sentences.

3 Look back at a piece of writing of your own and note some grammatical choices you intuitively made at the beginnings of sentences.

Subject and verb structure

You can now begin to look more closely at structures within the individual sentences of the text.

Below are listed the key structural elements of each sentence in the order that they occur. Three, however, have been deliberately omitted to see if you can recognise them for yourself:

... we were coming back ...
... Mrs B. found ...
Some children had gone in ...
... I was there ...
... Gary Destains said ...
... there's a pigeon ...
... Mrs B. shouted ...
Stop.
Come back.
... let me look ...
... I ... thought ...
... Dobbie said ...
... It's dead.
It was.
... Mrs B. picked (it) up ...
... it's neck ... flopped ...

... I said ...
She lifted ...
... they were ...
I didn't know ...
... we had gone in ...
... we were ... sitting ...
... (we were) telling ...
... Mrs B. came and held ...
... Mrs Sanderson was sad ...
... we all were ...

Read through the text again, noting the words just listed. Say the sentences aloud with the stress on these words. You should also be able to feel the rhythm of each sentence.
Did you spot the missing three?

We all rushed up ...
... it was resting ...
... Mrs B. came ...

What you have examined so far is a key structure of English grammar, the subject + verb structure (SV). 'Subject' here doesn't mean topic, it means the person or thing performing or receiving an action. The verb is the action, which is why verbs have traditionally been called 'doing words'. In the main they are 'doing words' but it is very important to recognise two verbs which are not 'doing words' in any obvious sense but which are used more frequently than any other verb in English. The different forms of these two verbs are set out below:

to be/am/is/are/was/were/will be/been/being

to have/have/has/had/will have/having

Not only do forms of the verbs 'to be' and 'to have' work on their own, they frequently combine with other verbs as well. When they do this they are called auxiliary verbs. Sometimes the two combine, as in the following examples:

will have been/has been/is having/having been/will be having

ACTIVITY

Look at the text again and list all the verbs. Note that verbs often use two or three words, as when they contain an auxiliary.

Check your list with the following:

were coming back; found; had gone in; was; said; There's; rushed up; shouted; Stop; come back; let ... look; what's happened; thought; was resting; said; It's; was; picked ... up; flopped over; said; lifted ... up; were; didn't know; were; had gone in; were; (were) telling; came; held ... up; was; was; were.

Did you notice the almost hidden verb 'is' in 'There's' and 'It's'? The apostrophe is there to signify the missing letter 'i'.

Now answer the following questions:

1 How often do the verbs 'to be' and 'to have' work on their own?

2 How often do they work as **auxiliaries**?

3 How many other verbs are there? (These are called lexical verbs.)

4 Are there any verbs that have another word attached to them?

5 Sometimes the verb 'to do' is used as an auxiliary. It is used once here; where?

If you remove all the verbs from your SV list, all you should be left with are the subjects that actioned the verb or received the action:

we; Mrs B.; Some children; I; Gary Destains, etc.

Sentences beginning 'There are' or 'There is' are slightly odd because they appear not to have a subject. Such sentences are however very common. Jokes and tales often begin with 'There was this bloke...'. They are called existential sentences because their purpose is to state quite simply that someone or something exists or existed.

Another term you will come across in reference grammar books is 'predicate'. This need not worry you. All it refers to is the very feature of language you have just been exploring. Predication means making a statement or a proposition about someone or something (or somewhere) using a verb.

All the verbs Lesley uses have the effect of moving her story along in our minds. They are called **finite** verbs because they have a definite location in time and space and because she tells us explicitly who did what. Verbs signify movement, action, energy. They don't have to be dynamic in obvious ways (run, jump, kiss, shout, dive, etc); they can express states (was asleep; is thinking; were worried). Above all they express commitment (I was ... He is ... They were ... It will be ...).

You may have noticed that some of Lesley's verbs do not appear to have an obvious subject. They are:

Stop.
Come back ...
... let me look ...

These are all command or imperative sentences; they tell someone to do something. Thus the subject is implied; it is 'you'. 'You' is the implied subject of all commands. Commands are frequently in the form of one- or two-word sentences.

Lesley's text is beginning to look like an English grammar in miniature, which should reassure you that grammar is not as complicated as you might have thought. It consists, in fact, of a small number of operations performed with extraordinary ingenuity by English users. However, before turning to the other grammatical features of this text we need to look again at Lesley's sentences.

Phrases and clauses

If you take as the definition of a written sentence 'everything between the initial capital letter and the full stop', you will notice that some sentences contain more than one subject and more than one verb. For example:

Today, at afternoon play, just when **we** *were coming back* into school, **Mrs B.** *found* a pigeon on the floor, next to the Haygreen Lane side.

I *was sorry* for it, poor thing, and **Mrs Sanderson** *was sad.*

The subjects are in bold type and their verbs are in italics.

To most people, the sentence is a common sense unit and so it should be. Certainly in writing it makes most sense to treat sentences as the main units of meaning and communication. There are, however, two important sub-units out of which sentences are made: **clauses** and phrases. Phrases are sometimes referred to as groups.
So far in this grammatical exploration of Lesley's text you have looked at clauses, those parts of her sentences containing a subject and a verb.
Clauses are thought or idea units, the core consisting of a subject and verb. You have already listed the cores of Lesley's clauses. Sometimes a clause will be the same thing as a sentence. The following sentence, for example, is a clause:

I didn't know wings were so lovely and big, with so many feathers especially.

There is one subject, 'I', and one verb, 'didn't know'. Notice that verbs may be expressed negatively as well as positively. The rest of the sentence consists of phrases.
'It was.' is also a clause functioning as a sentence, in this instance a rather dramatic one. There are no phrases in this sentence; indeed there are no other words at all.
You can conclude from this that phrases are groups of words (two or more) that work together but without a verb. They provide additional content to the meaning of the sentence. Here are the phrases from the last section of Lesley's narrative:

in our class; Mrs Sanderson and the others; about it; with its lovely, grey wings; poor thing; we all.

It is best to identify grammatical units as chunks rather than single words. That way, you do not lose sight of the wood for the trees. Usually, long phrases can be broken down into smaller phrases if you need to, for example:

our class; the others; grey wings.

ACTIVITY

Look at the first part of the text (down to 'It was') and list the phrases. Then identify some phrases within phrases, for example: 'on the floor, next to the Haygreen Lane side' contains 'on the floor'; 'next to'; 'Haygreen Lane'.

In the course of your investigation so far you should have discovered the following from Lesley's narrative:

- the human mind doesn't just think in words, it thinks in chunks of words (grammatical structures are recognisable as meaningful chunks of words)
- some chunks are phrases (short or long) which can consist of phrases within phrases (even something as simple as 'the cat' is a phrase, while 'cat the' isn't because it doesn't make sense; definite articles precede nouns)
- a short phrase may be extended into a long one by adding more phrases, as in 'the cat with a beautiful golden coat, fierce whiskers and white paws'
- if speech and writing consisted only of phrases, communication would be tedious and very limited
- the clause is the other 'think unit'; it gives energy and direction to the phrases.

Consider now, clauses in more detail.

Independent and dependent clauses

'The cat' is a short phrase, as is 'the mat'. Join the two together by means of a verb and you create a clause: 'The cat sat on the mat'. This clause can also be called a simple sentence or, to put it another way, it is a one-clause (one-idea) sentence.

Now look at one of Lesley's sentences cited earlier:

Today, at afternoon play, just when we were coming back into school, Mrs B. found a pigeon on the floor, next to the Haygreen Lane side.

There are two clauses here using two verbs: 'we were coming back' and 'Mrs B. found'. Thus the sentence contains two thoughts or ideas, together with phrases giving additional information. Notice, however, that one of the clauses is introduced by the word 'when', as follows:

when we were coming back into school

Lesley's intention here is to indicate time in terms of what the children were *doing* at the time in question. She also uses the word 'when' which is known as a subordinating conjunction. Statistically speaking, this is the first subordinating conjunction young children learn at an age when they are beginning to get a sense of past and present. It does an important job by connecting (which is all conjunction means) two clauses into one sentence. 'Subordinating' means that the clause is adding meaning to the main idea (clause) of the sentence which is that Mrs B. found a dead pigeon. The clause is also called 'dependent' because it cannot stand alone if it begins with a word like 'when'. 'Subordinate' and 'dependent' mean the same thing.

'Mrs B. found a pigeon', on the other hand, is an independent clause because it does make complete sense on its own.

The key grammatical words to watch out for when identifying subordinate or dependent clauses are:

when/if/because/whilst/where/while/until/although/whenever.

Note also that whilst these words are called conjunctions (joining words), they do not always appear between the two clauses. For example:

We are bad tempered because we are hungry.
Because we are hungry, we are bad tempered.

Now look at another of Lesley's sentences:

I was sorry for it, poor thing, and Mrs Sanderson was sad.

Here the connection between the two clauses is not a subordinating one. The two thoughts, 'I was sorry' and 'Mrs Sanderson was sad' are independent of each other, joined by the familiar use of 'and'. 'Poor thing' is a phrase conveniently inserted. Words like 'and', 'but' and 'or' are known as co-ordinating conjunctions because they simply join independent clauses together. When used in speech, co-ordinating conjunctions can imply subtler connections through intonation, but in writing they are unsatisfactory if overused. Children use them a great deal; notice the two at the end of Lesley's narrative. For comment on whether writers should or should not begin sentences with 'and' or 'but', see the later part of this chapter.

Earlier, one-clause sentences were referred to as simple sentences. Sentences that contain one or more subordinate clauses are referred to as **complex**. Do remember that all this means is that they contain a dependent clause; they are not necessarily complicated. Remember also that a sentence cannot be 'more complex'; it is either complex or it isn't. Sentences that contain two or more independent clauses (that is, no subordination) are referred to as **compound** sentences. Lesley's 'I was sorry for it, poor thing, and Mrs Sanderson was sad' is a compound sentence.

The terminology is not the important thing here; it is your ability to see how words work in groups that matters. When you come to the summary of English grammar at the end of this chapter you will find that Lesley has already caused you to consider the most important elements:

- sentence functions: statements, commands
- phrases: short ones and long ones
- clauses: independent and dependent (subordinate)
- sentence structures: simple, complex, compound
- verbs: 'to be' and 'to have' plus others
- grammatical subjects: a variety of nouns and pronouns.

Look now at some other grammatical elements in Lesley's writing.

Nouns

Nouns do, or receive, the actions of the verbs you have already identified. They are the names of persons, places and things; they signify the 'thingies' people talk about. Sometimes they label '**concrete**' objects and real people in the world (chairs, tables, Marilyn Monroe), sometimes they label **abstract** ideas that exist in the mind (freedom, love, happiness, management, education). Remember that it is the words that are abstract.

ACTIVITY
---

1 Use the abstract nouns just cited (in brackets, above) as headings and write underneath each one five associated 'concrete' nouns.
2 Now look through Lesley's text and list the words that you think are being used as nouns. Remember you are looking for names of persons, places and things.

The following is a list of the nouns and noun phrases used in Lesley's text:

play; school; Mrs B.; pigeon; floor; Haygreen Lane side; children; Gary Destains; pigeon; floor; Mrs B.; thing; Dobbie; Mrs B.; neck; thing; Dobbie; wings; fans; wings; feathers; class; Mrs Sanderson; the others; Mrs B.; wings; thing; Mrs Sanderson.

Notice how this list is a mixture of ordinary concrete nouns and proper nouns; not an abstract noun anywhere. Why not? Notice too, that the word 'thing' is a very handy, all-purpose noun along with 'stuff' and 'thingamajig'.

You are also likely to have observed that nouns rarely appear entirely alone; they like to keep company with other words and their favourite habitat is the noun phrase. Below are the nouns once again, but in their phrases (proper nouns have not been repeated):

afternoon play; into school; Mrs B. (a phrase in itself); a pigeon; the floor; the Haygreen Lane side; Some children; Gary Destains; a pigeon; on (the) floor; poor thing; its neck; poor thing; its wings; big, lovely grey fans; so many feathers; our class; the others; its lovely, grey wings; poor thing.

The kinds of words that most frequently work with nouns can be discovered from this data:

adjectives: afternoon, poor, big, lovely, grey
determiners: a, the, some, its, our, many
prepositions: into, on.

These need a little explanation.

Adjectives

An adjective describes a noun. The word 'afternoon' is most often used as a noun (it names a particular time) but here Lesley has used it as an adjective to describe which particular playtime. The same thing happens in phrases such as 'morning coffee', 'breakfast tea', 'motor show', 'coat rack', 'hat stand' and 'gun dog'. Many words function as nouns or adjectives, and even as verbs, according to the meaning intended. Don't let this confuse you; if you are not sure, asking the question 'What is the word doing to the next one?' usually gives you the answer.

Determiners

The word 'determiner' came into linguistic terminology in the 1930s. It is very useful because it draws attention to a class of words that do a vital job in grammar, namely making absolutely clear just what is being referred to. Some books use other or additional terminology but the different labels used can be grouped under the general heading of determiners, as follows:

definite articles: a, an (indefinite), the (definite)
demonstratives: eg this, that, those
possessives: eg my, our, your
some pronouns: some, many

If the determiners are missing, you will suddenly find yourself asking questions to establish the precise meaning of an utterance

Do you mean *the* car or *any* car?
Do you want *this* one or *that* one?
Shall we go in *your* car or *my* car?
Are they *all* coming or just *some* of them?

Hence the useful name, determiners.

Again, don't worry too much about the terminology at this stage; make sure you can spot the words themselves.

Pronouns

Among the determiners are some pronouns. These belong with nouns because their function is to stand in lieu of nouns. Behind every 'it' lies a noun; behind every 'he', 'him', 'she' and 'her' lies an individual person. The word 'it' is known as an impersonal pronoun and the others are known as personal pronouns. Personal pronouns are organised under three headings:

first person: I, me (singular)
we, us (plural)
second person: you (singular)
you (plural)
third person: he, she, him, her (singular)
they, them (plural).

ACTIVITY

Look at Lesley's text again and list the pronouns
she has used.

Notice how frequently 'it' is used and also the possessive form 'its' (not to
be confused with 'it's', which means something quite different). Note too
the possessive pronoun 'our'.

The first pronoun in the text is 'we' which sets it up as a first person
narrative straight away. The only way another first person can be
introduced into the text is via dialogue, as when Mrs B. says 'let me look'.

So far you have explored the following word classes: verbs, nouns,
conjunctions, adjectives, determiners and pronouns. You need now to
consider adverbs.

Adverbs

ACTIVITY

Opposite is a list of words and phrases used by
Lesley as adverbs. Look at where they occur in
the text and write a sentence or two saying what
adverbs do.

Today; at afternoon play; there; a bit; just (used
three times in all); so; especially.

Your description of what adverbs do, on the evidence of the data here,
should have included:

- telling the time (today; at afternoon play)
- locating a place (there)
- describing or modifying the verb (*just* flopped; *just* sitting) and
  indicating manner (often by '-ly' words such as especially as in 'they had
  so many feathers especially').

All the word classes are necessary; communication would become difficult
if one was lost overnight. Adverbs, however, are particularly interesting
from a stylistics point of view. On the one hand they signify precise times
and places and the manner of actions, but they are also little persuaders
that nudge meanings in a particular direction. Lesley is precise about time
and place but what does she mean by 'just flopped' and 'just sitting'? How
many is 'so many'? Clearly it means 'a lot' to Lesley. How long is 'a bit'?

There is no criticism intended here. People use adverbs like this every day, being very precise and explicit one moment, and leaving it to assumption the next. Why 'especially'?

You may have noticed in other contexts that 'just', along with 'only', is a favourite adverb of young children: 'It just broke!' It is probably a favourite of adults too. Other favourite adverbs, especially in informal speech, are 'right' and 'dead' used to intensify adjectives as in 'right little' and 'dead good'.

The '-ly' adverbs are worth looking at particularly closely. They are familiar enough, for example: 'she ran quickly'; 'he ate slowly'. In these, and countless more used every day, the adverb occurs very close to the verb it is modifying (all modifying means is adding a detail or a nuance of meaning). Some novelists avoid adverbs of this kind in the belief that writing should be vivid enough for the reader not to need '-ly' adverbs. Writers of instructions, however, need to use them often, as in 'turn lid slowly'; 'tap lightly'; 'stir briskly'; 'lift carefully'. Sometimes they need to use double adverbs, as in 'open *very carefully*'; 'fasten *really tightly*'; 'proceed *extremely slowly*'. Again, the verb and its adverb(s) are close together.

It is noticeable, however, that on other occasions adverbs are rather mobile words and can be separated quite a distance from their verbs. Look at the following examples:

I like fish and chips, actually.
I actually like fish and chips.
Actually, I like fish and chips.
I like fish actually, and chips.

Imagine how these would be spoken, and notice the subtly different meaning communicated by a different adverbial position.

In English, adverbs are frequently placed either at the very beginning of a sentence or as the last word. This strategy doesn't just affect the verb, it affects the way in which a reader or listener receives the whole of what is being said. This does not always mean that somebody is trying to pull a fast one; it often expresses the personal enthusiasm or other feelings of whoever is communicating.

ACTIVITY

Here are some examples of adverbial chasers and afterthoughts. Note the comma in writing (the slight pause in speech).

1 Decide for yourself what attitude or feeling is being imparted by each of the following:

Chasers
  a Happily, he hadn't started on the decorating.
  b Surprisingly, she won the game.
  c Amazingly, I came out of it all right.
  d Incredibly, they were not hurt.
  e Actually, I have to go early.
  f Regrettably, I cannot stay.
  g Loyally, they did everything to help.

Afterthoughts
  h He won't be there, sadly.
  i That's my suitcase, actually.
  j 'Give us a chip,' he said, cheekily.

2 Does it make any difference where the adverb is placed?

3 Lesley places her adverb 'especially' at the end of her sentence. Why has she used it in the first place? What grammatical choice might you have made here? Would you have used the word 'especially'?

Clearly, when writing about the pigeon's wings, Lesley is writing about something special to her, almost revelatory. Her surprise and pleasure are expressed in the adverb 'especially' and it is not surprising that it comes at the very end of the sentence (where the weight of the most important thing we want to say often falls). A critic might point out immaturity of expression here and that the writing is closer to speech patterns than writing structures. On the other hand, there is a charm and candour that only a ten-year-old could achieve.

Pre-modification and post-modification

Where speakers and writers choose to place information within a grammatical sequence, consciously or unconsciously, has certain effects on listeners and readers. You have already been introduced to the basic pattern of English sentences and utterances: subject + verb + anything else. Most of Lesley's sentences have the subject very near the beginning followed by its verb, for example: 'I just thought...' and 'I was sorry...'. But the existence of the SV pattern does not mean that we should use it all the time. The truth is that we often do, but equally we often break up that pattern. Every time a question such as 'Are you going?' is asked, the SV pattern is reversed, for example. The pattern is interrupted for all sorts of reasons. 'The dog ate the bone' could be interrupted as follows:

(i) The dog, a mongrel of indeterminate colour, ate the bone.
(ii) The dog greedily ate the bone.
(iii) The dog, only when she had left the room, ate the bone.
(iv) Creeping out of the cupboard, the dog, sniffing cautiously with an eye kept always on the door, ate the bone.

Lesley also knows how to modify the SV pattern. Look at her opening sentence:

Today, at afternoon play, just when we were coming back into school, Mrs B. found a pigeon on the floor, next to the Haygreen Lane side.

She delays the appearance of Mrs B., the subject, by twelve words. True, the pattern isn't exactly broken but it is delayed, and the delay is effective. Lesley has a storyteller's instinct for setting the scene and the time before introducing the centrepiece of the story. This is called **pre-modification**, which means giving descriptive and circumstantial information *before* telling the reader what it is you are writing about. If it is overdone it is called, in everyday terms, 'going round the houses' and provokes the response 'get on with it'.

Pre-modification is yet another of those intuitive grammatical choices. Here it sets the scene; it can create anticipation, and it can also predispose a reader toward whatever it is that is coming next. If someone says to you, 'I had an appalling experience just now', you are expected to share the feeling before you know the cause.

Post-modification means, as the name suggests, supplying descriptive and circumstantial information *after* introducing whatever it is you are talking about. Lesley adds post-modification to her first sentence with 'on the floor next to the Haygreen Lane side'. If the SV of this sentence were to be wholly post-modified, it would read something like this:

Mrs B. found a pigeon today, at afternoon play, on the floor, next to the Haygreen Lane side, just when we were coming back into school.

Wholly pre-modified, it would read:

Today, at afternoon play, on the floor, next to the Haygreen Lane side, just when we were coming back into school, Mrs B. found a pigeon.

Whichever way, there can be little doubt that Lesley's sentence is better than either of these.

Conjunctions

Another word class evident in Lesley's text is the conjunction. Conjunctions are used to join clauses. Look through the piece again and spot her favourite conjunction.

She uses 'and' five times to connect clauses; she also uses 'when' for the same purpose. Given that the word 'and' in writing does nothing special except join things, the word 'when' has more effect because its special job is to signify time sequence.

Notice how Lesley's narrative is strictly chronological, the 'when's' fairly evenly distributed throughout the text. Notice too, that all the verbs in the actual story told by Lesley (the narrative) are in the past tense, the most frequently used tense for storytelling (check this by looking at the opening section of ten stories). Some of the sentences in the dialogue, however, are in the present tense. This is quite proper, but why should it occur?

One final aspect of English grammar remains for you to investigate in Lesley's narrative.

Lexical and grammatical words

The English vocabulary consists of about half a million words in modern use, world-wide. The vast bulk of these are called *lexical* or *content words*. These are words that have reference outside themselves to things and actions in the real world or that can be thought. They are in fact all the verbs, nouns, adjectives and adverbs you have just been exploring in Lesley's text.

There is also a second, very much smaller, group of words, called *grammatical words* – a couple of hundred or so. These are the conjunctions, determiners, interrogatives (when? where? how?) and the prepositions (at, from, through, of, for, in, for example). Prepositions are chiefly concerned with location.

Lesley's text can be re-written excluding each of these types of words to show the difference. Pronouns have been classed as grammatical words. This is how it looks with the grammatical words removed:

Today, afternoon play, just were coming back school, Mrs B. found pigeon floor next Haygreen Lane side. children had gone was Gary Destains said,
'Hey's pigeon floor.'
all rushed Mrs B. shouted,
'Stop. Come back let look 's happened poor thing.'
just thought was resting bit Dobbie said,
's dead'.
was. Mrs B. picked neck just flopped.
'Poor thing,' said Dobbie.
lifted wings, were like big, lovely grey fans. didn't know wings were lovely big, feathers especially.
had gone were just sitting class telling Mrs Sanderson others Mrs B. came held lovely grey wings. was sorry poor thing, Mrs Sanderson was sad. all were.

Now look at the version with the lexical words deleted:

at when we into a on the to the Some in but I there when
up! There a on
We up but
and me what to it,
I it a but It It When it up, its over
I to
She it up with its and they like I so and with so many
When we in, we in our and and the about it when and it up with its I for it, and And we

You should be able to see clearly from these two versions that the function of the grammatical words is to fasten the lexical ones in meaningful structures. It should not surprise you to know that statistically, the grammatical words, though much fewer in number, are used far more frequently than any of the individual lexical words. Indeed, the top 20 most frequently used words in written and spoken English consist solely of grammatical words plus forms of the two most frequently used verbs, 'to be' and 'to have'.

ACTIVITY

To test this out, ask friends or members of your family to fill in the gaps in the two versions above.

Those doing the first will have only 200 or so words to choose from. You could space the text out to indicate the missing words. They have a very good chance of doing the puzzle.

Those trying to find the missing lexical words, however, will have very much more difficulty. You could, again, space out the text to indicate the missing words but your friends will still be faced with the problem of choosing from at least 30,000 words!

Some conclusions

Examination of Lesley's narrative should have given you an action picture of English grammar at work in an everyday context. It will have demonstrated what grammatical competence is and introduced you to some key grammatical concepts and their appropriate terminology.

So far as your general stylistic analysis of texts is concerned, you are not expected to look at the grammar as concentratedly as you have here. The activities you have just done should give you an idea of the grammatical structure of written sentences in whole texts. That knowledge should help you recognise a feature when it is distinctive or significant. Grammatical analysis isn't always useful, nor do you need to analyse everything every time.

Now that you have had an opportunity to investigate grammar in action, in the context of a whole text, there follows a summary of English grammar that makes reference where appropriate to the text you have already explored. You have done quite a lot of the jigsaw, as it were, and it is time to look at the picture as a whole.

English grammar: an introductory outline

English grammar consists of two principal areas of study: *morphology* and **syntax**.

Morphology

Morphology is concerned with the structure of English words. It is called morphology because it comes from the Greek word *morphos*, meaning 'shape' or 'form', and it studies the ways in which a basic word is altered in structure to enable it to do a different grammatical job. Early on in life, young children learn to add bits to words: an '-s' makes a noun plural; an

'-ed' signifies the past tense. These added bits are sometimes called inflections. Lesley, for example, intuitively understands the morphology of the following words:

flop – flopped
come – coming
happen – happened
love – lovely
sit – sitting
was – were (sometimes words change their internal structure).

If a word has a dependent bit attached, it is called a *complex word*, rather like a complex clause.

Many of Lesley's words are *simple words* in that they are complete in themselves with nothing attached, for example:

play; Lane; side; big; pigeon; class; grey; sad; poor; thing; neck; floor.

In addition to simple and complex words, there are *compound word* structures. These consist of two simple words joined together. Lesley uses two: 'afternoon' and 'Haygreen'. Other examples of compound nouns Lesley would be likely to know are 'playground', 'classroom' and 'headteacher'.

Syntax

The moment two or more words are strung together according to a rule or convention, they are said to be *syntactic*. The syntactic units you have been investigating are phrases, clauses and sentences.

The vital connection between morphology (word structure) and syntax (sentence structure) is the idea of *word classes*, or what used to be called parts of speech. A summary of word classes follows.

Word classes

Word classes are the specific jobs words do when they are put into syntactic units. You could only guess at the meaning of the word 'runs' if it were on its own, whereas in a sentence you would know exactly how it was being used, for example:

I am going to build two chicken runs (plural noun)
She runs faster than her sister (present tense, singular third-person verb)
They scored a hundred runs (plural noun).

There are all sorts of names for word classes, none of them contradictory, but word classes can in fact be divided into three groups, which has the advantage of helping you see the wood and not just the trees.

1 Nouns, adjectives, determiners and pronouns

The first group consists of nouns, adjectives, determiners and pronouns. They form the content of phrases, whether the phrases are subjects or objects. 'Subject' is a term you have explored in Lesley's story; 'object' is a term that has not been introduced yet because you need to get a clear idea first of the importance of the SV structure.

If subjects 'do' the verbs, objects receive the action. Look again at Lesley's story. The list of nouns in her story is in fact longer than the list of subjects because some of the nouns are acting as objects:

Mrs B. found *a pigeon*
She lifted *it*.

These are called 'direct objects' because the verb acts on them directly. Look now at two other sentences:

we were coming back *into school*
we were just sitting *in our class.*

Here the objects are called 'indirect objects' because the verb does not act on them directly. It is connecting words like 'into', 'in' and 'to' that make all the difference.

2 Verbs and adverbs

The second group of word classes consists of the verb and the adverb. Here, there are many sub-divisions because the verb does a great variety of work in English sentences. The following concepts and terms are useful:

- tense – signifies the time of the action
- participles – different forms (or parts) of the verb: '-ing', for example, signifies present participles which are very good for making adjectives with (eg walking boots; frying pan; looking glass); '-ed' signifies past tense and is also useful for making adjectives (eg boiled beef; fried bread)
- modal verbs – verbs added in front of other verbs (ie could, should, would, can, may, might, must, ought to, need to)
- auxiliary verbs – the addition of forms of 'to be', 'to have' and 'to do' to other verbs
- **passivisation** – verbs in the active form are performed by their subject; when they are put in the passive, the subject receives the action (eg 'he was attacked'). Note the use of an auxiliary verb to achieve this.
- phrasal verbs (or verb idioms) are a combination of verb plus preposition and are best treated as chunks of meaning (eg get off with; get by; get over; get on with; get up; go under; go over to; go off; go to; go for; go out with).

Adverbs give us more information about the verb, but they also modify themselves as in 'walk very carefully', and modify adjectives as in 'a really good book'.

3 The connectors

The third group of word classes can be called connectors because they connect words to words, phrases to phrases, clauses to clauses and all three permutations of these grammatical elements. They include prepositions and conjunctions in particular, which brings this grammar outline to a final point concerning Lesley's story. At the very end of it, there is an obvious emotional charge. Notice her use of the conjunction 'and'. Her last sentence begins with the word 'and', a practice some people find objectionable. From time to time, professional writers do it because it best fits both the rhythm and the sense of the writing. When you look later at Lesley's original, unpunctuated version, you will see that her word order has been retained but punctuation has been added. What decision would you have made?

This concludes a very brief outline of the structures of English grammar. The following diagram is another way of thinking about the three groups of word classes that form the 'grammar kit'.

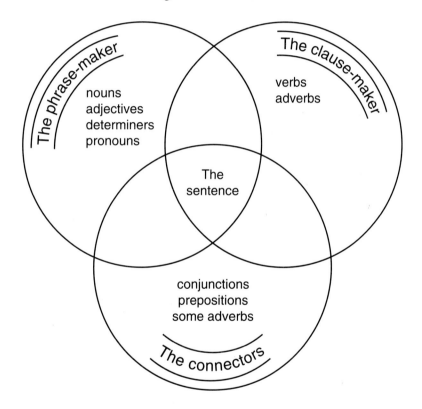

Comparing texts

This chapter concludes with activities based on two more texts. First, though, read a typed version of Lesley's text as she spelled and punctuated it herself:

Today at afternoon play when we was comeing back in to school Mrs B found a pidgin on the floor next to the Haygreen Lane side Some children had gone in but I was ther when Gary Desdains said hay up thers a pidgin on floor. We all rusht up but Mrs B showted "stop come back and let me look whats apend to it poor thing". I just thout it was resting a bit but Dobbie said its dead it was when Mrs B picket it up its kneck just flopped over poor thing I said to Dobbie She lifted it up with its wings and they were like big lovely grey fans. I didn't know wings were so lovely and big with so many fethers espeshily When we had gon in we was just sittind in are class and telling Mrs Sandison and the others about it when Mrs B came and held it up with its lovly grey wings I was sorry for it poor thing and Mrs Sandison was sad and we all was.

Now compare this with a piece by Martin in the same class.

The wood pigeon has a pees of red on its beak at the top and yellow at the end. When you look closely at it it isnt only grey and white it has litish green and purple just near the neck part. it has right little feathers on it head not long ones like the wings. Its head is very soft. The wood pigeon is a bird of the woods but since the spread of agriculture it has taken to feed on cultivated land it is a familiar bird in parks and gardens. It is quite tame in the parks. Its normal flight is fast and strong with quick regular wingbeats and occasional glides on the ground it struts. It roosts in trees and its voice can be heard at all times of the year but mainly in March and April. It is often said to coo. Cereal grains are the most important food. When we were in London my dad got a bag of seeds for me and Joanne and the pigens came right up to us. Joanne was scared. My dads friend Jim rases pigeons but not wood I don't think.

ACTIVITY

1 Punctuate Martin's piece of writing where necessary.
2 Look at its grammatical features.
   a What does it have in common with Lesley's? What significant differences are there?

   b What do you think happened in the middle of the piece?
   c What do the last three sentences have in common with Lesley's writing?

The next text was written as part of a response to a case study task requiring candidates to re-present material in the form of a booklet for European travellers.

Have you ever wondered just how many languages there are in the world? Language experts have long argued the exact number, and estimates vary between 2,700 and 6,000. The problem is not made easier by the fact that languages do not coincide with countries and nationalities. In Europe, for example, there are more languages spoken than there are countries. Most people in Spain speak Spanish, and most people in Britain speak English. Yet in Spain, Catalan, Asturian, Aragonese, Galician, Portuguese and Basque are also spoken, while in Britain, Welsh, Scots, Scottish Gaelic, Irish Gaelic, Manx and Cornish are also spoken quite apart from the many Eastern European, Middle Eastern and Asian languages that have arrived since 1945. In Belgium, people in the north speak Flemish, people in the south speak French. In Switzerland, the Swiss speak French, German or Italian depending upon which part of Switzerland they live. There are other so-called minority languages all over Europe, eg Yiddish, Romany, Luxembourgian, Faroese and Breton. Look at the map to find where these languages are spoken.
  With the coming of the European Economic Community problems have been caused by the number of majority languages let alone the minority ones. Its enlargement from twelve to sixteen countries means that the

European Parliament needs more translators to cover the 132 possible combinations of official languages. In an editorial *The European* newspaper (10.2.94) wrote: 'The Union must now confront the need to change a policy which was originally designed for a Community of six members and was barely workable for twelve, but will be an expensive administrative nightmare for sixteen.' It concluded: 'Historical accident and widespread accessibility – not linguistic imperialism – suggest that the one working language required will be English.' But how do the French or the Germans feel about that?

When you go backpacking or inter-railing across Europe you will no doubt be glad that so many people speak English as well as their native language but if the majority languages are still very sensitive politically, spare a thought for how minority language speakers must feel. They are as much a part of Europe as anybody else. Find out more about them. This booklet will introduce you to the basic facts. Now read on.

ACTIVITY

Compare the A-level student's text with those of Lesley and Martin for purpose and sentence length, type and structure. If you think the writing is more mature grammatically, what makes it so? Is it average sentence length? Sentence openings? Anything else?

7 Reading Texts

You are about to begin reading Italo Calvino's new novel, *if on a winter's night a traveller*. Relax. Concentrate. Dispel every other thought. Let the world around you fade. Best to close the door; the TV is always on in the next room. Tell the others right away. 'No, I don't want to watch TV!' Raise your voice – they won't hear you otherwise – 'I'm reading! I don't want to be disturbed!' Maybe they haven't heard you, with all that racket; speak louder, yell: 'I'm beginning to read Italo Calvino's novel!' Or if you prefer, don't say anything; just hope they'll leave you alone.

Find the most comfortable position: seated, stretched out, curled up, or lying flat. Flat on your back, on your side, on your stomach. In an easy chair, on the sofa, in the rocker, the deck chair, on the hassock. In the hammock, if you have a hammock. On top of your bed, of course, or in the bed. You can even stand on your hands, head down, in the yoga position. With the book upside down, naturally.

Adjust the light so you won't strain your eyes. Do it now, because once you're absorbed in reading, there will be no budging you. Make sure the page isn't in shadow, a clotting of black letters on a gray background, uniform as a pack of mice; but be careful that the light cast on it isn't too strong, doesn't glare on the cruel white of the paper, gnawing at the shadows of the letters as in a southern noonday. Try to foresee now everything that might make you interrupt your reading. Cigarettes within reach, if you smoke, and the ashtray. Anything else! Do you have to pee? All right, you know best.

These are the opening paragraphs of *if on a winter's night a traveller*, a novel by Italo Calvino. It's likely that you found this a rather unusual start, as most novels don't begin by suggesting how you should read them. But here, the author is directly addressing you, the reader, and encouraging you to find the best conditions possible to enable you to lose yourself in the reading of his work.

Whilst these may well be the best conditions for novel reading, there are many other types of reading that do not require such comfortable surroundings or such concentration. Nor are we always reading for pleasure as we are with a novel.

Consider these, for example:

- reading the back of a cereal packet at breakfast time
- reading the Highway **Code** in preparation for your driving test
- reading a holiday postcard from a friend
- reading your bank statement
- reading an advertisement on the side of a bus
- reading over the draft of an essay you've just written
- reading the titles of magazines in a newsagent's
- reading your horoscope in a magazine
- reading a textbook on one of your A-level subjects
- reading a recipe.

These are just a brief sample of the reading that someone might easily do in one day. Not only are there different types of text here – essay, horoscope, advertisement – but also different types of *reading*. Reading is used in each of these examples, but the *way* you read the texts is likely to be different from one to the next. You would not be expected to pay the same amount of concentrated attention to the back of a corn-flakes packet as you would to an A-level textbook. Looking at the titles of magazines on a newsagent's shelves is a different kind of reading than carefully following a recipe.

ACTIVITY

To show that there are many ways or strategies of reading, look at these **words** and expressions:

peruse   skim   bury oneself in   flick through   browse
study   wade through   piece together   glance over   dip into

Each of them refers to a different reading strategy.

1 List them in order, beginning with the word or expression that you think refers to the reading strategy demanding the greatest amount of concentration and ending with the one demanding the least.

2 The authors collected over 30 additional words or expressions. Can you beat this?

3 Slot your extra ones into the list you have just drawn up.

A reading autobiography

There are a number of factors involved in any piece of reading, some of which may require deliberate choices on the reader's part. For instance, he or she has to decide:

- the *subject matter* of the reading (eg the geography of Belgium; the breeding habits of guinea-pigs; the programmes on ITV next Tuesday evening)
- the *type of text* (eg advertisement, insurance policy, DIY magazine, anthology of short stories)
- the *context* for the reading (eg *where* will it take place? *with whom? when* will it take place?)
- the *reason* or *purpose* for the reading (eg to be entertained or amused; to find out information; to learn a new skill)

- the *type* of reading (eg skim, browse, study, glance at)
- the *length of time* spent on the reading
- the *effect* of the reading (eg learnt how to make an omelette; booked a plane ticket; gained pleasure).

ACTIVITY

In this piece of research you will be looking at your own pattern of reading and considering some general questions about the nature of reading.

1 Draw up a chart that will allow you to survey the full range of your reading pattern for a specified period. Two or three days would be a manageable period for you to deal with. You must ensure that you include everything that you read, otherwise you will not have an accurate record. There are some suggested headings in the table below.

2 When you have completed your survey, compare it with others in your group. Here are some questions to guide your discussions.
   a What, if any, general conclusions can you reach about your group's reading patterns?
   b What differences, if any, are there between individuals' reading habits?
   c What might be the reasons for any differences that exist? (Gender? Cultural?)

Subject matter	Type of text	Context	Purpose	Reading strategy	Amount of time spent	Effect

Your survey and discussions should have highlighted the variety of reading experiences that people have even over such a short period: the range of texts encountered; the reading strategies employed and the differing purposes attained. It is obvious that most of us are, to say the least, highly skilled and experienced readers.

Reading expertise

As you have seen, reading is an activity which requires the reader to use many different skills and strategies. Perhaps one of the most surprising things about reading, given the high level of skill involved, is that relatively few people encounter any difficulty with it. Most readers can recognise, almost at first glance, different types (or **genres**) of texts. It is easy to distinguish between, say, a diary entry, a newspaper editorial and the opening of a novel. Even the most challenging of texts presents few problems for those who are experts in that particular field. Some texts are *so* distinctive in their use of language that they can well be called 'restricted varieties' of English, and non-experts find them almost impossible to decode. What do you think are the expert audiences for these (admittedly extreme) examples of 'restricted Englishes'?

Text A

White: Alexei Shirov

Black: Boris Gelfand

1 e4 c5	22 Qg4 b5
2 Nf3 d6	23 Nf6+ Ke7
3 d4 cxd4	24 0-0-0 Qxg4
4 Nxd4 Nf6	25 Nxg4+ Kf8
5 Nc3 a6	26 Bh6+ Ke7
6 Be3 e6	27 Bg5+ Kf8
7 g4 e5	28 Bd8 -BxfS
8 Nf5 B6	29 Bxc7 NcG
9 g5 gxf5	30 Nh6 Bg6
10 exf5 d5	31 Rd6 Nb4
11 gxf6 d4	32 cxb4 Kg7
12 Bc4 Qxf6	33 h4 Rhc8
13 Nd5 Qc6	34 h5 Rxc7+
14 Bxd4 Bb4+	35 Kd2 Be4
15 c3 Qxc4	36 Rgl+ Kh8
16 Be3 Ba5	37 Ke3 Bb7
17 Nf6+ Ke7	38 Rgdl Re8
18 Nd5+ Ke8	39 Nf5 Bc8
19 Nf6+ Ke7	40 Rd8 BxfS
20 Bg5 Bc7	41 Rxe8+ Kg7
21 Ne4+ Ke8	42 RxeS 1-0

Text B

Murray Johnstone UT Mgmt (1000)H

7 West Nile St, Glasgow G1 2PR 0345 090 933

Acumen	1	106.10	108.60	40
Acumen Inc	1	98.18	100.50	40
Acumen Reserve	1	93.151	94.08	
Acumen Reserve Inc	1	75.16xd	75.91	
Americas Growth	1	65.63	67.53	+0.07
Blue Chip	1	53.28	54.49	−0.33
Blue Chip Ace	1	55.06	56.30	
Equity Income	1	101.20xd	103.80	
European	1	77.04	78.49	
Smaller Cos	1	84.04	88.08	+0.36
Worldwide Equity	1	75.01	76.92	+0.37
Global Bond	1	47.96	48.55	+0.04
UK Growth	1	106.20	108.90	
Pacific Growth	1	126.10	129.90	
Japan Growth	1	107.60	109.60	+0.80
Cash	0	54.23	54.23	+0.01
Cash Inc	0	50.21	50.21	+0.01
Corporate Bond Inc	1	51.58xd	52.17	
Corporate Bond Acc	1	52.79xd	52.69	

Text C

> **1st row:** Nil (2c., 1g., 1c., 1g.,) (7c., 1g., 1c., 1g.), 1c., 1g., 3c., 1g., 1c.,* 1g., 1c., 1g., 13c., 1g., 1c., 1g., 1c., 1g., 3c., 1g., 1c.; repeat from* until nil (5) (10) sts. remain, nil (1g., 1c., 1g., 2c.) (1g., 1c., 1g., 7c.).

There are plenty of other examples of 'restricted' English. Think of these, for example:

weather forecasts   shipping forecasts   sports scores   book indexes

CB radio talk   air-traffic control language   recipes

auctioneering language

It is quite likely that you will be familiar with some very specialised 'Englishes' yourself. Your group should collect as many as possible and bring in examples to the class. They will form a valuable data resource for further investigation.

Sixteen texts

In the next piece of work, you will be discussing your reading of a number of very different texts and deciding on the groups or categories in which to place them. Some of your discussion may well involve you in deciding on the intended audience for the texts, as in the previous exercise, but your discussion will probably range more widely. You might find it helpful to bear the following questions in mind as you read:

- what kind of text *is* this?
- what is the text about?
- what is the purpose or aim of the text?

But doubtless, you will find many additional areas on which to focus for yourselves.

ACTIVITY

1 In groups, discuss the texts and place them in the groups or categories they best seem to fit. You will, of course, have to decide on the categories themselves. Remember that there are no right or wrong answers in this investigation.

2 Make sure you have at least *two* texts in each of your categories. Do not take the easy way out by having a 'miscellaneous' category. Here is a suggested form on which you can record your decisions.

3 Appoint a group secretary who should briefly record how your decisions were reached.

4 When everyone in your group has agreed on the categorisation of the texts, you should discuss these questions:
   a How easy or difficult was it to agree on the categories?
   b Which texts were the most difficult to assign to a category? Why?
   c Which texts were the easiest to assign to a category? Why?
   d Choose any two of the texts and list any similarities or differences between them that you have noticed. For instance, you could pair Text D (on strong government)

Category	Brief description of your category	Texts in your category
(i)		
(ii)		
(iii)		
(iv)		

with Text O (bullseye) or Text P (scanner) with Text K (the Gallant).

5 When each group has finished its discussion, the group secretaries should report back to the whole class.

Text A

A Hi, Sue!
B Hi, John!
A Hi, Charlie! Had your dinner?
B I've fed the animals already.
A Been home long?
B Just a few minutes. I was out in a school all afternoon.
A Ah! We eating at home?
B Could, I suppose.
A No. Let's go out. I've got to look for a book.
B OK. Give me a few minutes to get changed. By the way . . .
A Yes?
B Oh, nothing. Chinese food?
A Yeah. If you want. I'll take the dog out for a walk while you get ready. Rufus!

Text B

CURTIS – Karen. In memory of a dear
sister, Karen, died January 18 1996.
Dear sister up above,
The lovely girl we all know and love:
God knew you had to say goodbye.
Never a day passes by,
You will always be a twinkle in our eye.
  – From all your family.

Text C
IT REALLY MEANS SOMETHING
SOCIALLY TO LIVE IN A FILTHY OLD
GEORGIAN HOUSE IN FASH ISLINGTON.
Liverpool Rd, N.1 is one of the filthiest
we have had for a long time & must be a bargain.
Base: 2 rms 15 × 12 & 12 × 10. Grnd: Front rm 16 × 10 & even a bathrm! Rear:
STUDIO 2 intercom rms 30ft & W.C. All a *real* artist needs.
1st flr: 2 rms wld make Grand 24ft Draw rm.
2nd flr: 2 rms 15 × 13 & 11 × 11. Also 2 store-
rms. If you've ever wanted to live on the Set of
a Sean O'Casey play, here's your chance. PATH-
ETICALLY CHEAP £9,955 EVEN TRY
OFFER.

Text D
government should be very strong to do those things which only government can do
it has to be strong to have defence because the kind of Britain I see would always
defend its freedom and always be a reliable ally so you've got to be strong to your
own people and other countries have got to know that you stand by your word then
you turn to internal security and yes you HAVE got to be strong on law and order and
do the things that only governments can do but there it's part government and part
people

Text E
and there's two slips and a gully they go down now as Julian is on his way to bowl to
the England captain Graham Gooch who nibbles onto the front foot a little reluctantly
but plays the ball off the middle of the bat towards Merv Hughes at mid off Gooch
takes a deep breath and goes for a stroll around the crease pacing around now he
knows the importance of this match I talked to him yesterday at the press conference

Text F
ON THE ninth day of December in the
Year of Our Lord Nineteen Hundred and
Eighty-Eight, hereinafter to be referred
to for purposes of clarity as 9 December
1988, and pursuant to Command 42,
Paragraph 13, Section c, of the Sub-Com-
mittee of the Secretariat of Oratorical
Peregrination (see Ministry of Obfusca-
tion directive number 2344/g/89, 20 December 1979, marked 'For Cabinet Office
Eyes Only'), such Command to be referred to hereinafter as 'Section c', the
manifestation of incomprehensible verb-
alisation, as indicated today (hereinafter
referred to without prejudice as 10 December) by the so-called Plain English
Campaign (see Department of Employment: Special Social Psychology Unit
Command Number 13, dated 22 December 1979) continues to make unprece-
dented advances as envisaged in the Secretary of State's memorandum *Gobble-*

degook: The Way Forward annotated in the said 'Section c' and being conditional upon the requisite directive remaining undisclosed for a period not exceeding 22 calendar months or part of one calendar month.

Text G

THE VOICE of King Alfred may have been discovered on a unique fragile wax cylinder which has lain undisturbed for some eleven hundred years.

Only a few words can be deciphered on the crude recording believed to have been made in Winchester during the last decade of the ninth century. King Alfred – if indeed it is he – speaks for all of 43 seconds, but so far the only section recognisable with any certainty is the opening: *Aelfred kyning hatath gretan Aerhelwaerd ealdormann.* ('King Alfred commands nobleman Athelward to be greeted.')

The cylinder was discovered last July during excavations in the Winchester area.

Stringent security measures are being observed to maintain secrecy over the exact location in order to prevent possible spoliation of the site by intruders.

Dr James Sherrington, a specialist in Anglo-Saxon art and technology made the astounding find while excavating what is thought to be the site of a late ninth century royal administration building. At that time Winchester was the most important West Saxon centre; King Alfred (871–899) is known to have spent much time there during the latter part of his reign.

Few persons to date have seen, let alone examined, the ancient artefact. In an attempt to stem the flow of recent wild rumours, the Antiquities Department of the British Museum, where it is currently being studied, has released a tantalisingly brief and factual description without any speculation on the historical and cultural consequences.

The wooden cylinder, coated with a now much darkened mixture of beeswax and resin – the latter probably acting as a hardening agent – is described as similar in appearance to the early recording of cylinders manufactured at the end of the nineteenth century.

Text H

In 1981 the World Health Organisation (WHO) adopted an International Code of Marketing of Breast Milk Substitutes. The Code required all baby-milk companies to refrain from advertising and aggressive marketing of infant foods. There was to be no promotion of baby foods within hospitals or to health-care workers and no free samples or supplies. Since 1981 there have been amendments and clarifications to the Code.

This Code, and the amendments, have not been respected by companies. Monitoring suggests that no baby-milk company fully adheres to the International Code. Nestlé have been singled out as the main British supplier and thus is the target of a boycott campaign. Some of their products are listed overleaf. The main target of the boycott in the UK is Nescafé.

Text I

Sweet as the ambrosial air,
With its perfume rich and rare;
Sweet as violets at the morn,
Which the emerald nooks addorn;
Sweet as rosebuds bursting forth
From the richly laden earth,
      Is the 'FRAGRANT FLORILENE'

The teeth it makes a pearly white,
So pure and lovely to the sight;
The gums assume a rosy hue,
The breath is sweet as violets blue;
While scented as the flowers of May,
Which cast their sweetness from each spray,
      Is the 'FRAGRANT FLORILENE'

Sure, some fairy with its hand,
Cast around its mystic wand,
And produced from fairy's bower
Scented perfumes from each flower;
For in this liquid gem we trace –
All that can beauty add and grace –
      Such is the 'FRAGRANT FLORILENE'

Text J

Hiyamac.
Lobuddy.
Binearlong?
Cuplours.
Ketchanenny?
Goddafew.
Kindarthay?
Bassencarp.
Enysizetoum?
Cuplapowns.
Hittinard?
Sordalite.
Wahchoozin?
Gobbaworms.
Fishanonaboddum?
Rydonaboddum.
Igoddago.
Tubad.
Seeyaround.
Yeatakideezy.
Guluk.

Text K

How a Gallant should behaue himselfe in a Play-house

Mary let this obseruation go hand in hand with the rest: or rather like a country-seruingman, some fiue yards before them. Present not your selfe on the Stage (especially at a new play) vntill the quaking prologue hath (by rubbing) got culler into his cheekes, and is ready to giue the trumpets their Cue that hees vpon point to enter: for then it is time, as though you were one of the *Properties*, or that you dropt out of ye Hangings to creepe from behind the Arras with your *Tripos* or three-footed stoole in one hand, and a teston mounted betweene a forefinger and a thumbe in the other: for if you should bestow your person vpon the vulgar, when the belly of the house is but halfe full, your apparell is quite eaten vp, the fashion lost, and the proportion of your body in more danger to be deuoured, then if it were serud vp in the Counter amongst the Powltry: auoid that as you would the Bastome.

Text L

HIGHWAYS ACT 1980
THE A556(M) MOTORWAY
(M6–M56 LINK)
AND CONNECTING ROADS
(SIDE ROADS) (NO. 2) ORDER
1994
THE SECRETARY OF STATE FOR TRANSPORT hereby gives notice that he proposes to make an Order under sections 12, 18 and 125 of the Highways Act 1980, in relation to the A556(M) Motorway (M6–M56 Link) which will be situated between Over Tabley and Bowden in the County of Cheshire, which will:
(1) authorise him to –
(a) improve highways,
(b) stop up highways,
(c) construct new highways,
(d) stop up private means of access to premises,
(e) provide new means of access to premises, all on or in the vicinity of the route of the Motorway mentioned above; and
(2) provide for the transfer of each new highway to the Cheshire County Council as highway authority as from the date on which he notifies them that it has been completed and is open for traffic.
COPIES of the draft order and the plans referred to in it, and of the environmental statement which the Secretary of State has published in relation to the construction of the new highways and the improvement of existing highways referred to in the draft Order, may be inspected free of charge at all reasonable hours from Wednesday 24 February 1993 until Friday 9 April 1993, or within six weeks from the date of first publication of this notice if that period expires later, at the Department of Transport, 2 Marsham Street, London SW1P 3EB; at the offices of the Director, North West Construction Programme Division, Sunley Tower, Piccadilly Plaza, Manchester M1 4BE.

Text M

So, we'll go no more a-roving
    So late into the night,
Though the heart be still as loving,
    And the moon be still as bright.

For the sword outwears its sheath,
    And the soul wears out the breast,
And the heart must pause to breathe,
    And love itself have rest.

Though the night was made for loving,
    And the day returns too soon,
Yet we'll go no more a-roving
    By the light of the moon.

Text N

ONCE upon a time and a very good time it was there was a moocow coming down along the road and this moocow that was coming down along the road met a nicens little boy named baby tuckoo...

His father told him that story: his father looked at him through a glass: he had a hairy face.

He was baby tuckoo. The moocow came down the road where Betty Byrne lived: she sold lemon platt.

O, the wild rose blossoms
On the little green place.

He sang that song. That was his song.

O, the green wothe botheth.

When you wet the bed first it is warm then it gets cold. His mother put on the oilsheet. That had the queer smell.

Text O

er / I remember once when I were at school / I was about six or seven at the time / it were our first biology practical / our teacher / his name were / er / I can't remember his name now / told us he was goin' t'cut up a bull's eye / because we were doin' work about eyes and things / anyway / he went to the small fridge in the corner of the lab / and / pulled out a small dish / and put it on one of the tables in the lab / we all crowded round the table / then he picked up this eye from the dish / ooomgh / it were awful / all shiny and bloodshot / then / he / er / put it down on a bit of newspaper / and he / calm as you like / he picked up a scalpel / and cut the eye in two / an' all the stuff in the eye glooped out onto the newspaper / magnifying the text on it / you know / but by this time my stomach was doin' cartwheels / an' I 'ad a lump in me throat / so I ran out o' the lab an' straight into the toilet / an' brought up all me cornflakes back into the toilet / if them toilets were any further away / I don't know what I'd've done / an' I got called by me mates fer weeks after / right

Text P

Follow your scanner manufacturer's instructions to install the scanner, interface card and device driver. Test the scanner using the manufacturer's software before using it with Wordlinx.

1 Turn the scanner on.

2 Double-click the Scanner Set-up icon.

3 Select your scanner from the list box and click OK to accept your selection and exit from the dialog box.

If you change scanners at any time, repeat the above steps to select a different scanner.

If you have problems using Wordlinx with your scanner, double-click the Readme icon and review the configuration information for your scanner.

You should have learnt not only that some texts are difficult to categorise, but also that it is possible to place texts into more than one category. For example, you can assign texts to categories on the basis of their audience, purpose or intention, genre (or form), date, topic or subject, and mode (written or spoken).

Genre

In the previous investigation into texts you may well have chosen to assign some of them to categories on the basis of genre. For example, you could well have grouped together 'Florilene' (Text I), 'So we'll go no more a-roving' (Text M) and the *In Memoriam* piece (Text B) as examples of verse; or 'Florilene' and the estate agent's piece (Text C) as examples of advertisements. If so, you would have categorised these texts on the basis of their genres.

What is genre? It is a term that has been used for a long time in literary criticism to denote different kinds of imaginative literature. For instance, the classical Greeks recognised three genres: the epic, the poetic and the dramatic, whilst the Elizabethans understood the term 'genre' to cover tragedy and comedy.

We too distinguish between different genres, sometimes without even thinking about it. For example, every time we go to a library or bookshop and choose books labelled 'Detective Fiction', 'Romance', 'Thrillers', 'Science Fiction', 'Fantasy' and so on, we are making choices between genres.

The concept of genre has, in recent times, broken through the 'literary' barrier and is now used 'to refer to any formally distinguishable variety (of language) whether of speech or writing' (David Crystal). So it is now quite legitimate to regard not only such types of writing as spy novels and comics as genres, but also such types as, for instance, letters, sermons, examination papers, news bulletins, official forms, etc.

One of the consequences of this is that most of us, as skilled readers, can assign a text to a specific genre on the basis of what may be no more than a cursory glance. We can quickly distinguish between a junk-mail circular and a court summons without much more than a scanning of the contents. Only after this scanning do we decide whether we wish to read the text more carefully. Of course, when the writer is playing games with text types and parodying them, our skills of immediate genre recognition are a little more severely tested. Did you spot which texts in the categorisation investigation were not genuine examples of their supposed genre?

Look at the three very brief texts below and consider the characteristics that allow you to make an almost instant recognition of their genre. You should have little, if any, difficulty in doing this.

Text A
IRA smash ceasefire

Text B

Once upon a time there was a rabbit whose name was Edward, but his friends called him Teddy Bun-Bun.

Text C

BRITISH RAILWAYS BOARD

This ticket is issued subject to the conditions shown in the Board's current Passenger Conditions of Carriage and also in any other of the Board's publications and notices appropriate to its use.

Below are listed some of the features of the language that are likely to have made the recognition of genre an easy task for you.

Text A: Newspaper headline

- only three words in total
- bold print and large-size letters
- omission of 'unnecessary' words such as 'the'
- use of a vivid, aggressive verb – 'smash'
- assumption that readers will be familiar with the context – no need to explain 'IRA'.

Text B: Children's story

- use of formula 'Once upon a time' signalling opening of specific type of story
- animals depicted as having human characteristics – names and friends
- setting likely to be familiar to children
- use of third-person narrator.

Text C: British Rail ticket

- **lexis** from semantic field of travel ('ticket', 'passenger')
- very formal lexis ('Conditions of Carriage', 'publications and notices appropriate')
- frequent use of capital letters
- official heading in capitals
- repetition of the noun 'the Board' rather than the use of the pronoun substitute 'it'
- heavy **post-modification** of nouns eg '*conditions* shown in the . . . to its use' and '*notices* appropriate to its use'
- use of the passive 'This ticket is issued' rather than the active 'British Rail issues'

It is sometimes helpful to think of genres as being similar to families in that most family members share certain characteristics. Hair colour, build and facial features are some of the factors that can help in identifying people as belonging to the same family. It does not follow, of course, that family members are identical.

Genres and sub-genres can share characteristic features. You have seen, for example, how the novel can be divided into detective fiction, romance, historical fiction and so on. These will all be recognisable as novels, in that they are likely to share distinguishing features (characters, plot), but are sufficiently distinct from each other to be a genre (or sub-genre) in their own right. Like families, genres can have 'trees'. Below is a suggested 'family tree' for newspapers. It is necessarily incomplete and you may not agree with the categories chosen, but it does attempt to show the relationship between genres and sub-genres.

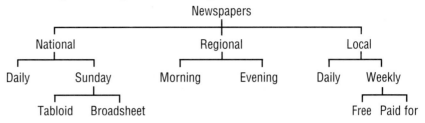

ACTIVITY

Draw up 'genre trees' of your own. You can choose your own categories, expand on the newspaper tree or choose from the following:

fiction
persuasive writing
magazines
notices

newspaper articles
drama
jokes
letters

A framework for looking at texts

When you are examining texts, it is often useful to have a set of questions that you can ask, almost as if you were interrogating the text! These should help you both to establish exactly what kind of text it is that you are encountering (ie its genre) and to indicate many of its distinguishing features. This aspect of language study is covered in more depth in the chapter on stylistics but the questions here form a useful starting point.

What is the text about?	*People? Things? Events? Ideas?*
What is the author's aim or purpose?	*To entertain? To report? To inform? To describe? To instruct? To…? A mixture of these?*
Who is the text written for?	*The writer him/herself? One individual reader? A friend? Experts? Novices? Old people? A teacher? People with shared interests?*
What is the relationship between the writer and the intended reader?	*Distant? Friendly? Bullying? Formal? Diffident?*
What does the text look like on the page?	*Layout? Print size? Fonts?*
How has the writer structured the text?	*Headings/sub-headings? Links between sentences? Links between sections? A sequence of events? A succession of points? References backwards and forwards through the text?*
What sort of vocabulary is used?	*Everyday words? Taken from specialised areas?*
Does it remind you of similar texts?	

Here are three texts for you to consider using the framework outlined above. A suggested approach for the first text has been provided.

Text A

An increasing number of subjects now include a project as part of the course. In many cases this project is assessed and the mark contributes to your examination result. Most projects fall into the following categories:

Library-based projects
Laboratory and workshop projects
Creative projects
Fieldwork
Community projects

All the above have common features:

(i)   They tend to be based on problems and therefore give you an opportunity to apply your knowledge.
(ii) The topics covered can often be selected by the student.
(iii) They may involve team work.
(iv) They test communications skills.
(v)   The end product should be useful for revision purposes.

Your first task is to choose the theme for your project. You should make an early start, giving yourself time to think about the options open to you. Ask for advice and look at past projects.

The framework applied to Text A

The text is clearly about project work for examinations and has twin aims: to inform and to advise the audience (potential examination candidates) on how to prepare for this work. The writer, who assumes the role of a knowledgeable expert, directly addresses the reader, at times in a relatively friendly manner ('you should make an early start') though the relationship is kept quite formal ('there are a number of factors'; 'the student'). The text uses layout to ensure clarity of information presentation (separate lines are used for 'categories' of project and their 'common features' are numbered). As a piece of informative writing, the topic is stated in the first sentence and cohesion (the way in which a text is 'tied together') is ensured by frequent repetition of 'project' or substitutes for it ('all the above'; 'they'). The writer aims for clarity by making general statements ('most projects fall into the following categories'; 'all the above have common features') and by exemplifying the categories or features in a list. The lexis (vocabulary) is quite specialised, taken from the fields of education and examinations ('library', 'laboratory', etc). In sum, the text is a good example of its genre, as many of these features can be found in similar passages in textbooks or student guides.

Text B

The average person doesn't need a car with twin airbags and power steering.

The average person doesn't need a car with a high-level brake light and a coded key pad immobiliser.

The average person doesn't need a car with electric front windows and three rear-point safety belts.

The average person doesn't need a car with a driver's door mirror with built in blind-spot eliminator.

The average person doesn't need a car with a six-speaker remote-control stereo radio cassette.

The average person doesn't need a car with a steering column with height and reach adjustment.

The average person has 2.4 children.

Text C

The magic Paintbrush

One Nigth a boy lay in bed wen he saw a paintbrush so in the morning he painted a picture the picture came alive so he let the budgie go then he went for a walk then he saw a girl wishing she had a cockral the girl was very pleased then he went home one day he heard about the crown jewel had been stolen so the boy painted a horse and went to look for it just then he saw some gold he went over to hav a look and there was the crown jewel

If you want more practice in identifying the characteristics of genres, the class should collect lots of different texts and bring them in for groups to work on. Here are a few suggestions of genres that could provide valuable practice, but you will have no difficulty in finding lots of examples of your own.

children's textbooks	newspaper sports reports
problem-page letters	tourist guides/holiday brochures
film reviews	TV listings
school reports	junk mail
insurance policies	limericks
minutes of meetings	astrology predictions

Genre bending

Writers can sometimes create unexpected and amusing effects by subverting genres. There are at least two ways of doing this. Firstly, a writer can take a genre and, by changing one of its features whilst retaining most of its others, create oddly disturbing effects. This can force us to look at the genre with fresh eyes. To illustrate this, read the following story.

The Other Frog Prince

Once upon a time there was a frog.
One day when he was sitting on his lily pad, he saw a beautiful princess sitting by the pond. He hopped in the water, swam over to her, and poked his head out of the weeds.
'Pardon me, O beautiful princess,' he said in his most sad and pathetic voice. 'I wonder if you could help me.'
The Princess was about to jump up and run, but she felt sorry for the frog with the sad and pathetic voice.
So she asked, 'What can I do to help you, little frog?'
'Well,' said the frog. 'I'm not really a frog, but a handsome prince who was turned into a frog by a wicked witch's spell. And the spell can only be broken by the kiss of a beautiful princess.'

The princess thought about this for a second, then lifted the frog from the pond and kissed him.

'I was just kidding,' said the frog. He jumped back into the pond and the princess wiped the frog slime off her lips. *The End.*

ACTIVITY

1 What features of the fairy-story genre has the author
   a retained?
   b changed?
2 What is the effect of the change(s)?
3 Try writing your own alternative fairy tales. Here are some suggested titles, but you are free, of course, to choose your own.

The Really Ugly Duckling
Little Red Running Shoes
The Princess and the Football
The Three Rather Obnoxious Pigs
Coal Black and the Seven Vertically
   Challenged Males

The second method a writer could use is to mix the **style** and **structure** of one genre with the subject matter of another. This provides plenty of potential for humour, whilst at the same time focusing on the characteristics of the genre in question, as the reader's attention is drawn to the absurdity of the mixing. Think, for example, of a weather forecast in rap, the story of the Good Samaritan retold by *Sun* journalists or a Valentine's card written as an A-level essay.

To show you what can be done by mixing genres, here are three amusing illustrations. They are all based on the nursery rhyme 'Jack and Jill', but you will notice that it is not the short version most of you will be familiar with, but a nineteenth-century one, with additional verses. The three pieces based on it were all written by A-level English language teachers.

The Adventures of Jack and Jill and Old Dame Gill

Jack and Jill
Went up the hill
To fetch a pail of water;
Jack fell down,
And broke his crown,
And Jill came tumbling after.

Then up Jack got,
And home did trot,
As fast as he could caper;
Dame Gill did the job,
To plaster his nob
With vinegar and brown paper.

Then Jill came in,
And she did grin
To see Jack's paper plaster;
Her mother, vexed,
Did whip her next,
For laughing at Jack's disaster.

This made Jill pout,
And she ran out,
And Jack did quickly follow;
They rode dog Ball
Till Jill did fall,
Which made Jack laugh and halloo.

Then Dame came out
To enquire about,
Jill said Jack made her tumble;
Says Jack, I'll tell
You how she fell,
Then judge if she need grumble.

Dame Gill did grin
As she went in,
And Jill was plagued by Jack;
Will Goat came by,
And made Jack cry,
And knocked him on his back.

Though Jack wasn't hurt,
He was all over dirt;
I wish you had but seen him,
And how Jill did jump
Towards the pump,
And pumped on him to clean him.

Which done, all three
Went in to tea,
And put the place all right;
Which done, they sup,
Then take a cup,
And wish you a good night.

Mix A: Sociology textbook

Case study: Jack & Jill (after Langsten 1992)

Genetic versus skewed deviance
In this particular case we may observe the nature of sibling rivalry and its inevitable consequences on the regrettable phenomenon of anti-social and deviant behaviour.

Case commentary
The incident which follows has been selected from a number of similar instances in which the impact of the deprived living conditions experienced by the two subjects, coupled with what Durkheim termed 'the incorrigible wickedness of man', are manifest in the way in which simple tasks, ie the collection of water from the public water supply, are interrupted by lack of direction and discipline: inability to organise and share tasks in an atmosphere of co-operation also play a part.

The case
The two individuals (who for the purpose of this case will be referred to as

Jack and Jill) had been sent to collect water from a public supply, 200 metres away uphill. What should have been a comparatively simple task, but one which was of importance and should have been executed easily, efficiently within the capacity of the two young people, was not completed. The two quarrelled violently about division of labour until their inability to negotiate the task in hand resulted in physical violence. That is to say, Jill expressed dissatisfaction at not being allowed to fill the said pail, whereupon a physical wrangle resulted in Jack falling and striking his head on the tap. Jill's attempt to save the bucket had the consequence in her 'tumbling after'. Let us make no mistake, the incident, seemingly trivial, is born of the siblings' fundamental inability to communicate co-operatively.

The next stage is perhaps more disturbing in that Jack quickly recovered and returned home to attend his injuries: he not only left his sister injured but also abandoned the only means of obtaining water for the household: in short, the pail.

To quote Durkheim (1946, p. 377):

'In short, labour is divided spontaneously only if society is constituted in such a way that social inequalities exactly express natural inequalities.'

Mix B: American 'hard-boiled' detective novel

The big kiss-off of Jack and Jill

It was a Thursday morning and I had lots to do, like stare out of my window. I heard my outer office door open, and turned to see a blonde girl, maybe 25 years old.

'You can come right in,' I called.

She straightened her skirt and walked in very quickly. She was tall and composed, with a perfect nose, absolutely perfect.

'You're Levine, P.I.?'

'I am if you want me.'

'My man Jack needs your help.'

I couldn't have cared less. I cared more when she slowly crossed her legs.

'I hardly know where to begin, Mr Levine.'

'Begin at the dirty part. It's been a slow week.'

'Jack and I are co-starring in *The Grand Old Duke of York*. We were shooting the hill scene. You know he's a big matinee star but he's been drinking more lately. He's got something on his mind.'

'Blackmail?' I interposed. Her open blue jacket revealed a tight sweater that was being stretched to its limits.

'That's for you to find out. He's playing the king and he was real tipsy last night. When it got to the bit when we had to fetch a pail of water, he fell down and broke his crown. And I just fell right down there with him.'

The thought of those long lithe limbs intertwined with Jack's drove me crazy.

'Then up Jack got. And I rushed him to the condom. in a cab. Fortunately we'd got in a stock of vinegar and brown paper. And I got on with the job of plastering his nob.'

'You did what?'

Mix C: Report of court case

In re: Dame Gill and 2 minors v Acme Bucket Co.
Hearing in the Court of Appeal.
Lord Justice Cochtehund presiding, before Lords Y and Z.

The defendants Acme Bucket Co. appealed against the verdict of negligence, and against the award of damages in the case of Jack, a minor, who had injured himself in a fall while collecting water in a pail manufactured by Acme.

It was contended that the fall was occasioned by the pail becoming unstable when only half full. Damages of £200,000 were awarded in compensation for personal injury and trauma to family.

Delivering judgement, Lord X had taken due note of the evidence offered by the defendants that their product had been widely used for a number of years without any similar circumstance arising.

Their Lordships felt that due weight had not been given in the Lower Court to the precedent (Harry v Eliza, 1923) where it had been claimed that the pail had been repaired with inappropriate materials. Manufacturer's liability had been reduced for subsequent mishap.

This clearly established a *prima facie* defence. As the receptacle in this case had been in continuous use for a number of years the precedent applied. Their Lordships gave no weight to the evidence offered by the plaintiff, and having granted the appeal, the damages were waived.

Judgement was reserved on the matter of cash. Leave to appeal to the House of Lords was granted.

ACTIVITY

Try out some of the following suggestions for genre-bending experiments of your own, based on 'Jack and Jill'. You should attempt to be as accurate as possible when using the features of the new genre. Don't strain for comic effects, though some may occur naturally as a result of the mismatch of subject and genre.

- The script for a local TV news programme focusing on the incident.
- An advertisement for 'Gripwell', a new brand of children's non-slip shoes.
- A report in the *Sun*, highlighting the series of violent incidents affecting the family.
- Jill's letter to 'Confidential', *Just 17*'s problem page, and the reply.
- A leaflet advertising the Jack and Jill Heritage Theme Park.
- An article in a broadsheet newspaper revealing a breakthrough in the treatment of head injuries.

- A script for a talk to be given to children in an infants' school as part of a safety campaign.
- Questions for a physics examination paper based upon the incident.
- A review of a steamy new novel *Jack and Jill*, written by a well-known TV and film sex symbol, together with a short extract from the novel.
- A profile in a glossy film magazine of the exciting new star who plays Jack/Jill in new Hollywood blockbuster.

There are lots of other possibilities for re-writing nursery rhymes in different genres. Think about 'Little Miss Muffet', 'Little Jack Horner', 'Old King Cole' and 'The Cat and the Fiddle'. Then, of course, you could re-write well-known children's stories: 'The Three Billy Goats Gruff'; 'Cinderella'; 'Goldilocks and the Three Bears'. Or poems: 'The Pied Piper'; 'The Owl and the Pussycat'...

8 The Language of Literature

Advertising language

Here is the text of an advertisement for Royal Mail promoting Airpack, 'easy-to-use, pre-paid envelopes for sending your presents abroad'. Read it carefully.

Christmas comes but once a year, thank heavens. We've been up and down Oxford Street more times than a No. 25. My heart's set on a plastic terracotta soapdish for cousin Alfie in Turkey. But of course they only had it in the Russian Yellow. No way would that go with the Burgundy hand towels I got him last year. I knew I should've got that one my Jack spotted at that car boot sale in Rhyl, back in July. You live and learn. My feet are killing me, and my Jack's gone to feed the meter, muttering something about his angina. I was about to give up too! Get Alfie a bottle of peppermint foot rub and have done with it. It was at that moment I spotted them. A set of countryside coasters. So what if they were the last ones and the box was a bit flaky? I had that nice man in Homewares wrap it up. Then after I got home, I popped it into an Airpack and posted it. Simple.

ACTIVITY

What are the central features of this text? Discuss the suggestions below and supply the textual evidence in support of each one. You may, of course, want to add to this list of features.

- A narrative about a Christmas shopping expedition.
- One speaker (presumably female) directly addressing an unseen listener.
- Informal language.

- The language reveals the personality of the speaker, who doesn't realise the impression she is creating of herself.

An interesting question to think about is whether a novelist would consider this text to be a poor piece of writing and if so, why.

In groups, discuss these next two advertisements and again identify the type of text that each is meant to be by commenting on (i) its central features and (ii) the evidence for your decisions. Text A is part of the text of a newspaper advertisement for a National Savings product, whilst Text B is part of a script for the long-running series of TV advertisements for Gold Blend coffee.

Text A

Is the National Savings Capital Bond for me?

As a housewife I keep as busy as anyone, but like many other housewives I don't have a paid job, and I'm a non-taxpayer: I've a lump sum to invest. What are the advantages of Capital Bonds for a non-taxpayer like me?

There are quite a few. For a start, all the interest you'll get is added on gross – nothing is taken off for income tax before you get it, so as a non-taxpayer you'd keep the lot.

Is there any risk?

None whatsoever. Capital Bonds carry a cast-iron guarantee. Your return is absolutely guaranteed for a full five years, whatever happens to other interest rates in the meantime.

So as a non-taxpayer I'd know exactly how much money I'd end up with at the end of five years?

Precisely, and you'll get the best return if you keep your money in for the full five years. And Capital Bonds offer another very particular benefit for housewives in your situation, because of the change next April in the way you'll be taxed on your investment income.

What's that?

Well, after April 1990 husbands won't have to pay tax on the income from their wife's savings. As a wife, you'll have your own tax allowance, and all the interest on your Capital Bond will count against your allowance, not your husband's.

So why should Capital Bonds be better than saving with my local bank or building society?

With Capital Bonds the interest is taxable annually. But you'll be credited with every penny of your interest. Because, unlike your local bank or building society, which have to take tax off your interest, National Savings will add on the interest in full. So if you are a non-taxpayer you'll keep the lot.

Text B

(*doorbell rings*)
(*first woman*) Hi.
(*man*) Laura
(*first woman*) You always did stay up late.
(*man*) How long have you been back?
(*first woman*) About a day and a half. I was just(.) passing by.
(*man*) At this time of night?
(*first woman*) Are you alone? (*turns round*)
(*man*) (.) er (.) No(.) Look, I'm expecting someone.
(*first woman*) At this time of night?
(*man*) It's (.) a neighbour.
(*first woman*) Well, do we have time for a coffee?

(*male announcer's voice*) GOLDEN ROASTED RICHER. SMOOTHER. NESCAFE GOLD BLEND
(*doorbell rings again*)
(*second woman*) Hope I didn't get you out of bed.
(*first woman*) The coffee tastes good.
(*man*) (*sighs*)
(*second woman*) (*astonished gaze towards camera/first woman*)

You will find helpful information on conversations in Chapter 3.

This next group of texts contains a number of slogans and one complete advertisement (for the Volvo 850 TDI). Discuss how the advertisers have tried to ensure that each slogan sticks in your mind. The first one has been done for you.

1 Something plump to put on your plate. (sausage)
   (i) Uses alliteration: **p**lump/**p**ut/**p**late
   (ii) Heavy rhythmic stress: **some**thing **plump** to **put** on your **plate**.
2 Alliance and Leicester for the smarter investor. (building society)
3 Gillette – the best a man can get. (razor)
4 For the whitest, brightest, just-from-the-dentist polished feeling. (tooth cleaner)
5 Peugeot – the Drive of your Life. (car)

6 Timotei – a breath of fresh air in skin care. (hair shampoo)
7 Sainsbury's – Special Food at Everyday Prices. (supermarket)

8 THE NEW VOLVO 850 TURBO DIESEL. AN INCREDIBLE RATE OF NOTS.

Not slow: 0–60 in 9.9 seconds. Not sluggish: delivers 140bhp. Not dull: capable of 125mph. Not boring: 215lb/ft torque for swift overtaking. Not thirsty: 64mpg at a constant 56mph. Not smoky: lean-burn catalytic converter. Not heavy handed: has all the classic Volvo 850 driving characteristics. Not beyond reach: prices start at £21,975. Not your ordinary diesel. The new Volvo 850 TDI. A car you can believe in.

You will have recognised that the writers of all these advertisements and slogans are employing some of the characteristics and conventions of language that are in use everyday. They rely for their success partially on the fact that potential customers will recognise these familiar features and conventions and are likely then to be at ease and relaxed when reading or viewing the advertisements. They may even be entertained by them. This is not to suggest, of course, that the language of advertising mirrors exactly the language people use as they go about their daily lives, but that there are many similarities.

You will have identified that the slogans, catchphrases and the Volvo advertisement all use phonological patterning to create their effects. The sausage slogan employed both alliteration and heavy rhythmic stresses. There are further examples of alliteration and of assonance and rhyme in the others, some quite subtle, as in the Timotei slogan, and others more obvious, as in the Alliance and Leicester slogan. The Volvo advertisement uses a repeated grammatical **structure** 'Not...' to achieve its effects.

Where, then, in everyday life are these patterns – alliteration, assonance, rhyme, rhythm and repeated structures – used?

1 What phonological patterns can you identify in these football chants? Can you think of any to add to the list?

   a *Come on you Blues!*

   b *2 – 4 – 6 – 8
      Who do we appreciate?*

   c *B – O – L – T – O – N!
      BOLTON!!*

   d *Play up, Pompey!*

   e *Ev – er – ton!*

   f *We are the Wanderers!*

2 What patterns are being used in the following extract from a baptismal service?

   The Minister says to the parents or guardians of the *child*:

   You have brought *this child* to be baptized, and you will receive *him* again to be trained in the doctrines, privileges and duties of the Christian religion. I ask you therefore:

Will you provide for *this your child* a Christian home of love and faithfulness?

Answer: With God's help we will.

Will you help *him* by your words, prayers and example to renounce all evil and to put *his* trust in Jesus Christ *his* Saviour?

Answer: With God's help we will.

Will you encourage *him* to enter into the full membership of the Church, and to serve Christ in the world?

Answer: With God's help we will.

If there are sponsors, the Minister says:

Will you, who have come to support these parents, help them in the Christian upbringing of *this child*?

Answer: With God's help we will.

3 What is the effect of the patterns used here?

Collect as many other examples as you can of everyday language that uses strong patterns.

Questioning and answering

The National Savings advertisement on page 125 uses the technique of question and answer that is frequently found not only in advertisements, but in other genres as well. You will be able to think of many for yourself, but a quick trawl through material collected over a very short period revealed this technique used in an information pack about drugs, a leaflet explaining the differences in hi-fi equipment and a guide to the best methods for hair-care. Questioning and answering is, of course, very much part of everyday communication, from the classroom and courtroom to ordinary conversations. Advertisers have appropriated this method, but there are a number of significant differences between their use of it and its use as part of an ordinary conversation. Foremost amongst these, of course, is that the questions asked are not genuine ones. In everyday conversations the questioner normally seeks information and usually sets the agenda. It might be what time the train leaves or what clothes would be suitable to wear for a particular occasion. In the National Savings advertisement, however, the 'questions' are not genuine because the 'questioner' is not setting the agenda at all. It has been pre-set by the writer to provide a third party, *you*, with the information that the advertiser wishes to provide. There are no off-the-cuff questions allowed!

What everyday equivalents can you think of for the narrative **discourse** used in the Royal Mail Airpack advertisement? Anecdotes and jokes would be two obvious ones to begin with. But can you think of any more?

Models for examining the structure of narrative

Linguists have developed a number of ways for studying the structure of narrative. You will be looking at two of these. The first model to consider is known as the Problem–Solution pattern and it was developed by linguist Michael Hoey. There are four basic elements:

Situation	What was the situation?
Problem	What was the problem?
Solution	What was the solution or response?
Evaluation	How successful was the solution?

If the solution was not successful, then another attempt could be made, of course.

This model can be applied to the Airpack advertisement as follows:

Situation	Christmas shopping in Oxford Street
Problem	To find a suitable present for Cousin Alfie in Turkey
Solution	Buy a set of countryside coasters and post them in an Airpack
Evaluation	'Simple'

Another well-known way of looking at narrative structure was developed by William Labov during his investigation of oral story-telling in Harlem. In Labov's model, there are six elements:

Abstract	What is the story about?
Orientation	What? Who took part? Where and when did it happen?
Complicating action	Then what happened?
Evaluation	What's the point of the story? Why have you been telling me this? So what?
Resolution	What was the final outcome?
Coda	The story's over and I'm returning to the present situation.

Not every element has to be present in every narrative and they do not have to be given equal weight. The coda, for example, if present, may be no more than a single line or a brief remark, if the story is an oral one.

ACTIVITY

1 Analyse the Airpack advertisement in terms of Labov's narrative structure.
2 Apply *either* the Problem–Solution model or Labov's to this *Urban Myth*.

A friend of a friend's mum was on her way back from her daughter's new house and had stopped to top up with petrol at a motorway service station. She had just finished and was about to rejoin the main carriageway when her eagle eyes spotted a microwave oven glinting on the hard shoulder, seemingly abandoned.

Figuring it must have fallen off the back of a lorry, the overjoyed woman screeched to a halt and hoicked the modern technological marvel into her hatchback. Even if it was damaged, her handyman husband would soon get the gadget up and cooking.

The woman couldn't believe her luck: her conventional cooker was on its last legs, and for months she'd been jealous of her neighbours, who never stopped gassing about their microwave marvel. Eager to get home and excited by her good fortune, she put her foot down. But shortly after she'd set off, a police motorway patrol car came haring up behind her, sirens wailing. The driver flashed her and indicated she should pull over.

As the officers sauntered over towards her, the poor woman began perspiring heavily and just couldn't help looking horribly guilty.

Deciding honesty was the best policy, she was ready to blurt out the whole sorry tale about the microwave when one of the officers jammed his head through her open window.

'I'm terribly sorry to bother you, madam, but could you please tell us why you've just stolen this object,' he oozed.

Through floods of tears, the woman explained everything: 'I just wanted to use it to cook my family's dinner,' she sobbed.

'You'd be hard-pushed to cook for anyone with that thing,' smirked one of the officers. 'You see, it's a radar speed-trap box.'

3 Are there any other ways that you could divide either the Airpack advertisement or the *Urban Myth* into sections? How would you label them?

Myths, legends and folk tales, like this *Urban Myth*, have been a source of rich material for Russian linguists, too. One of them, Vladimir Propp, unearthed the common patterns that controlled the narrative in Russian fairy tales. Here is one example from Propp's work. What is the constant element (or common pattern) in these tales he quotes?

- A tsar gives an eagle to a hero. The eagle carries the hero away to another kingdom.
- An old man gives Súcenko a horse. The horse carries Súcenko away to another kingdom.
- A sorcerer gives Iván a little boat. The boat takes Iván to another kingdom.
- A princess gives Iván a ring. Young men appearing from out of the ring carry Iván away into another kingdom.

ACTIVITY

Look at a volume of short fairy stories yourself. Choose three that you think exemplify a narrative structure that you have detected in them. Be original. You can then formulate your own theory of narrative structure and call it 'The Raymond Wagstaff Theory' (or whatever your name is!).

These, and the other models that have been proposed, suggest ways that you can examine any narrative, but, of course, it is more complicated if you are studying a long narrative, such as a novel, which can consist of a number of narratives and sub-narratives. If you are interested in this subject, you might like to read *Narrative: A Critical Linguistic Introduction* by Michael Toolan (Routledge), though it is quite difficult in places.

So far, you have seen that advertisers use the techniques and conventions of everyday language, but that they use them in rather specialised ways. They may slightly alter, adapt or emphasise and in so doing, of course, they establish their own conventions. You have seen too that advertising language is used to persuade and often to entertain, though this latter is not the primary purpose of an advertisement. In the advertisements examined in this section, the writers have used

- narrative
- dialogue
- phonological and grammatical patterns.

These, as you will know, are the staples of literature. Novelists use narrative; dramatists, dialogue and poets, phonological patterns. This is not to suggest that such elements are mutually exclusive: novelists also use dialogue, poets can tell stories and playwrights use phonological patterns. But whereas advertisers may *incidentally* wish to entertain their potential customers, writers of literature will have entertainment as one of their primary goals.

Literary language

You will remember the ten-year-old girl who, as part of a classroom project, was asked 'What can you do with language?' She came up with quite a long list ('shouting at people; cheering on your team; swearing; being cheeky...'; you might like to try the same activity yourself. How long would your list be?). She was then asked 'What can't you do without language?' and 'lie' was her response. It is an interesting notion that literature could be viewed as licensed lying, because literature is something that depends entirely on language. Without language, there would be no literature. Without lies, there would be no fiction.

The writers of literature, then, are using language in a specialised way in order to invent and entertain. But they cannot afford to use language which is so divorced from the way it is used in normal situations that it becomes incomprehensible to their intended audiences. The techniques and conventions of literary language, just like the techniques and conventions of advertising language, have to be very firmly rooted in the way that language is used by people every day. The language of literature is not a language completely separate and divorced from any other. People tell stories, have conversations and make imaginative comparisons as they go about their everyday lives. But it is not *quite* everyday language.

It is impossible in a short chapter to cover all of the ways in which writers of literature use language, one reason being that many literary texts are longer than this whole book! But it is important to get some idea of a literary whole to understand better the extracts set in examination papers.

The two case studies that follow are designed to help you discover how writers use specific features and conventions of language in their literary works.

Case study 1: Talk in *Othello*

You will need to have read or seen *Othello* and to have a copy of the text available as you explore this case study.

Read the first scene. The substance of the immediate opening is political gossip, itself a well-known form of talk. Notice how the very first line refers to speech:

Tush, never **tell** me.

This is followed very soon by further references:

'Sblood, but you will not **hear** me Thou **told'st** me

In Iago's speech beginning on line 8, there are two further references to varieties of speech: 'bombast' and 'prattle'.

Who is in control of the conversation between Iago and Roderigo (lines 1–82)? How do you know?

ACTIVITY

Begin a thesaurus of all the words and phrases to do with speaking and listening that you collect as you go through the play. You have already collected 'tell', 'told', 'hear', 'bombast', 'prattle'.

How would you describe Iago's manner of talking in this opening scene?

In line 94, Roderigo calls up to Brabantio 'do you know my voice?'. Brabantio assumes that Roderigo is wooing his daughter, Desdemona, and says:

In honest plainness thou hast heard me say
My daughter is not for thee

How effective do you think spoken prohibitions are? What gives them their force or authority? What is the dramatic effect in this instance?

ACTIVITY

1 Find the following remarks in Act 1 Scene 2. They are arranged in sequence.

   a Nay, but he prated
   And spoke such scurvey and provoking terms
   Against your honour

   b My services … shall out-tongue his complaints

   c … when I know that boasting is an honour
   I shall promulgate

   d I will but spend a word here in the house

   e Where will you that I go
   To answer this your charge?
   To prison, til fit time
   Of law and course of direct session
   Call thee to answer.

2 Find out who spoke these remarks and in what context, and make sure that you understand the meaning of any unusual **words** or phrases.

3 Of the many threads running through the play, one has to do with gossip, hearsay, private conversations and backbiting; another has to do with public speech – as in a court of law, for example. To which of these threads or themes do the quotations above contribute? What, for instance, is the significance of the verb 'to answer'?

ACTIVITY

1 Now find the following remarks in Act 1
   Scene 3.

   a How say you by this change?

   b We lacked your counsel and your help tonight

   c … corrupted by spells …

   d Rude as I am in my speech
      And little blessed with the soft phrase of peace

   e … little of this great world can I speak

   f And therefore little shall I grace my cause
      In speaking for myself

   g I will a round unvarnished tale deliver

   h But Othello speak

   i Say it Othello

   j This to hear
      Would Desdemona seriously incline

   k … and with a greedy ear
      Devour up my discourse

   l She wished she had not heard it

   m She thanked me
      And bade me, if I had a friend that loved her
      I should but teach him how to tell my story,
      And that would woo her. Upon this I spake.

   n I think this tale would woo my daughter too.

   o I pray you hear her speak

   p Let me speak like yourself and lay a sentence

   q But words are words. I never yet did hear
      That the bruised heart was pierced through the
      ear

   r Let her have your voice

2 Identify the speaker and the context of these
   quotations.
3 What is said (and sometimes what is not
   said) is as important in love as in politics.
   Sort out these remarks under the headings.

   ■ Lovers' talk
   ■ Political talk
   ■ Other talk.

What do you make of Othello's remarks about himself? How accurately
does he refer to his own speech? How well does Othello answer the charge
against him? Notice that Desdemona shifts the real focus of her love onto a
hypothetical 'friend that loved her'. Why does she do this? How does
Othello respond to the hint?

ACTIVITY

1 Think about situations in life when people
   want to talk about themselves but deflect the
   talk onto a hypothetical person. What are the
   advantages of doing this?
2 Think of ways in which people talk to each
   other, not plainly or directly, but in hints

and implications. What advantage is there in
communicating in this way? What is the
danger? Desdemona's hint was a fairly
unsubtle one; what about Iago's hints? List
the occasions so far on which he has hinted
or implied meanings to his listener.

Turn to Act 2 Scene 1. Look at the meeting of Iago, Cassio, Emilia and
Desdemona that begins at line 100 and continues to 'O fie upon thee,
slanderer!' This is the kind of comic banter, rather sharp edged in this
instance, that Shakespeare frequently inserts into his plays. There is
another, more vulgar example, at the beginning of Act 3. It would be
described nowadays as a male sexist put-down. In Elizabethan times the
language would have been more immediately accessible and the humour
more obvious.

What is ironic about Desdemona calling Iago a 'slanderer'? Note that 'slanderer' is another addition to the talk thesaurus.

Make sure you understand the Elizabethan meanings (eg 'housewifery' means what we would call 'housekeeping money'). Re-write the conversation as a brief exchange in a modern TV sitcom.

Continue through Act 2 Scene 1, identifying the speaker and the context of the following:

O my sweet
I prattle out of fashion

First I must tell thee . . .
Mark me with what violence she first loved the Moor, but for bragging and telling her fantastical lies; and will she love him still for prating?

Look particularly at Iago's speech from which the last quotation is taken. How does he tell his lies?

Your investigation of the play so far will have shown you just how central are ideas about the role of speech in human affairs. The American linguist, Dwight Bolinger, described language as a loaded weapon that can do a great deal of damage whether intended or not. You could continue through the remainder of the play and you would find many other such speech references.

Here are a few quotations from Act 5 to demonstrate both the richness and the sustained preoccupation with talk:

Nay, guiltiness will speak Though tongues are out of use.

O, good my lord, I would speak a word with you.

I will not charm my tongue; I am bound to speak.

From this time forth I never will speak word.

All that is spoke is marr'd.

Myself will straight abroad, and to the state
This heavy act with heavy heart relate.

The whole play is, ironically, framed by an opening and final reference to talk:

Tush never **tell** me . . .

. . . with heavy heart **relate**.

Note too, the irony of Iago's very last words.

Case study 2: Dialect and dialogue

Writers use dialogue in novels and short stories for a variety of purposes. It can be used:

- to further the plot
- to describe the setting
- to describe the atmosphere
- to present a moral argument or point of view
- to present and develop character.

The speech of a character in a novel will often mark him or her out as an individual and thus distinguish him or her as unique. It would be difficult, say, to mistake the middle-class Mrs Morel in D H Lawrence's *Sons and Lovers* for her miner husband. Look at this short exchange between them as they discuss their young son, William.

'I'll learn 'im!' said Morel. 'It none matters to me whose lad 'e is; 'e's none goin' rippin' an' tearin' about just as he's a mind.'
' "Ripping and tearing about!" ' repeated Mrs Morel. 'He was running after that Alfy, who'd taken his cobbler, and he accidentally got hold of his collar, because the other dodged.'

Note how Mrs Morel uses Standard English, except for her use of the dialect term 'cobbler' and how she mocks her husband for his pronunciation.

Nor would Mrs Morel ever utter words like this:

'You mun get me a drop o' laxy vitral,' he said. 'It's a winder as we canna ha'e a sup i' th' 'ouse.'

Lawrence is giving Mr Morel a Nottinghamshire working-class dialect here.

Many writers have used dialect in their novels to identify characters with particular regional, social or occupational classes. You need only think of Thomas Hardy and Charles Dickens and of how they used dialect speech for characters such as the rustics in *The Mayor of Casterbridge* or Sam Weller, the Cockney, in *Pickwick Papers*. Dialect, you will remember, can be defined as a regional, social or occupational variety of English.

Dialect speech and narration has often been used by novelists not only to identify their characters with particular groups, but also:

- to provide comedy
- to depict unaffected simplicity in a character
- to depict integrity in a character
- to depict natural warmth in a character
- to depict intimacy and tenderness.

Remember, though, that the speech of any individual is as unique as his or her set of fingerprints. You have already encountered the term '**idiolect**' for this. Each person will have his or her favourite words and expressions, idiosyncrasies of pronunciation, and particular mannerisms of stress and intonation that mark him or her out as being different from anyone else. Thus, whilst you may be part of a group (of people from Huddersfield, of young mothers, of football fans, of public-school educated students...) you are, at the same time, a unique individual who has his or her own 'voice'.

Characters in fiction can also be both individuals and representative of a group and their speech can mark them out as such. Though, for example, Lady Bertram and Mrs Norris in Jane Austen's *Mansfield Park* are sisters, nonetheless their speech is not a carbon copy of each other's, they have their own idiolect. Dr Watson and Sherlock Holmes speak differently, though they share the same age, sex and interests.

Writers of literature try to avoid stereotyping their characters and usually want to create an individual, unlike the writers of advertisements who wish deliberately to create stereotypes so that the advertisements will appeal to *all* young mothers who want a cleaner, brighter wash or to *all* upwardly mobile young professionals who aspire to a new, faster, sleeker car.

What do the writers of TV soaps like *Emmerdale* or *Brookside* wish to create?

You are now going to examine the specific use of dialect in extracts from four novels.

Hard Times *by Charles Dickens*

Hard Times is set in industrial Lancashire in the mid-nineteenth century. In this extract, Stephen Blackpool, a mill worker, is defending the striking workers against their employer, Mr Bounderby, who accuses them of being 'a set of rascals and rebels'. Stephen himself has felt unable to join the strike. Louisa is Mr Bounderby's young wife. Note that Dickens comments on how Stephen's 'rugged earnestness' is reflected in his dialect speech.

'Nay, ma'am,' said Stephen Blackpool, staunchly protesting against the words that had been used, and instinctively addressing himself to Louisa, after glancing at her face. 'Not rebels, nor yet rascals. Nowt o' th' kind, ma'am, nowt o' th' kind. They've not doon me a kindness, ma'am, as I know and feel. But there's not a dozen men amoong 'em, ma'am – a dozen? not six – but what believes as he has doon his duty by the rest and by himseln. God forbid as I, that ha' known an had'n experience o' these men aw my life – I, that ha' ett'n an droonken wi' 'em an' seet'n wi' 'em, and toil'n wi' 'em, and lov'n 'em, should fail fur to stan' by 'em wi' the truth, let 'em ha' doon to me what they may!'

He spoke with the rugged earnestness of his place and character – deepened perhaps by a proud consciousness that he was faithful to his class under all their mistrust; but he fully remembered where he was, and did not even raise his voice.

'No, ma'am, no. They're true to one another, faithfo' to one another, 'fectionate to one another, e'en to death. Be poor amoong 'em, be sick amoong 'em, grieve amoong 'em for onny o' th' monny causes that carries grief to the poor man's door, an' they'll be tender wi' you, gentle wi' you, comfitable wi' you, Chrisen wi' you. Be sure o' that, ma'am. They'd be riven to bits, ere ever they'd be different.'

'In short,' said Mr Bounderby, 'it's because they are so full of virtues that they have turned you adrift. Go through with it while you are about it. Out with it.'

'How 'tis, ma'am,' resumed Stephen, appearing still to find his natural refuge in

Louisa's face, 'that what is best in us fok, seems to turn us most to trouble and misfort'n and mistake, I dunno. But 'tis so. I know 'tis, as I know the heavens is over me ahint the smoke. We're patient too, and wants in general to do right. An' I canna think the fawt is aw wi' us.'

'Now, my friend,' said Mr Bounderby, whom he could not have exasperated more, quite unconscious of it though he was, than by seeming to appeal to anyone else, 'if you will favour me with your attention for half a minute, I should like to have a word or two with you. You said just now that you had nothing to tell us about this business. You are quite sure of that, before we go any further?'

'Sir, I am sure on't.'

ACTIVITY

Dickens had visited Preston before writing *Hard Times* and therefore had some familiarity with the dialect of the area. How does he represent Stephen's local speech? Think about:

- spelling
- **syntax**
- **lexis**.

Wuthering Heights *by Emily Brontë*

In the first edition of *Wuthering Heights*, published in 1847, Emily Brontë represented the servant, Joseph, as speaking with a very broad Yorkshire **accent** which, for many non-Yorkshire readers, proved almost incomprehensible. Her sister, Charlotte, felt this too and wrote:

It seems to me advisable to modify the orthography of the old servant Joseph's speeches; for though as it stands it exactly renders the Yorkshire dialect to a Yorkshire ear, yet I am sure Southerns must find it unintelligible; and thus one of the most graphic characters in the book is lost on them.

So Charlotte modified Joseph's speech when she edited the second edition of the novel in 1850. Here is one of the revisions, together with Emily's original.

'Noa!' said Joseph ... 'Noa! that manes nowt – Hathecliffe maks noa 'cahnt uh t'mother, nur yah norther – bud he'll hev his lad; und Aw mun tak him – soa nah yah knaw!' (1847)

'Noa!' said Joseph ... 'Noa! that means naught. Hathecliff maks noa 'count o' t'mother, nor ye norther; but he'll hev his lad; und I mun tak him – soa now ye knaw!' (1850)

ACTIVITY

1 What changes did Charlotte make?
2 Why do you think she made these particular alterations?
3 Do you think she needed to have made the alterations?
4 Here is a further sample of Joseph's speech from the 1847 edition. What changes would you make to ensure it became more intelligible? You can check your version with Charlotte's by looking at Chapter 9.

'Und hah isn't that nowt comed in frough th' field, be this time? What is he abaht? girt eedle seeght!' demanded the old man, looking round for Heathcliff.

It can be quite difficult to get dialect right. Bill Owen, a Cockney, who plays Compo in *The Last of the Summer Wine*, the TV comedy set in a small West Yorkshire village, tells in his autobiography how difficult it was to get his 'thees' and his 'thous' in the right place. There is a complex set of rules that govern when 'thee' and when 'thou' should be used. It wasn't till the second series of the programme that Bill Owen felt he'd got them right!

Thomas Hardy

Hardy was attacked by a number of critics at the time he was writing for using what they considered to be unreasonably obscure dialect. But was it so obscure? Here are two passages, one from Hardy's novel *The Return of the Native* (1878) and the other a record of actual rural speech from the same period made by William Barnes, a Dorset dialect poet and contemporary of Hardy's. The extract from the novel is part of a discussion on marriage, whilst the other is the reply Barnes received from a countryman to a question about his new waggon.

Text A: *The Return of the Native*
'Couldst sign the book, no doubt,' said Fairway, 'if wast young enough to join hands with a woman again, like Wildeve and Mis'ess Tamsin, which is more than Humph there could do, for he follows his father in learning. Ah, Humph, well I can mind when I was married how I zid thy father's mark staring me in the face as I went to put down my name. He and your mother were the couple married just afore we were, and there stood thy father's cross with arms stretched out like a great banging scarecrow. What a terrible black cross that was – thy father's very likeness in en! To save my soul I couldn't help laughing when I zid en, though all the time I was as hot as dogdays, what with the marrying, and what with the woman a-hanging to me, and what with Jack Changley and a lot more chaps grinning at me through church window. But the next moment a strawmote would have knocked me down, for I called to mind that if thy father and mother had had high words once, they'd been at it twenty times since they'd been man and wife, and I zid myself as the next poor stunpoll to get into the same mess ... Ah – well, what a day 'twas!'

Text B: The countryman's reply
'Why, the vust thing I do vine fate wi' is the drats; tha be too crooked; and the tug-irons be a-put in mwore than dree inches too vur back. An' jis' look here, where the rudge-tie and breechen rings be: why, nar a carter in the wordle can't put a hoss into en. I don't call the head and tail a-put out 'o han' well. They be a-painted noo-how. Why'e woon't bear hafe a luoad; tha've a meade en o' green stuff a-shook all to pieces. The vust time 'e 's a-haled out in the zun, e'll come all abrode. The strongest thing I do zee about en is the mainpin; and he is too big by hafe.'

1 Has Hardy made his version of dialect intelligible to the general reader? How?
2 Why is the countryman's speech about his waggon so difficult to understand? List some of the features of nineteenth-century Dorset dialect that this extract reveals.

Billy *by Albert French*

In this short extract from an American novel published in 1993, Billy Lee, a ten-year-old black boy, is trying to persuade his friend Gumpy to come with him to a pond usually frequented by white children.

The distant pondwater sparkles through the silent shade of the trees. Gumpy shouts, 'Ah ain't goin down there, Billy Lee. Ah ain't goin down there. We can'ts go down there, that's where them redhead boys be, we can'ts be goin down there. They chase us, they's big. Ah ain't goin down there. Ya knows what theys do before, ya remembers. They almost git us. Theys can beat us up bad if theys git us.' Billy sighs, but still looks through the trees and bushes to the quiet waters of the pond. He turns and whispers to Gumpy, 'Theys ain't be down there. Theys ain't goin ta see us. Come on, Gumpy, let's go. Ah ain't scared. Ah goes first. Come on wit me.' Billy keeps his eyes on Gumpy's eyes, but they don't move. Gumpy just stares at the pond. Billy quickly whispers, 'Ya scared. Ya be scared of everythings, ya more scared than an old lady be. Ya scared all the time of everything.'

'Ah ain't be scared,' Gumpy yells back.

What features of black American speech does the author represent here?

9 Stylistics

It would be as well to clarify what is meant by stylistics in a chapter that uses the term as its title! So what *is* stylistics? (Or should the question be 'what *are* stylistics?')

The word has obvious connections with **style**. What then do we mean by 'style'? We use it in two senses. Firstly, when we talk about someone having 'style', we are usually passing a complimentary comment on the way that person dresses or behaves, for example. We are measuring him or her against a particular standard, whether it is of dress, social behaviour or ability at batting. To push the cricketing analogy a little further, the former England Test captain, David Gower, was often described as a 'stylish' batsman. This didn't necessarily mean he scored more runs than anyone else (though he often did so) but that he scored them in a way that people found attractive. He had 'style' in that he scored his runs in an aesthetically pleasing way. His batsmanship was thus measured against a standard which other batsmen may not have met.

The second sense of 'style' does not have any value judgement attached to it, as it is purely descriptive. Thus we can say of someone that he or she has, for example, his or her own distinctive 'style' of dress. If we note that Jane habitually wears a sweatshirt, jeans and trainers, whereas Suzi habitually wears a black dress, then we are merely observing differences in their style of dress. We are not valuing one above the other. David Gower has a different batting style than Mike Atherton. In this sense then, style simply describes the set of distinctive characteristics that identifies people, places, periods or whatever.

When we talk about the style of a piece of writing (or speech) we are using the word in its second sense outlined above. We are saying that the writer or speaker has, consciously or unconsciously, selected a certain set of language features from all those that are available to him or her and has rejected others. Thus we can refer to the style of a particular individual's writing (Jane Austen has a different style than that of Charles Dickens) or speech (Richie Benaud has a different commentary style than Geoff Boycott).

A distinction needs to be made here between **register** and style. Though style is often loosely used when people refer to the style of sets of writing or speech – chemistry textbooks, wedding invitations, after-dinner speeches, wills, examination questions, job interviews and telephone conversations, for example – a more accurate word to describe this would be the 'register' of chemistry textbooks, wedding invitations, after-dinner speeches and so on. The clothes analogy should help to make this distinction clearer. There are, for instance, certain occasions when it is expected that men will wear a suit – formal dinners, weddings, job interviews, for example. There are other occasions when both men and women would be expected to wear a t-shirt and jeans. We could say, then, that the 'register' of some occasions is a suit and of others, a t-shirt and jeans. But there are many variations possible within the 'suit register' – double-breasted, single-breasted, with or without turn-ups, for instance. Similarly, there are variations possible within the 'jeans register' – blue, black, straight, flared, frayed . . . These variations can be called different styles. Similarly, with texts: there are recognised and appropriate registers for all chemistry textbooks or all wedding invitations, but there are variations within these registers that allow the reader to see that a chemistry textbook written by x differs in style from one written by y, but they are both within the register of chemistry textbooks.

Stylistics, then, is the study of language style. In it, we are asked to do two things: first, to *describe* the style of a particular language variety or individual's language, and second, to *comment* on the effects that these linguistic choices have. These effects may be consciously intended by the speaker or writer or may indeed be accidental.

You will have realised that as stylistics asks you to describe and comment on the style of language, then you have already covered a great deal about the subject in this book. The sections on:

- **grammar**
- phonology
- **genre**
- the language of literature
- reading
- original writing and re-writing

all contain material that is relevant to stylistics.

Remind yourself of the diagram on page 33. You will remember that it stresses that at the centre of all language study is the *text*. The diagram focuses attention on texts (as does stylistics) and shows us that we can investigate them not only for what they reveal about the 'big issues' in language (the boxes along the top row) but also that we can investigate their **structure**, organisation and other important linguistic features (the boxes along the bottom row). We can thus take a 'top-down' or a 'bottom-up' approach to the linguistic study of a text.

Stylistics, then, can be seen as where your knowledge about language comes together, as you consider the **lexis**, semantics, phonology, morphology, **discourse** and **pragmatics** of a particular text. This close investigation of the style of a text may well lead you to reach conclusions about how it reflects something about the 'big issues' in language study. Stylistics is essentially investigative.

Lest stylistics begins to seem a very daunting discipline, you should remember two things, especially when you are in an examination. First, you can't say *everything* about a particular text. Second, some texts will, as it were, leap out at you and say: 'You've *got* to comment on these important features here; if you don't, you'll be missing the crucial way this text works; there *are* other features, but in this particular text, they are less important, so comment on them only if you have time.' These 'other features', of course, may be the crucial ones in a different text. For example, whereas you might be foolish if you neglected to examine the ways sentences are connected in a young child's story, these might be of less importance in a poem, where the essential features could well be phonology and lexis. The child could have written his or her story without considering phonological effects at all. Of course, some important features of a text may be more subtle or less obvious.

The focus of this chapter, then, will essentially be practical. You will be:

- examining a variety of texts and discovering ways of looking at them that will reveal their important stylistic features
- looking at examination questions and evaluations of candidates' answers, so that you can improve your own chances of success.

Text A

MEETING AT NIGHT
The grey sea and the long black land;
And the yellow half-moon large and low;
And the startled little waves that leap
In fiery ringlets from their sleep,
As I gain the cove with pushing prow,
And quench its speed i' the slushy sand.

Then a mile of warm sea-scented beach;
Three fields to cross till a farm appears;
A tap at the pane, the quick sharp scratch
And blue spurt of a lighted match,
And a voice less loud, thro' its joys and fears,
Than the two hearts beating each to each!

In this investigation, you will be closely examining three features of the first verse of the poem. Read through the poem very carefully to ensure that you know what it is about. Who is meeting whom? When? Where? With what result?

Noun groups

Begin by looking at the noun groups. Here is a list of them with the head word highlighted:

- the grey **sea**
- the long black **land**
- the yellow **half-moon** large and low

■ the startled little **waves** that leap / In fiery ringlets from their sleep / As I gain the cove with pushing prow / And quench its speed i' the slushy sand.

Notice how they progressively lengthen:

sea has only one pre-modifier: 'grey'
land has two pre-modifiers: 'long, black'
half-moon has both pre- and **post-modification**: 'yellow' and 'large and low'
waves has two pre-modifiers: ('startled' and 'little') and two post-modifying dependent **clauses** which contain other noun groups: fiery ringlets; their sleep; the core; pushing prow; its speed; the slushy sand.

What effect does the poet achieve by using this syntactical scheme?

Phonology

Now look at the phonology of the first verse. You should be able to notice how the poet uses sound patterning to good effect. For example, look at all the |l| sounds. Remember to concentrate on sound only. Not every word with 'l' in it uses the |l| sound.

Can you find any examples of alliteration?

How does the writer use sound in lines 1 and 2 to slow the movement down? And how does sound help speed up the movement in the next two lines? Why should he want to do this?

Notice the prevalence of the |sh| sound in the last two lines:

As I gain the cove with pu**sh**ing prow,
And quen**ch** its speed i' the slu**sh**y sand.

Is this, do you think, an example of onomatopœia? Are there any other sound patterns in this verse?

Semantic fields

There are two main **semantic** fields that the poet draws on here. Note the use of colour terms: 'grey', 'black', 'yellow' and arguably 'fiery'. What do you think the other semantic field is?

You will remember that it has been suggested that it is difficult to say everything about a text in the time you have available. This is as true for the authors of this book as it is for you. Your attention has been drawn to the three most important stylistic features of this verse – the noun groups, the phonology and the semantic fields used – but there is more that could be said about it. A fourth very significant grammatical feature has deliberately been ignored. What is it? You will be looking at it later.

The other aspect of stylistics that this analysis should have alerted you to is that it isn't enough merely to *identify* linguistic features and patterns. You should always try to explain the *effect* of these features on the reader or listener. In poetry, as here, the effect is probably the result of conscious effort on the part of the writer, but in many other texts, this might not always be the case. Some effects can be unintentional.

ACTIVITY

1 Investigate the second verse under the same headings as you did with the first: noun groups, phonology and semantic fields. You will find there is plenty to discuss.
2 Here is a second version of 'Meeting at Night'.

The grey sea and the long black land
Lay before me,
And the yellow half moon was large and low.
The startled little waves leaped
In fiery ringlets from their sleep,
As I gained the cove with pushing prow
And quenched its speed i' the slushy sand.

Then I walked a mile of warm sea-scented beach
And crossed three fields till a farm appeared,

I tapped at the pane,
Heard the quick sharp scratch
And saw the blue spurt of a lighted match.
Then came at last a voice less loud
Thro' its joys and fears,
Than the two hearts now beating each to each.

a What is the major grammatical difference between this and the first version that you have been investigating?
b Does this difference change the effect of the poem at all? Which do you prefer?
c One of the two versions was written by the Victorian poet, Robert Browning, the other was an adaptation of it by a student. Which is which?

Text B

This poem, by the American writer, Theodore Roethke, gives you a further opportunity to look closely at **syntax**, phonology and semantics.

CHILD ON TOP OF A GREENHOUSE

The wind billowing out the seat of my britches,
My feet crackling splinters of glass and dried putty,
The half-grown chrysanthemums, staring up like accusers
Up through the streaked glass, flashing with sunlight,
A few white clouds all rushing eastward,
A line of elms plunging and tossing like horses,
And everyone, everyone pointing up and shouting.

ACTIVITY

Divide into groups, each group making itself responsible for a close investigation of one of these three language areas: syntax, phonology and semantics. Report back to the class on the results of your investigation.

Text C

The third text is another literary one, this time a complete short story by the American writer, Ernest Hemingway, called 'One Reader Writes'. It shows how different voices or points of view can be found in one short text. A young wife is worried that her husband has contracted syphilis and is seeking advice from a doctor who writes a syndicated newspaper column. There are three sections to the story:

(i)   The narrator sets the scene and describes her actions
(ii)   The letter that she wrote to the doctor
(iii) Her thoughts after she had written the letter.

She sat at the table in her bedroom with a newspaper folded open before her and only stopping to look out of the window at the snow which was falling and melting on the roofs as it fell. She wrote this letter, writing it steadily with no necessity to cross out or rewrite anything.

Roanoke, Virginia
February 6th, 1933

Dear Doctor,
May I write you for some very important advice – I have a decision to make and don't know just whom to trust most, I dare not ask my Parents – and so I come to you – and only because I need not see you, can I confide in you even. Now here is the situation – I married a man in U.S. service in 1929 and that same year he was sent to China, Shanghai – he stayed three years – and came home – he was discharged from the service some few months ago – and went to his mother's home in Helena, Arkansas. He wrote for me to come home – I went, and found he is taking a course of injections and I naturally ask, and found he is being treated for I don't know how to spell the word but it sounds like this 'silfilus' – Do you know what I mean – now tell me will it ever be safe for me to live with him again – I did not come in close contact with him at any time since his return from China. He assures me he will be OK after this doctor finishes with him – Do you think it right – I often heard my Father say one could well wish themselves dead if they once became a victim of that malady – I believe my Father but want to believe my Husband most – Please, please tell me what to do – I have a daughter born while her Father was in China – Thanking you and trusting wholly in your advice I am

and signed her name.

Maybe he can tell me what's right to do, she said to herself. Maybe he can tell me. In the picture in the paper he looks like he'd know. He looks smart, all right. Every day he tells somebody what to do. He ought to know. I want to do whatever is right. It's such a long time though. It's a long time. And it's been a long time. My Christ, it's been a long time. He had to go wherever they sent him, I know, but I don't know what he had to get it for. Oh, I wish to Christ he wouldn't have got it. I don't care what he did to get it. But I wish to Christ he hadn't ever got it. It does seem like he didn't have to have got it. I don't know what to do. I wish to Christ he hadn't got any kind of malady. I don't know why he had to get a malady.

You will notice that each section has a distinctly different style, the second and third clearly revealing the woman's character and feelings, not only through what she writes and says to herself but also by the style in which it is expressed.

ACTIVITY

1 Look at the style of the second section of the story. Below are some key stylistic features and one or two examples of each. Your task is to find further examples of these features.

- Uses letter format: address, salutation and formal opening
- Formal lexis: 'decision', 'confide', 'situation'
- Intrusion of spoken language features: 'do you know what I mean', 'OK'
- Euphemisms: 'close contact' (meaning 'have sex')

- Loose **co-ordination** of clauses and sentences: 'He assures me . . . of that malady'.

2 Now, in pairs, investigate the stylistic features of the other two sections of the story.

3 Finally, two questions for you to discuss about the story as a whole:
  a What impression do you gain of the wife's character and feelings?
  b What purpose does the opening section serve? How would the story have been different had this section been omitted?

Text D

One way of identifying the style of a passage and assessing its effectiveness is to write a piece of your own in the same style. You have already had some practice at this in the work you did on 'Jack and Jill' (page 123). Here is a further opportunity. This short extract from James Joyce's 'Ulysses' presents part of the inner conversation of Leopold Bloom, the main character, as he walks through Dublin one day in 1904.

He crossed at Nassau street corner and stood before the window of Yeates and Son, pricing the field glasses. Or will I drop into old Harris's and have a chat with Young Sinclair? Wellmannered fellow. Probably at his lunch. Must get those old glasses of mine set right. Goerz lenses, six guineas. Germans making their way everywhere. Sell on easy terms to capture trade. Undercutting. Might chance on a pair in the railway lost property office. Astonishing the things people leave behind them in trains and cloak rooms. What do they be thinking about! Women too. Incredible. Last year travelling to Ennis had to pick up that farmer's daughter's bag and hand it to her at Limerick junction. Unclaimed money too. There's a little watch up there on the roof of the bank to test these glasses by.

ACTIVITY

Write a passage using as many of Joyce's stylistic features as you can, in which you record your thoughts as you walk through your home town. When you have finished, write a brief commentary in which you identify the features you have used.

Text E

A very revealing way to investigate the style of a text is to examine the beginnings and ends of its sentences. Here, for example, are the opening three and closing three **words** of the first 26 sentences of an article written in the *Daily Telegraph* in 1937 by J B Firth, a famous linguist, entitled 'Americanisms which Vulgarise the English Language'.

Beginnings	**Ends**
One does not	pure and undefiled
Indeed, it is	quite inadequate allowance
It is a	is becoming Americanised
The worst faults	possible, laboriously copied
The result –	of superior wisdom
Today the opposite	for their models
They imitate freely	most potent ally
It is a	is spoken and written
For nothing is	sacred to them
The rules of	not bind them
They have a	usage and convention
They mock at	correct and academic
It is as	to attract attention
Attempts are sometimes	the American paragraph
That, however, is	is rarely achieved
The results are	bastard and mongrel
Reporters have suddenly	of the Atlantic
Members of the	most hideous cacophony
London's most sought-after	Throb No. 1.'
A boy messenger	a grotesque hyperbole
Sentences are made	sought-for jolt
I do not	bunch of chorines'
It would be	and attractive slang
A country as	of its own
It was no	and his laws
Instead of chiding	to be broken

What can be learnt about the passage from just these fragments?

Beginnings
- Only one beginning uses the personal pronoun 'I'.
- Other personal opinions are disguised either by the use of the formal and universal pronoun 'one' or by openings such as 'it is', 'it would be', 'for nothing is'. This gives a magisterial and authoritative feel to the writing.
- The use of 'it' delays the information that is the focus of the sentence and thus gives this information extra emphasis.
- Most of the lexical (as opposed to the functional) words are quite formal and neutral in tone: 'result', 'opposite', 'nothing', 'rules', attempts', 'reporters', 'sentences', 'country'.
- Only a few of the lexical words suggest the writer's opinion: 'worst faults', 'freely', 'mock', 'chiding'.
- Some of the words suggest that the writer is engaged in the construction of an argument: 'indeed', 'the result', 'however', 'instead of'.

Ends
- There are many words and phrases that clearly indicate the writer's opinion. They are anything but neutral in tone: 'pure', 'sacred', 'undefiled', 'superior', 'bastard', 'mongrel', 'hideous cacophony', 'grotesque', 'quite inadequate'.
- There are far more lexical words here than in the openings of the sentences, which contain a greater number of functional or grammatical words.

Here is the passage in full. You will see how the writer blends what appears to be rational argument with very emotive feelings.

One does not expect the sensational or 'tabloid' Press to be a 'well of English pure and undefiled'.

Indeed, it is a mistake to apply too exacting a standard of literary purism to any form of popular journalism, the practice of which is governed by certain inescapable conditions for which the literary purist makes quite inadequate allowance.

It is a matter of everyday observation that English 'Journalese' is becoming Americanised. The worst faults of Victorian 'Journalese' were directly derived from the tradition that the best literary models should be, as far as possible, laboriously copied. The result – in the hands of indifferent exponents – was long-windedness, rotundity of diction, redundancy, and an addiction to polysyllabic words which were supposed to smack of superior wisdom. Today the opposite extreme is favoured and the exponents of the latest school of 'snappiness' have gone to America for their models.

They imitate freely and borrow without a blush and in the American films they find their most potent ally. It is a combination dangerous to the English language, as it is spoken and written.

For nothing is sacred to them. The rules of grammar do not bind them. They have a contempt for established literary usage and convention. They mock at what is correct and academic. It is as if the aim of the writers were to jab the reader in the eye or ear in order at any cost to attract attention.

Attempts are sometimes made to borrow together with the words the general style and atmosphere of the American paragraph. That, however, is more difficult, and success is rarely achieved. The results are bastard and mongrel.

Reporters have suddenly become 'newshawks' in certain English papers because they are so styled for the moment on the other side of the Atlantic. Members of the advertisement departments of newspapers have become 'ad-men' a most hideous cacophony. London's most sought-after visitor, Mr Robert Taylor, of Hollywood, is 'Heart Throb No. 1.' A boy messenger who came to London on some trivial errand was thrust forward into the notice of the British public as 'No. 1 Office Boy of New York' – a grotesque hyperbole.

Sentences are made to open starkly without the customary article to supply the sought-for jolt. I do not mind saying a long farewell to that favourite Victorian Cliché 'ladies of the ballet', but it is still pleasanter to eye and ear than the new Americanism 'a slick bunch of chorines'.

It would be churlish, of course, to deny our manifold obligations to

America for a host of valuable additions to the English vocabulary, especially in the way of racy and attractive slang. A country as big and self-assured as the United States and composed of so many nationalities, was bound to develop a language of its own. It was no more likely to be tamely content with the language of King George III, than with his Constitution and his laws. Instead of chiding the Americans for evolving a language separate from English, we should rejoice that the connection between literary English and literary American is so intimate and fundamental that it is never likely to be broken.

Text F

The subject of American influence on the English language has been a source of fascination for many writers. Here is a passage written in 1980 by Philip Howard on the same subject. You will find it revealing once again to look at the beginnings of the sentences in this passage. Notice how many declarative openings there are. The first three sentences are such: 'The language is'; 'Almost everybody has'; 'Slang has always'. What is the effect of this?

The language is changing because there are many more sources of new slang, and because slang spreads instantly around the world. Almost everybody has access to such media of mass communication as trannies. Slang has always been around. Most language starts as slang, the vernacular of ordinary people in the cave or on the Clapham omnibus, if they can catch one. If slang is successful, it is adopted into the language. It should therefore not vex us or worry us that the American Young today use 'bad', pronounced 'ba-a-ad', to describe something or somebody easy on the eye; 'foxy' as a sexy compliment for a pretty girl; 'dynamite' to mean super; 'brick house' to mean a good-looking, well-stacked girl; and 'buns' to mean bum. No doubt young Brits, influenced by television, films, and magazines, will pick up the slang. But other terms will soon become fashionable, as the old ones become boring. Chesterton said that all slang was metaphor, and all metaphor is poetry.

 English is changing because many more people are speaking it as a first or second language. The grammar is becoming simpler and coarser, as it is taught by teachers for whom it is not the native language. 'Whom' will be as old-fashioned as wing collars and corsets by the end of the century. The distinction between 'will' and 'shall' is dying. Under American influence the difference between 'I haven't got' and 'I don't have' is dead. 'I haven't got indigestion' means that I am not suffering from a belly-ache at the moment. 'I don't have indigestion' means that I am not dyspeptic. 'We haven't got any bananas' means that there happen to be none in the shop, but we usually have them. 'We don't have bananas' means that we don't stock them, blackberries and breadfruit yes; bananas never.

ACTIVITY

Discuss this passage and the previous one (Text E) and compare the attitudes of the two writers.

How do they use language to achieve their effects?

One of the features of Text E was the way that certain words seemed to signal steps in the construction of an argument. Such words can provide cohesion in a text. Cohesion has been defined as 'the formal links that mark various types of inter-clause and inter-sentence relationships within a text' or, to put it more simply, the way that a text is tied together. Think about cohesion as if it were a series of direction signals that the writer has provided to guide you through a text so that you don't lose your way. These *cohesive ties* can include the way that sentences are sequenced, how one thing can lead to another in, for instance, an argument or in a narrative and so on. Cohesion can be provided by the grammar, the lexis or sometimes even the phonology of a text. You have already seen how Browning used phonology as a cohesive tie in 'Meeting at Night'.

It is important not to confuse cohesion with coherence, though they are, of course very closely linked. For a text to be coherent, all the ideas and relationships that the writer (or speaker) is dealing with must make consistent sense to the reader (or listener). The ideas and relationships should be relevant to each other. The linguist Noam Chomsky's famous example illustrates the difference:

Colourless green ideas sleep furiously.

This sentence is quite *cohesive*, but not *coherent* in that its meaning is nonsense.

The next textual investigation will lead you to consider the cohesive ties that bind it together.

Text G

You are now going to look at a *complete* story by Ernest Hemingway, which consists of only eleven sentences. Here they are, but not in the order in which Hemingway wrote them.

All the shutters of the hospital were nailed shut.
When they fired the first volley he was sitting down in the water with his head on his knees.
There were pools of water in the courtyard.
They tried to hold him up against the wall but he sat down in a puddle of water.
One of the ministers was sick with typhoid.
Two soldiers carried him downstairs and out into the rain.
There were wet dead leaves on the paving of the courtyard.
Finally the officer told the soldiers it was no good trying to make him stand up.
They shot the six cabinet ministers at half past six in the morning against the wall of the hospital.
It rained hard.
The other five stood very quietly against the wall.

ACTIVITY

1 Either individually or in groups, reconstruct Hemingway's original story, which is about a political execution. Part of your discussion will probably focus on the cohesive ties in the text.
2 Explain to the other members of the class how you reached your decision. Were there other reasons besides the cohesion you found to help you? Which sentences seemed to fall

naturally into groups? Which were the most difficult to place? Why?
3 You might like to compare your version with Hemingway's which you can find on page 152. Please don't look at it until you have completed your discussion. What differences are there between your version and Hemingway's? Which is the more effective? Why?

Texts H–L

In this next section, you are going to look at three short texts, each one chosen because there are important lexical features to comment on. Remember that in an examination you probably wouldn't have time to write about every stylistic feature in a text, but that there are some that simply demand attention. The lexis in these texts demands it. Don't think, though, that there is nothing more you could comment on. After each text there are some very brief notes for you to study.

Text H

Lecturer Appraisal aims to . . .

provide a means by which individual members of staff, in conjunction with a trained appraiser, can review their skills, experiences, strengths and weaknesses and their current responsibilities and role within the college, and identify ways in which the two might more effectively be combined to improve delivery. The review process will consider how professional development can be supported and enhanced both as a means of increasing job satisfaction and the quality of provision within institutions.

(from *A Strategy for Staff Development Training and Appraisal*, CCDU, Leeds University)

- preponderance of nouns or noun groups to verbs or verb groups: 21 to 7
- majority of nouns are **abstract**: 'conjunction', 'skills', 'experiences', 'weaknesses', 'delivery', 'process', 'development'
- many polysyllabic nouns
- some hidden **metaphors**: teaching and lecturing is seen as 'delivery' or 'provision'.

Text I

The photolytic decomposition of phenylazotriphenylmethane in benzene apparently follows a similar course to the pyrolytic decomposition discussed above. It has been investigated by Homer and Naumann (1954) and Huisgen and Nakaten (1954) and was found to involve a primary dissociation into phenyl and triphenylmethyl radicals and nitrogen, in the manner indicated in equation (8). The phenyl radicals are capable of effecting arylation, and the arylation is inhibited by the presence of an excess of p-benzoquinone, which traps the radicals efficiently. Nitric oxide similarly prevents the formation of triphenylmethane by uniting with triphenylmethyl radicals, as also does iodine in the presence of ethanol.

(quoted in Crystal and Davy: *Investigating English Style*)

- much technical and specialised lexis from field of chemistry: 'photolytic decomposition', 'triphenylmethyl', etc
- contrast between this and more everyday lexis: 'follows', 'discussed', 'similarly', 'prevents'
- technical words formed by adding morpheme to morpheme: 'tri' + 'phenyl' + 'methane', 'tri' + 'phenyl' + 'methyl'
- many nouns indicating processes indicated by the '-tion' morpheme: 'decomposition', 'arylation', 'dissociation', 'formation'.

Text J

Ed's letter

When I was a nipper, I saw a horror movie
in which a Frankenstein-style monster hid
in the wardrobe then attacked its sleeping victims.
Even now I can't sleep with my wardrobe door ajar.
   Not convinced? Feast your eyes on Spook Zone,
J17's guide to the scary and supernatural. Inspired
by witchy chick flick The Craft – think Clueless with
spells – we bring you real-life spooky-types in
'Spellbound' (p2), a Satan-possessed mum (p9)
and witchy style tips (p11) so you can look kooky
while you're feeling spooky. And if you're still not
scared, check out the new Upside Down video!
Watch out for those wardrobe doors!

(Just 17: Spook Zone Supplement)

- many words connected with ghosts, horror and witchcraft:
  'Frankenstein', 'spook', 'scary', 'supernatural', 'witchy', 'Satan'
- very informal: 'nipper', 'chick flick', 'spooky', 'kooky'
- use of hyphenation to combine lexical items: 'Frankenstein-style', 'real-life', 'spooky-types', 'Satan-possessed'
- words chosen for phonological pattering: 'witchy chick flick', 'look kooky … spooky'.

Here are two more examples for you to discuss, this time without any notes.

Text K

Antarctica – the White Continent – is the most spectacular travel destination on earth. Now you can experience the dramatic beauty of this glacial wilderness on a unique Christmas voyage aboard the luxury liner Marco Polo. In eighteen days, you'll view shimmering icebergs sculpted by nature, vast colonies of frolicking penguins, whales spouting off the side of the ship, and awe-inspiring ice cliffs. You'll spend three nights in vivacious Buenos Aires, and get a taste of Victorian England in the charming Falklands. And you'll enjoy the comforts and amenities of one of the most elegant cruise ships afloat. Including festive holiday celebrations on board.

Text L

Subscriptions
(a) The Annual Subscription shall be the amount decided by the General Committee and shall be payable on or before 1st April.
(b) Each member shall pay his subscription immediately on notification of his election, and should he fail to pay within one month, the Secretary shall report to the General Committee who may cause his name to be removed from the books of the Club unless satisfactory reasons are given for the delay.
(c) The payment of the subscription by a member shall be understood as a distinct acknowledgement of him of his acquiescence in the rules and regulations of the Club.
(d) That senior members of 60 years and over having been a fully paid member over three years or more to enjoy a 50% payment of normal subscriptions.

Collect texts that illustrate some striking lexical features and bring these into the class so that you can investigate this aspect of stylistics further.

Finally, here is the correct version of the Hemingway story (Text G). Check your version against it.

They shot the six cabinet ministers at half past six in the morning against the wall of the hospital. There were pools of water in the courtyard. There were wet dead leaves on the paving of the courtyard. It rained hard. All the shutters of the hospital were nailed shut. One of the ministers was sick with typhoid. Two soldiers carried him downstairs and out into the rain. They tried to hold him up against the wall but he sat down in a puddle of water. The other five stood very quietly against the wall. Finally the officer told the soldiers it was no good trying to make him stand up. When they fired the first volley he was sitting down in the water with his head on his knees.

Examination questions

In the final section of this chapter, you will be looking at two essays written by candidates in response to a stylistics question set in a recent A-level examination. Here is the question in which they were asked to compare two texts.

The first of the following texts, Strange Fruit, a poem by Seamus Heaney, was published in 1975. The 'girl's head' referred to in the poem was discovered in a peat bog in Denmark, perfectly preserved by the acid in the soil since the Iron Age. The girl had evidently been executed.

The second text, an article entitled Warm Hearts in a Cold Land, was published in the science journal New Scientist in March 1995.

Comment on ways in which language is used on the poem and in the article to express information, ideas and attitudes.

In your answer you might comment on vocabulary, figurative language, grammar, overall structure and any other linguistic matters you think are relevant to meaning and tone.

Passage A

Strange Fruit
Here is the girl's head like an exhumed gourd.
Oval-faced, prune-skinned, prune-stones for teeth.
They unswaddled the wet fern of her hair
And made an exhibition of its coil,
5 Let the air at her leathery beauty.
Pash of tallow, perishable treasure:
Her broken nose is dark as a turf clod,
Her eyeholes blank as pools in the old workings.
Diodorus Siculus confessed
10 His gradual ease among the likes of this:
Murdered, forgotten, nameless, terrible
Beheaded girl, outstaring axe

And beatification, outstaring
What had begun to feel like reverence.

Glossary

Diodorus Siculus – a Greek historian who lived in the 1st century B.C.

Passage B

Warm Hearts in a Cold Land

The corpse of a girl discovered in Alaska last summer after being frozen in permafrost for 800 years has revealed the compassionate nature of Arctic people of the time, say anthropologists.

Medical examination of the body suggests that the girl suffered from a debilitating genetic disease called alpha-1-antitrypsin deficiency. The disorder is rare, affecting about one in 10 000 people today. Those with the faulty gene are unable to produce the enzyme alpha-1-antitrypsin, which is needed to ward off lung infections. The girl was probably unable to care for herself or even walk, says Michael Zimmerman, an expert on frozen bodies at the Mount Sinai Medical Center in New York, who conducted the post-mortem.

It would have been obvious to her parents that she would not live to lead a normal adult life, says anthropologist Glenn Sheehan of Bryn Mawr College in Pennsylvania. But despite their bleak existence in the Arctic, he says, the family apparently cared for the girl until she died, aged between four and eight.

That she survived so long is testimony to the care she received. She was carefully buried along with a whalebone toboggan, on which she might have been towed around the village. 'She had little hope, yet her family and her friends took care of her,' says Sheehan. 'This may give us new insights into their social organisation.'

The girl's body was discovered last August near Barrow, Alaska, when a beachcomber noticed part of the head sticking out from a bank overhanging the Arctic Ocean. At the request of local tribal elders, Sheehan and his colleagues – who were already working nearby – excavated the body. They used hot water to melt the permafrost and release the body, which was moved to Providence Hospital in Anchorage.

The cause of death was clear. 'She starved to death,' says Zimmerman. The girl's stomach contained dirt and bits of animal fur. 'She was being given whatever they could to fill her poor little belly,' he says. 'In the past, hungry children in the region were often given pieces of animal fur to chew,' says Zimmerman.

'Microscopic examination of the girl's lungs and liver showed scarring that is characteristic of alpha-1-antitrypsin deficiency,' Zimmerman says. The diagnosis still has to be confirmed by genetic testing, but Zimmerman says the scarring is virtually conclusive proof.

Before you look at the candidates' answers to the question, it may help you to consider, very briefly, the concepts and ideas a good answer could cover.

The poem is a personal response to the discovery of the girl's head and the poet is reflecting on what her fate implies about human nature. It is a bleak vision, possibly summed up by the word 'terrible'. The poem is meditative and very metaphorical. The writer of the prose passage has a more positive view of human nature, stressing the compassionate nature of the people who cared for the handicapped girl. Unlike the poem, which is reflective, the prose text narrates, explains and speculates.

The examiner's comments on each essay have been provided for you to study.

Essay 1

The poem 'Strange Fruit' is about a perfectly preserved head found in acid soil in Denmark. The scientists traced it back to the Iron Age and also found that the girl had been executed.[1] The poem describes the girl's head in detail.[2] The poem consists of fourteen lines and does not possess a rhyming pattern.[3]

The title of the poem 'Strange Fruit' links in with the poem on the second line
'prune-skinned, prune-stones for teeth'
with the idea of fruit and the prune.[4] It also links in with the overall idea that the head has been preserved unlike fruit[5] – strange.

She is now like a dried fruit – a prune.[6] The poet uses lists of metaphors[7] to describe the girl
'nose is dark as a turf clod'
'eyeholes blank as pools in the old workings'
This gives you a mental image or illustration of what she actually looked like.[8]

He expresses attitudes in the form of lists
'murdered, forgotten, nameless'
This is the attitude of the people that didn't know her.[9]

The poet has also linked the first part of the poem with the last part of the poem with the word 'beauty'
'leathery beauty'   beauty of the girl
'beautification'   bettering herself[10]

'Warm Hearts in a Cold Land', an extract from a science journal, expresses information about a corpse of a girl found in Alaska and how it revealed much about Arctic people of the time.[11] The information is set out in short[12] paragraphs. It contains scientific language but they are defined which means that the average reader could understand the journal and it isn't just for a selective audience of scientists.[13] Ideas are expressed by extracts of speech which makes it more interesting and lightens the tone as information is mostly factual.[14]

Examiner's comments
1 Repeats information already given in question. Not really necessary.
2 Yes, but it does more than this. Look at lines 10–14.
3 It's a sonnet.
4 Yes, but mention that prunes are *dried* plums.
5 Prunes *are* preserved fruit. It's not therefore 'strange'.
6 Yes.
7 These are similes, not metaphors.
8 Be more specific. Mention the similes used are from peat digging.
9 Yes.
10 Read the poem carefully. It doesn't say 'beautification'.
11 Again, repeating information already given in the question.
12 How short is 'short'?
13 Poor syntax, but I know what you mean. Need to give some examples to support your assertion.
14 Again, where's the evidence?

Overall comment
The candidate shows some general understanding of the two texts. However, there is little reference to any linguistic terminology and she recognises only a few language features. A very limited treatment of the prose passage and there is no attempt to compare the two passages at all.

Grade: E

Essay 2

The poem 'Strange Fruit' is so titled because it is a parallel to the metaphor which describes the exhumed head as a prune. The poem can be effectively divided into three sections: the first five lines describe how the group exhumed the head and what they did with it, the next three lines describe the appearance of the girl and the last six lines Diodorus Siculus's 'gradual ease' at how the girl appears, and here there is further elaboration of description of the head.[1]

There is evidently a lot of lexis from the semantic field of death and violence. The verbs 'exhumed' and 'beheaded' convey the violence which this body has encountered. The adjective 'broken' premodifies 'nose' and the noun 'eyeholes' presents an image to the reader of a vacant staring look. This imagery is continued with the verb 'outstaring'. It is used twice within one sentence to emphasise the lasting impression which Siculus has taken in.[2]

The essence of how personal this passage is can be seen through the use of possessive pronouns and other features. The introduction is a blunt 'here' – where the imagery does not have any descriptive premodification. The fact that the girl has been buried for so long means that the people exhuming her do not know her identity. This is shown when she is identified as 'the girl' – an identity which conveys her youth and the tragedy of her execution, and also the fact that she is nameless to the world. The possessive pronoun 'her' is also neutral in terms of identification and is used to premodify characteristics such as 'broken' and 'eyeholes' which emphasise the tragedy further.[3]

The use of a list is one linguistic technique designed to show the images running through the mind of Siculus: it is an awful thing he has seen and the poem presents the observations which he makes as 'murdered', 'forgotten', 'nameless', 'terrible'. The awkward nature of Siculus is also conveyed: the verb 'confessed' is used to describe how he communicates his dreadful observations and 'gradual ease' strengthens the feeling further. The 'likes of this' continues this impersonality relating to the girl, where 'this' is the only description of her he can muster – it consigns her to being merely an object.[4] Metaphorical language is prominent. The metaphor 'blank as pools'[5] describes effectively the emptiness of her eyeholes. 'Dark as a turf clod' compares the misshapen and blackend mass of turf to the girl's nose. In addition, hyphenated descriptions like 'oval-faced', 'prune-skinned' and 'prune-stones' continue the 'strange fruit' parallel.[6]

We can also see one final feeling conveyed by the passage. The people who have discovered the body are awe-inspired by this magnificent find: the verb 'unswaddled' can be compared to 'swaddling' for a baby and the careful way in which they unwrap her hair. The phrases 'leathery beauty', 'perishable treasure' and 'reverence' all show how privileged the group feel.[7]

The 'Warm Hearts' passage is very matter of fact. The introduction opens with 'the corpse of a girl' which sets the tone for the way in which the description will be factually presented. Statistics are used to support assertions – '800 years', '10 000 people' are figures which are presented.[8]

There is a strong association to the semantic field of medicine – 'gene', 'infections', 'enzyme', 'diagnosis' and 'examination' are related to genetic medical study. Medical practitioners' names are used to make the evidence presented more credible and tangible.[9]

The language used to present the facts is often certain but with some nature of being unsure.[10] The strong term 'conclusive proof' is premodified by the ambiguous 'virtually' and verbs such as 'may' and 'might' demonstrate how historical study is, in part, speculation.

The grammatical structure of the piece is quite complex. The sentences begin with a clear statement such as 'The disorder is rare' but then go on to describe in subordinate clauses the nature of the situation.[11] The factual nature of the piece is heightened by the concentration on stative verbs with little use of the progressive aspect. This is a report given without any progressive aspect so it does not have the same reality as that inspired by a poem which uses dynamic verbs to demonstrate how events are occurring in real time.[12] The passage is firmly in the past tense. In terms of relating layout to grammatical structure, the text is divided into a number of separate pieces which each describe one aspect of the discovery from the cause of death to her activities when she was alive.[13]

The use of concrete and abstract nouns is mixed. The quoted speech uses feelings such as 'hope' and colloquialisms like 'belly' rather than stomach. The narrative uses some abstract nouns like 'care' to elaborate on the girl's experiences.[14] However, the core of the text concentrates on concrete nouns which describe the technical aspects, such as postmortems and scientific developments. Words such as 'permafrost' and 'alpha-1-antitrypsin deficiency' are specifically related to the scientific field. Place names also feature to give perspective: Alaska and Arctic, for example.[15]

Examiner's comments

1 A good start. Deals accurately with the overall structure and organisation of the sonnet.
2 Accurate use of linguistic terminology. Comments about semantic fields and notes the effect created. Slight niggle: 'exhumed' and 'beheaded' are being used as premodifiers, not as verbs.
3 Very good. Close textual examination. Comments on grammar are well linked to the effect created.
4 More close attention paid to the effects of linguistic choices. Excellent.
5 Should have written about the whole metaphor, not just the beginning.
6 Very good insight.
7 Yes. Should have pointed out *exactly* how these words 'show' the 'privilege'.
8 Yes. Point backed up by textual evidence.
9 Deals convincingly with semantic fields.
10 An unclear assertion. The explanation follows in the next sentence.
11 This is vague, especially as the sentence quoted does not contain a subordinate clause.
12 Textual evidence needed to support this assertion. He is making an attempt to compare the two texts.
13 He would have done better to have begun his piece on this text with these comments about the overall structure and organisation. Needs to be more specific.
14 So what? What's the effect?
15 Candidate has run out of time. These last two points needed fuller treatment.

Overall comment

This is an excellent answer, which demonstrates good linguistic understanding and an ability to relate his observation of language features to the effect these have. Some errors made and some points left underdeveloped.

Grade: A

10 Writing Texts

The aim of this chapter is not to teach you to write, because you are well able to do that already. You wouldn't be following an A-level English Language course if you hadn't demonstrated some proficiency in writing. It is hoped, however, that the chapter will help you become a *better* writer and, specifically, to write for coursework and in original writing examinations with success.

There are many different types or modes of writing. Throughout this book, you have had opportunities to study some of them. The work that you did on **genre** was one of these opportunities, for example. Of course, all of us write frequently and have been doing so since we first learnt. Some of you may feel driven to write and gain considerable enjoyment from it: short stories, poems, articles for the college newspaper, lyrics for the band you play in, slogans for competitions, letters to friends or a diary. Sometimes you may write because you have to: taking the minutes of a meeting, writing a letter of complaint, writing up a science experiment or an essay in sociology or even an examination answer. Sometimes our writing is simply concerned with helping us organise ourselves. This can range from writing shopping lists or notes of things to remember to filling in a UCAS form and producing a personal statement or applying for a job.

ACTIVITY

Keep a writing log to see just how much writing you do. You should record both its purpose and its audience. Record everything that you write over a period of, say, a week. Here's a suggested grid with two examples of one of the author's own entries.

Date and time	Type of writing	Purpose	Audience
2/10/96 7.30 pm	Draft of chapter on writing for an A-level text book	Teaching and advising	A-level English Language students
2/10/96 7.50 pm	Note of telephone conversation	Reminder to ring back tomorrow	Myself

Some questions to ask after you have completed your grid:
1 What type of writing do you do most frequently?

2 How many different purposes and audiences have you written for? Which are the most common?

3 When do you do most of your writing?

4 How many of your pieces involved planning, drafting and redrafting?

5 Which type of writing required most planning and thought?

6 Did you receive any feedback on or response to your writing? Who from?

7 Compare your writing pattern with that of others in your group.

You have just been thinking about different purposes and types of writing and if you did keep a log, you will have perhaps realised that there are all kinds of ways of classifying writing. Your work here and elsewhere in the book should have convinced you that writing forms a huge network of audiences, purposes and different types of text.

One way of sorting out the many varieties of writing as practised in modern life is to classify them according to *mode*. Indeed, there is a useful, though advanced, critical book called *The Modes of Modern Writing* by David Lodge. The word 'mode' when used about writing means more or less the same as it does when used with reference to a digital watch or a computer. Press the right button in the right way and a watch can become a calculator, a stopwatch or an ordinary timekeeper. Similarly a computer when acting as a word processor (which is itself a computer mode) can be in text-production mode, editing mode or spellcheck mode.

A mode, then, is a purpose for writing that will determine the kind of language a writer will use and how she or he will use it.

The four most familiar modes, and the ones in which you will most frequently be asked to write for A-level English Language, are:

- writing which entertains (the entertainment mode)
- writing which persuades (the persuasive/argumentative mode)
- writing which informs (the informative mode)
- writing which instructs or advises (the instructional/advisory mode).

Obviously, there will be many texts that use more than one mode. It is rare that a text remains solely in one mode. Like computers, texts may be multifunctional. For example, a magazine article might set out to entertain and inform at the same time. Or an advertisement might seek to persuade and entertain simultaneously. Think about the Gold Blend script that you looked at earlier in the book (page 125).

Which modes are operating in the following text?

Tropical Trifle (serves four)

1 Jamaican Ginger Cake
225g/8oz canned pineapple in its own juice
568ml/1 pint fresh milk
2 level tablespoons custard powder
25g/1oz sugar
2 size 3 eggs, separated
100g/4oz caster sugar
Selection of fresh fruit (optional)

1 Cut the cake into slices and arrange in a heatproof dish. Soak the cake with the pineapple juice. Chop the fruit and place over the cake.

2 Blend the custard powder with 25g/1oz sugar, the egg yolks and a little of the milk. Bring the remaining milk to the boil.

3 Stir hot milk into the blended mixture, return to the saucepan, heat until custard boils. Simmer for two minutes. Pour over fruit and cake.

4 Whisk the egg whites until stiff, gradually whisk in the caster sugar. Spread or pipe over the custard, brown under a hot grill. Serve immediately.

5 Alternatively, pipe meringue round the edge of the dish, brown quickly, allow to cool. Fill the centre with a selection of hot fruit.

For a selection of recipes using fresh milk, send a 9" × 7" SAE to Dept RLJZ, The National Dairy Council, 5–7 John Princes St, London W1M 0AP

**Good food's
gotta lotta bottle when your
cooking's gotta lotta milk**

ACTIVITY

Here are extracts from two texts written by A-level students as part of their English Language coursework. The writers intended them both to be primarily instructional or advisory.

Text A

Emile Woolf
College of Accountancy
Notes for Administration Staff

1 *Answering the Phone*
- After picking up the receiver, your opening statement should be: 'Good Morning, Emile Woolf College'. Use 'Good Afternoon' or 'Good Evening' where appropriate.
- Always try to be as helpful as possible and if in doubt over a situation, ask the caller if you can put them on hold and then consult another member of staff.
- Never leave a caller on hold for longer than two minutes.
- If an incoming call is for the Director of Studies or another senior member of staff, tell the caller that you will try to put them through. Then press the hold button and the line extension which you require. Wait for a reply on the other phone to see if the person is busy or not.
- Always ask the caller for their name, and if they need further assistance than is available, take their phone number.
- Record every incoming call into the specific book.

Text B
'Does your Barry Manilow sound as though he's

singing through a blanket? Has your Pavarotti highlights lost its shine? Do Wet Wet Wet sound as though they're singing outside on a windy day?'

It's not likely to be the tape that's at fault, and you probably don't need a new cassette player.

When did you last clean the tape heads? If you cannot remember, read on because a simple clean will make a world of difference to your listening pleasure.

You could run a head-cleaning tape through and that might make an appreciable difference, but if you want a really good job done, there is a simple technique that is very thorough.

Don't buy a commercial preparation. They are usually expensive and you can buy better stuff at your local chemist, believe it or not.

Ask them to make up a small bottle of isopropyl alcohol. It'll cost you about a pound. You may get a funny look, but explain what you want it for and then they won't think you are a druggie or a sniffer.

You will also need some cotton buds: the sort for cleaning out babies' ears and noses. And that's all you need for a really professional job!

1 Which text remains solely in instructional mode and which is multifunctional?

2 What other mode(s) are present in the multifunctional text? Identify examples of them.

3 Which, in your opinion, is the more effective piece of instructional writing? Why?

4 Here are some particular features of writing that can be expected in instructional writing:

- **command**-form verbs are likely to be frequent, and likely to occur right at the beginning of sentences: 'Ask ...', 'Open ...', 'Remove ...', 'Take ...' 'Start cleaning ...'
- statements of fact are blended into the text at appropriate points
- the sequencing of sentences follows practical needs
- occasional sentences of advice or recommendation occur, frequently employing adverbs as in 'They are usually expensive'
- diagrams often accompany the written word.

Can you identify any of these features in the two pieces of writing you have been considering? Are they present in the 'Tropical Trifle' text? Collect other examples of writing whose primary purpose is instructional and identify the features.

5 Closely linked to instructional is advisory writing. Collect some examples of texts whose intention is to advise the reader. Texts such as guides to choosing a place in higher education or how to look after a pet, for example. How does the language used in these texts differ from those in instructional mode? Look at the use of modal verbs (like 'should' ... 'need to' ... 'may' ... 'could') in the first instance.

Choosing a subject

It is very important when you are writing for A-level English Language, whether in an examination or for a piece of coursework, that your piece of writing should have a 'real' equivalent. Much of the writing you will have done up to now, say, for GCSE will have been in the form of an essay on a subject unlikely to have been of your own choosing. 'Write me an essay on ... and have it finished by Tuesday' will probably have been familiar to you. By contrast, in A-level English Language your writing should have, wherever possible, a real equivalent. The original writing questions found in examinations are framed in this way. Look at this one:

Many people belong to organisations, clubs or societies and take a full part in their activities. These can range from large international or national organisations like Greenpeace or Amnesty International to smaller local ones. They cover a huge range of interests and activities: charitable (Save the Children Fund, Scope), community service (St John's Ambulance Service, The Samaritans), pressure groups (Friends of the Earth, Campaign for Real Ale) and leisure activities (Scouts/Guides, local sports clubs, fitness centres or theatre groups). You will be able to think of many more examples and may even belong to one or more of these types of group yourself.

However, people are often wary of joining, as they are unsure or apprehensive of just what is involved and what commitment they may be expected to make. To overcome this problem, many organisations produce a short booklet that is intended to inform prospective members in a friendly and approachable way about the activities or opportunities that are offered.

Using your own knowledge and experience, write the first draft of such a booklet for an organisation, club or society which you are a member of, or have considered joining. Be as specific as possible and think about the sort of information you yourself would like to have had before deciding whether to join.

Remember that your intention is not to persuade people to join, but to help them reach an informed decision about whether this is the organisation or group for them.

Your booklet should be about 750 words in length.

This question asks you to write in informative mode, using a real genre, that of a booklet, for a purpose that is as real as it is possible to provide under examination conditions. It is also asking you to use knowledge that you yourself possess.

There are, of course, a wide range of 'real' genres you can choose from in your writing: horoscopes, feature articles, reviews, scripts for radio programmes, instruction manuals, guidebooks, learning packs, poems and so on. You will find that you will always produce a better piece of writing if you make it as realistic as possible.

To give you an idea of the range of possibilities open to you, here are just a few suggestions about the sort of writing that could fit into each of the four modes. These are not exhaustive lists, because it is important for you to supplement them.

ACTIVITY

Writing to entertain

This is a very wide category. Don't be misled by the word 'entertain'. You don't have to be amusing in order to entertain your readers.

short stories	autobiographies
scripts	children's stories
collections of verse	travel writing
letters to a magazine	comedy sketches
articles for fanzines	chapters from a novel

Writing to persuade

campaigning speeches	newspaper editorials
political leaflets	advertising campaigns
stories with a moral	

Writing to inform

study packs	scripts for a tape to guide someone round a museum
reports	biographies
documentary scripts	guides to tourist sites in your locality

Writing to instruct/advise

how to organise something	instruction leaflets or manuals
recipes	advice packs

Working in groups, discuss how many other sorts of writing you can add to these suggestions.

The stages of writing

Magazine articles don't just appear magically from nowhere; books don't just slip unnoticed into bookshops overnight and an advertisement doesn't attempt to alter your buying habits without someone somewhere having carefully planned how to persuade you to part with your hard-earned cash. In other words, there are always a number of stages that a piece of writing has to go through prior to its appearance before its intended audience. If your own writing for A-level English Language is to be successful, then it, too, has to go through these stages or processes. These may well be familiar to you. You will have to:

- define your task
- prepare

- plan
- draft
- edit
- proof-read
- present or publish.

These were the stages that this book went through before you were able to read it, as you are now doing.

- We (the authors) *defined our task*: our audience (you); purpose (to teach and help you to get good grades in examinations); genre (a textbook) and mode(s) (instructional, informative and, we hope, both persuasive and entertaining).
- We *prepared* our material through reading, research, discussion and testing it out in classes and seminars.
- We *planned* the shape, **structure** and approach of the book. We decided on the number of sections and chapters and how we would treat each topic. We submitted our plans to the publisher who sought the opinions of experienced teachers of English about the proposed book, before giving us the green light to write it.
- We *drafted* the book, working carefully through it, section by section and then submitted our draft to more testing by very critical audiences. In other words, we tried out the material in class and in the light of its success or failure in these test-bed conditions, rewrote and redrafted where necessary.
- We *edited* the drafts. Had we included everything necessary? Did we need to cut anything? Was the material presented in the best order? Had we expressed it as clearly as possible?
- We *proof-read* the drafts, checking for grammatical and punctuation errors. Admittedly, we had help in checking our spelling, in the form of Microsoft Word's Spellcheck!
- We sent our final version to the publisher, who submitted it to more rigorous scrutiny. Here it was prepared for publication by being *copy-edited, designed and illustrated, typeset* and then sent back to us for any revisions and cuts deemed necessary and for final *proof-reading*. Then, and only then, was it *published*!

These, then, were the stages that a real piece of writing went through before publication. It has been stressed to you already that success in original writing at A level depends largely upon your viewing what you write as a real, professional piece of work and not merely as an academic or theoretical exercise. Before you look at some of these stages in detail, there are three points to note.

(i) Don't regard these stages as trial runs before you begin your 'real' writing. They are an essential part of the whole process. It's *all* for real.

(ii) Though these stages have been separated from each other and presented as if you had all the time in the world to deal with them, occasionally you haven't got this time and you may find yourself combining the stages. You will be familiar with at least one situation in which time is at a premium – the examination hall. Nonetheless, or perhaps *especially* in that situation, it is vital you go through the stages if you are to produce a good piece of work.

(iii) You will often find that during the actual process of writing, you depart from your original plans. Often you get new and good ideas whilst you are actually putting pen to paper. Don't ignore them just because they weren't in your plan. Inspiration can arrive at any time!

❶ *Defining your task*

Before you begin, you must have very clear answers to the following questions because the answers you give will determine how you write.

Who am I writing for?
What am I writing?
Why am I writing?

For example, if you were writing a recipe for a spaghetti sauce, you would write it very differently were it to appear in *My First Cookery Book* rather than in *Mastering the Art of Italian Regional Cuisine.* You must research your audience, purpose, subject matter and genre thoroughly before doing anything else.

Writers' guidelines

Many publications produce guidelines for writers who aspire to seeing their work in print. For instance, Mills and Boon, the publishers of romantic novels read mainly by women, issue very detailed advice to their authors on exactly what is required in their novels. Such guidelines are, of course, very useful both to writers and to editors. It saves an editor having to wade through a great deal of unsuitable material and it gives potential authors a much better chance of being published, if they can target their work very precisely.

Here are the guidelines for short-story writers for the teenage girls' magazine *Just Seventeen*:

Stories should be around **1000 words long**. Please send an SAE with your story. Although we publish a lot of stories about relationships, there's also lots of scope for other types of story. Stories that have a romantic element as part of a larger plot are fine, and so are stories about totally different issues. I very much want to receive stories addressing all kinds of different, original issues. I'm also happy to receive occasional genre stories, eg horror, suspense.

The very best thing a contributor can do is to read the magazine over at least a few issues to absorb the style, content and language of what we publish. Bear in mind that the average reader of *Just Seventeen* is age 15. So the main characters of the stories should be 14, 15, or 16 at most. Stories can be about small things – everyday scenarios, family relationships, emotions. Large dramatic events aren't necessary. Stick within realistic boundaries: keep in mind what might actually happen in the life of a 15-year-old *Just Seventeen* reader.

Original, lively use of language, with a contemporary and colloquial feel, is what I'm looking for.

Stories need to be self-contained, but a slick, obvious ending or 'twist in the tail' is not always the best device. A satisfying ending, or even a slightly open-ended one, is what's needed, without it being pat.

The format of the 'bitch' character who gets her come-uppance usually in a fight over a boy, is predictable and can often be unnecessarily venomous. Try to avoid strong competition between girls, if possible.

A strong moral message is often much too obvious. It can be implied, but try not to drive the moral lesson slant too hard – it tends to make a story very unsubtle.

Main female characters should be realistic, with normal fears or vulnerabilities, but don't make them too passive or reliant on what boys think. No doormats!

Above all, think about what is **realistic!** Many stories submitted tend to be a little old fashioned and obvious. We're on an anti-cliché drive! Try to reflect the content of the rest of the magazine – trendy, realistic but optimistic and very contemporary. Include current references if possible. While stories are like a warm bath – there to immerse yourself in and enjoy – keep an eye on what's real and what's not. Avoid clichés and think about whether something would *really* happen or not. For example, would a 15-year-old boy really ask a girl out the first time he met her? If you can basically guess at the beginning of the story who's going to end up with who, think again.

We do publish a story a week, so there's plenty of scope for good writers. Let your imagination go, and don't think you've only got to write about romance! I'm looking for original ideas, and stories that speak to and mean something to the reader.

You will have noticed that these guidelines are quite specific on such matters as:

- length (1000 words)
- subject matter (what might actually happen in the life of a fifteen-year-old *Just Seventeen* reader)
- language and **style** (original, lively, contemporary and colloquial feel).

ACTIVITY

Produce a guideline sheet for a publication that you know well. Remember, if you are writing for one that includes many different kinds of writing (like *Just Seventeen*, for example) you should concentrate on only one section, because the requirements for a 'Reader's True-Life Story' will be rather different from those for a review of some technical equipment. You will need, of course, as the *Just Seventeen* guidelines suggest, to read a number of issues of the magazine (or whatever) carefully to absorb its style, content and language.

❷ *Preparing*

Before you set pen to paper (or finger to keyboard) you obviously will need to prepare what you are going to write. This may involve you in researching the topic by visiting libraries, interviewing people, reading other relevant material or viewing it on film, video or TV. The nature of your preparation will vary according to the type of writing you are engaged in. It may be that you need to generate ideas rather than going out to research before you begin, and there are many ways of doing this. Some of the best ones are outlined in Alison Ross's useful pack of materials,

Original Writing (Framework Press). Once you have gathered together all your materials and ideas, you will need to plan what you are going to write.

❸ *Planning*

It is important not only to know what you want to say, but also to know the order in which you want to say it, because any piece of writing needs a shape and structure if it is to be effective. Your reader mustn't feel at sea when he or she is reading what you have written. It is your responsibility, whether you are writing an article, leaflet, short story, speech or recipe, to take the reader metaphorically by the hand and guide him or her through your piece. You can't do this properly unless you plan thoroughly and clearly.

ACTIVITY

Here are three plans that examination candidates wrote as they prepared to answer the question on pages 161–2. Discuss them and rank them in order from the most to the least effective. Consider which is the clearest to follow and would have provided the most help to the writer as she or he set about the task.

Text A

> friends of Bury Portage
>   What portage is
>   Where Portage Centre is
>   What friends has to offer
> Coffee mornings, Advice, Support
> someone To Talk To   Music Therapy
> soft Play area ball pool
> Sensory room   Toy library
> Aromatherapy   Trips (where?)

Text B

> Audience : v. wide range from young to old – quite simple but patronising
> Purpose: to INFORM about Greenpeace (being member of)
> Specific Info: cost, activities – diff. levels of involvement
>   \annual subs (diff. rates/payment)
> Tone : Friendly + approachable = informal
> TIME involved   boycotts, protest marches
>   activities/opportunities eg Brent Spar MONTHLY BULLETINS
> INTRO : Greenpeace as an international organisation (can send info/pics)
> brief aims
> LAYOUT : sub headings, bullet points for easy read
> INTRODUCTION : Greenpeace as international org = aims (awareness of...)
> FINAL PARA: make reader feel relaxed about joining although don't persuade/pressurise
> CONTENT
> ACTIVITIES : A lot of people immediately picture sitting in a dingy on the ocean round Brent Spar eg... Not all like this You make decision as to how much you're involved
> GP send info monthly – read/ignore   Write to local MPs, PM
> Protest marches – peaceful
> boycotting eg Shell petrol stations   just by recycling/raising helping
> pass on info to friends/family   GP aims
> Catalogue – Xmas cards, Tshirts with logo advertising for them

Text C

> ACTIVITIES   ADVANTAGES
> Shooting   New people
> Flying / gliding   boost confidence
> Camouflage
> Duke of Edinburgh / hiking / camping
>   career
>   AIR TRAINING CORPS   cadet profiles
>   with personal opinions/
>   stories
>   Explaining uniform
>   MILITARY ORGANISATION
>   Formal link with RAF/MOD
>   How disciplined, uniformed, ranked
> Explain motto – Venture Adventure
> Commitment – the higher rank you get the more is involved
> Funding – funded by Cadets (subs 50p), Parents Committee + MOD
>   ATC Headquarters
>   What Cadets have to pay for – camps, shoes, subs
> Thus expected to help with   (Free) – uniform
> fund raising for \yourselves → good time
>   → community
> OPPORTUNITIES
>   • Career • Travelling/going abroad on camp • Flying
>   • Getting a rank (responsibility) • New people

④ *Drafting*

Having planned your work, you are now ready to begin the actual process of writing. You *may* be one of those lucky people who can sit down with a blank piece of paper or word-processor screen and write a perfect version of what you want to say first time. But it is unlikely! That talent is given to very few writers. Most will tell you that writing is a hard process of drafting and redrafting and editing and re-editing until they have a piece they feel happy to offer to an audience. The writer Robert Graves claimed that his wastepaper basket was his best friend. Some computers even have as one of their icons a wastepaper basket for you to dump all your drafts into!

So *you* mustn't be satisfied with your first draft. You may find that a second, third or even fourth draft is needed before you are content with what you have produced. Of course, if you are writing your piece in an examination, you will have time for only one draft, but you will then be expected to comment on what you have written and to suggest any changes or improvements that you think should be made to subsequent drafts.

All writers, even the greatest, draft and redraft their work. In the activity below, you have the opportunity to view some changes at first hand and to comment on their effect. It will complement what you have learnt in the chapter on Stylistics, but remember that *all* writing benefits from the drafting and redrafting process. For instance, it can be very helpful to set up your class or group as a writers' workshop in which you can all offer helpful suggestions on each others' writing in progress. Second or third opinions can be very valuable!

ACTIVITY

1 Here are two versions of the eighteenth-century poet William Blake's poem 'London'. The first is an early draft, whilst the second is the final version.

Draft
I wonder thro' each dirty street,
Near where the dirty Thames does flow,
And see in every face I meet
Marks of weakness, marks of woe.

In every cry of every Man
In every voice of every Child
In every voice, in every ban
The german mind-forg'd links I hear.

But most the Chimney-sweeper's cry
Blackens o'er the churches' walls,
And the hapless Soldier's sigh
Runs in blood down Palace walls.

From every wintry street I hear
How the midnight Harlot's curse
Blasts the new born Infant's tear
And hangs with plagues the marriage hearse.

Published version
I wander thro' each charter'd street
Near where the charter'd Thames does flow,
And mark in every face I meet
Marks of weakness, marks of woe.

In every cry of every Man,
In every Infant's cry of fear,
In every voice, in every ban,
The mind-forg'd manacles I hear.

How the Chimney-sweeper's cry
Every black'ning church appalls,
And the hapless Soldier's sigh
Runs in blood down Palace walls.

But most thro' midnight streets I hear
How the youthful Harlot's curse
Blasts the new born infant's tear,
And blights with plagues the marriage hearse.

In pairs discuss as precisely as you can the changes that Blake made and comment on the effects of the revisions. Here are some questions to guide your discussion.

  a Why is 'dirty' replaced by 'charter'd?' What does 'charter'd' mean?

  b Why did Blake change 'see' to 'mark' in line 3?

  c Why has 'infant' replaced 'child'? What are the connotations of each word?

  d Are Blake's changes to line 8 an improvement?

  e What is the effect of the grammatical change of 'blackens' to 'black'ning' in line 10? Can a cry 'blacken'?

  f Comment in detail on the changes Blake made to the last verse.

2 George Orwell extensively redrafted and rewrote *1984*. Here is the published version of the beginning of the novel, together with Orwell's original opening. In what ways does the rewritten version differ from the original?

Published version

It was a bright cold day in April, and the clocks were striking thirteen. Winston Smith, his chin nuzzled into his breast in an effort to escape the vile wind, slipped quickly through the glass doors of Victory Mansions, though not quickly enough to prevent a swirl of gritty dust from entering along with him.

The hallway smelt of boiled cabbage and old rag mats. At one end of it a coloured poster, too large for indoor display, had been tacked to the wall. It depicted simply an enormous face, more than a metre wide: the face of a man of about forty-five, with a heavy black moustache and ruggedly handsome features. Winston made for the stairs. It was no use trying the lift. Even at the best of times it was seldom working, and at present the electric current was cut off during daylight hours. It was part of the economy drive in preparation for Hate Week. The flat was seven flights up, and Winston, who was thirty-nine and had a varicose ulcer above his right ankle, went slowly, resting several times on the way. On each landing, opposite the lift-shaft, the poster with the enormous face gazed from the wall.

Draft

It was a cold blowy day in early April and a million radios were striking thirteen. Winston Smith pushed open the glass door of Victory Mansions, turned to the right down the passageway and pressed the button of the lift. Nothing happened. He had just pressed a second time when a door at the end of the passage opened, letting out a smell of boiled greens and old rag mats, and the aged prole who acted as porter and caretaker thrust out a grey, seamed face and stood for a moment sucking his teeth and watching Winston malignantly.

'Lift ain't working,' he announced at last.

'Why isn't it working?'

'No lifts ain't working. The currents is cut orf at the main. The 'eat ain't working neither. All currents to be cut orf during daylight hours. Orders!' he barked in military style, and slammed the door again, leaving it uncertain whether the grievance he evidently felt was against Winston, or against the authorities who had cut off the current.

Winston remembered now. It was part of the economy drive in preparation for Hate Week. The flat was seven flights up, and Winston, conscious of his thirty-nine years and of the varicose ulcer above his right ankle, rested at each landing to avoid putting himself out of breath. On every landing the same poster was gummed to the wall – a huge coloured poster, too large for indoor display. It depicted simply an enormous face, the face of a man of about forty-five, with ruggedly handsome features, thick black hair, a heavy moustache.

❺ *Editing*

Editing is very much part of the process of drafting. You are editing your draft whenever you read through what you have written to see:

- whether you have included everything you ought to have done
- whether some part of what you have written should be omitted
- whether it is in the best order
- whether it is expressed in the most suitable way for your audience and purpose.

Much editing is done by the writer poring over his or her work without anyone else reading it, and this can sometimes make it a very lonely occupation. Often your writing will benefit from someone else reading it and offering their opinion as to its effectiveness. Your group or class should get into the habit of reading and commenting on each others' work. *Constructive* criticism should always be welcome.

ACTIVITY

You will need to be in groups of three or four for this activity as you are going to act as an editorial board whose job it is to choose between a number of pieces of writing that have been submitted to you.

The RSPCA is planning to visit primary schools and give a series of talks targeting junior pupils (age eight to eleven). These talks are designed to raise awareness of the responsibilities of pet ownership by providing advice and information on how to look after a pet. One of the talks in the series is to be on guinea-pigs, and people have been invited by the RSPCA to submit a script for this talk. Having read all the scripts, the RSPCA will choose *one* which they will then issue to everyone who is to deliver this talk to pupils. The RSPCA is keen to ensure that the same talk is given to all schools, even though different individuals will deliver the talk to different schools. The opening sections of eight of the scripts submitted are given below.

By the end of this activity you will have:
1 decided on the criteria for a successful opening to the talk
2 carefully read the scripts submitted
3 made notes on each one
4 chosen the successful script
5 written an explanation for their rejection to

the unsuccessful writers and offered each one some advice on how to improve their submission.

Script A
Hello. My name is . . . and I'm here today to talk to you about how to care for a guinea-pig properly. My talk will include: how to tell if it is a boy or a girl, the appearance of a guinea-pig, what they eat and how they should be fed, sounds they make, body language and the meaning of each sound, choosing a guinea-pig, what to do if they get ill and breeding. When I have finished talking, I will be happy to answer any questions you may have.

Script B
Hi. My name's . . . As your headteacher said, I'm from the Royal Society for the Prevention of Cruelty to Animals, or the RSPCA for short. Today I'm going to talk to you about guinea-pigs. Most of you will have seen a guinea-pig at some time in your life. It might have been at your own house, a friend's or even here at school. But by the time you leave here this afternoon, all of you will know much more about guinea-pigs and how to care for them as pets.

Script C
Hello everyone, I'm . . . and I'm here to talk to you today about these (picture of guinea-pig). Does everybody know what it is? Yes, good. I work for the RSPCA, the Royal Society for the Prevention of Cruelty to Animals. I see hundreds of sick guinea-pigs every year and it makes me very sad when I hear that it's

their owners that make them sick. That's why I'm here to tell all you children how to look after your guinea-pigs.

Script D

The Guinea-Pig is a member of the rodent family. This is why it has 'gnawing' or 'cutting' teeth, two each in the upper or lower jaw. These teeth grow continuously, and so need to be worn down by constant chewing of hard foods. The Guinea-Pig's food intake can actually be prevented by the teeth if they are not worn down! Although a rodent, the Guinea-Pig does have a visible tail like the mouse or rat – but the skeleton of a guinea-pig does not have a tail extension.

Script E

Hello everyone, my name's . . . and I've come to teach you a Golden Rule – Guinea-Pigs need Love, Care, Food and Attention and they can only get that from you! I've come to talk to you today about caring for a particular pet which some of you may already have at home. It is a very special kind of pet which needs lots and lots of love, care and attention. I've brought with me a very special friend of mine, a black and white smooth-haired guinea-pig called Trotters.

Script F

Hello, my name is Mr/Mrs . . . and I've come here today from the RSPCA, which some of you might know is the Royal Society for the Prevention of Cruelty to Animals. The RSPCA tries to look after all sorts of animals from lions to birds, from elephants to pigs and tries to stop them from being treated badly or hurt unfairly. The RSPCA also sends people like me to schools all around the country to talk to boys and girls like you about keeping and caring for pets, and today I'm here to talk about a pet some of you might have thought about getting, or some of you might already have got. Today I'm here to talk about these little creatures here (point to OHP of guinea-pigs) guinea-pigs.

Script G

Good morning/afternoon. My name is . . . and I'm here to talk to you about having a guinea-pig as a pet and how to look after it. Now, hands up anybody who has a guinea-pig at home. Good, perhaps you'll be able to help me later in my talk. If you'd all like to have a look at the OHP now, you'll be able to see a picture of a guinea-pig. As you can see, they're really cute but what is important to remember is that you should *never* buy any animal, even a guinea-pig, just because it looks cute or sweet. I'm sure you've heard all those stories about pets being bought for Christmas or birthdays and then being found abandoned. Never forget, treat a pet as you would like to be treated.

Script H

I am from the RSPCA and I will be talking to you about the responsibility of pet ownership by providing advice and information on how to look after a pet. I would like to show you the different varieties of guinea-pigs but most importantly – how to care for them, feed them and keep your guinea-pigs hygienic. Owning a pet can be a rewarding and educational experience. It can teach you to be considerate to others, respect for all creatures and in return others (including your pets) will be affectionate towards you.

All these scripts were written by students following an A-level English Language course.

Commentaries

In addition to producing a number of pieces of original writing either as coursework or in an examination, many A-level syllabuses require you to write a 'commentary' on your work. In this section, you will be looking at:

- what a commentary is
- examples of poor commentaries
- examples of good commentaries.

A commentary is a genre of writing, and like any other it has a purpose, audience, **form** and content.

Purpose

The purpose of a commentary is to record the process of your writing, reflect on it and thus, it is hoped, enable you to become a better writer. It should illuminate all the choices you made as you were producing the piece of writing.

Audience

The audience for your commentary is quite a tricky one, because in a sense, there are two, or maybe even three, audiences each with different agendas.

The first and most obvious audience is the examiner. You will probably think of him or her as a somewhat remote figure whose sole aim in life is to knock as many marks as possible off your work, taking great delight in doing so. Well, the authors of this book certainly hope that this isn't the case, but it does remain true that examiners are a tricky audience.

It is probably more helpful for you to think of the examiner as part of the second audience – that of other writers. If you think of yourself when writing a commentary as writing for other (apprentice) writers, then you are more likely to get both the tone and the content of your commentary absolutely spot on.

The third audience may well be yourself. One way of thinking about your commentary is to see it as a log or journal of your writing whose purpose is to help you become a better writer. As in a diary, when you record events and reflect on them, so in a commentary you are reviewing and reflecting on the stages, processes and decisions you made during the process of composition.

Form

There is no set form for a commentary. If you are writing it on a piece of coursework, then there are many forms it could take. Here are some suggestions, but you should use any form that is most suitable or comfortable for you:

- a log or journal of your writing in which you record your comments throughout the process of writing from planning to publication
- a pre-commentary in which you write about what you hope to achieve, followed by a commentary at the end of the writing on whether your aims have been achieved
- an essay written after publication in which you reflect on the stages of composition and the choices you have made.

Content

Nor is there a set content for a commentary. You are free to choose what you wish to focus on, but, of course, much will depend on what you have written in your original piece and its drafts. Your commentary on a short story for six-year-olds is likely to focus on very different issues than one on a leaflet for senior citizens on the welfare and benefit rights available to them. Nevertheless, you should focus on how you have composed your piece to suit its audience, purpose and context.

Here are some possible questions your commentary could answer:

- Who is my intended audience?
- Where did I get my ideas from?
- What research or prior reading did I do?
- What help did I get from others (teachers, parents, fellow students)?
- Did I base my writing on any particular model?
- What did I change, omit, add, revise during the writing? Why?
- What was the response of people who read it in draft form?
- Did I adapt it in the light of these responses or comments?
- What particular language choices (**lexis**, tone, **register**, etc) did I make and why?
- How did I organise and structure my material?

Examples of commentaries

It is now time to look at some examples of commentaries.

First of all, here are some short extracts from commentaries, together with some examiners' comments:

I could have used better words. *('Better' in what way? Explain what you mean. Give some examples.)*

I could have put more into it. *(What? Be specific! More effort? More words? More humour?)*

My story is called 'The Haunted House'. It's about this girl and her boyfriend. They go away for the weekend. *(I know all this – I've just had to read your very boring story!)*

The second draft is better ... I put 'stomach' instead of 'guts'. *(Is this all you have to say about the changes you made?!)*

I decided to make my final piece of writing an instructional piece. I have written an instructional piece on 'How to throw a successful party' not only to help people organise a party but to write an instructional piece that was light-hearted. *(Yes, I think we know you're writing an instructional piece by now!)*

None of you reading this are likely to write such commentaries! However there are three mistakes that are frequently made and you should try to avoid them at all costs.

1 Don't be anecdotal

An anecdote is a short narrative from one's private life and it can be quite easy to slip into one when writing a commentary. Anecdotes can be interesting and amusing when told in the right circumstances, say at a party or in a pub, but they are not really suitable for reflections on a piece of writing. This extract continues the final commentary above:

I went to a party where a friend of mine spilt a brightly coloured drink – blue curaçao – all over the light-coloured carpet and we had a problem getting the marks out of it. We tried everything – soap and water, washing-up liquid, dry cleaner – and it just made the mess worse. There was blue everywhere…

This might have been the germ of a piece of entertaining writing, but it is not a commentary. It is clear she was trying to explain the source for her ideas for her instructional writing piece, but she has badly misjudged the purpose of a commentary.

2 Don't describe

This Picasso piece is targeted at children between eight and twelve years old. It can be obtained in school classrooms, libraries and public libraries.

It contains informative information, my own personal opinion of the artist will not be taken into consideration. The information was presented in a simple form, with a contents page, numbered pages, this would give the reader an idea of the content and give the reader quick access to what they would like to read with a glance.

I have used short paragraphs, lots of headings, lots of pictures and lots of colourful writing to attract the reader's attention, hopefully they would find the piece an easy read. Example 'Where was Picasso born?' is a heading used with a short paragraph answering the question.

You will notice that all this writer has done in this badly written commentary is to tell us what we have already read in her 'Picasso piece'. If we have read it carefully, we will have noticed that she has used 'short paragraphs, lots of headings, lots of pictures'. There is no need to tell us what we already know! We know that there are contents pages and numbered pages. She is describing what she has written, not giving us any insight into the processes of thinking, planning and drafting that went into the creation of the published piece. It is therefore not a commentary.

3 Don't be superficial

In the extracts from this commentary, the writer is dealing with a biographical piece on George Orwell. He fails to illuminate any of the processes involved in its composition, merely observing that he had to change his first draft. The reader demands some detailed illustration and justification for the changes he refers to.

This piece of writing was without doubt the easiest and quickest to write. The idea was successful and needed only one redraft. The ease with which I was able to write makes the commentary harder to write, because there is little I can highlight about the piece. The material was not difficult to organise into an informative leaflet and everything was straightforward. It has to be said though that I did change my first draft. Originally I had intended that the piece would be an obituary, but as my teacher suggested, it was not a good idea because Orwell had been dead for nearly fifty years.

4 Good Practice

Finally, an extract from an excellent commentary. The writer had produced an instructional poster on 'How to Print a Black and White Negative' for beginners to photography and wrote an extremely thorough and detailed commentary. There is not enough space to reproduce all of it here as it runs to four pages, but here is the opening section.

I decided to produce a poster in the instructional register to teach a beginner in photography how to select equipment, set up a dark room and produce a satisfactory print from a black and white negative. I have developed my own negatives for several years and in that time I have seen relatively few books which explain clearly how to print a negative. Most of them use long, complicated words and technical language which beginners would find difficult to understand. Therefore, they are of little use to them. I noted down everything that I had learnt from my experience of printing negatives and some information from some sheets that I was given in an art lesson at high school (included in my Bibliography) then compiled it in instructional form.

I chose to present the piece in poster form, as it would be easier to handle. It is useful, especially for beginners, to have their hands free in a dark room. A poster will keep clean and dry on the wall and the working surfaces will be free from loose papers. If I made a further draft, several changes to the format would be made. Firstly, I would use thinner paper so it would be easier to fold. Also, the paper needs to be light red or orange in colour in order to avoid too much reflection of light, which may affect the photography paper. The writing would need to be much darker and bolder so that it could be easily read and the size would need to be altered to unclutter the different sections. Also, a plastic covering would ensure that it was waterproof.

Other changes could also be made concerning the format. After finishing the poster I realised that the first side could be included in a separate booklet or sheets because it is not used during the printing process and a booklet would be easier to read. One advantage of the poster, however, is that all the information and instructions are kept neatly together. The only separate sheet is the summary of the method. This is separate because once the beginner knows and understands the process, it will be all that is needed to trigger off the process in the person's mind.

The SUMMARY OF METHOD simplifies the process into ten easy stages. This avoids any confusion that the audience may feel when he or she is told to *use the same process of developing as with the test-strip* (Section D, side 2). It also prevents the audience from having to work through sections B and C once more to extract the relevant details. The audience can then continue to print, referring only to this sheet and the poster for any diagrams when necessary.

I place the poster in a realistic context by making it a part of a series, as it would be in the developing process. This piece is stage 2 in the series. Stage 1 is mentioned in the 'negatives' section on side 1 of the poster. It describes how to develop the negatives once the picture has been taken. This connected with my aim to make the layout visually interesting and easy to read. I experimented with the layout, before choosing which to use. I consulted my audience on whom I tested my first draft.

The process on side 2 is divided into four stages. A – SETTING UP THE NEGATIVE, B – MAKING A TEST-STRIP, C – DEVELOPING THE PAPER and D – THE FINAL PICTURE, plus a diagram of the enlarger. I had planned to have the diagram in the middle of the poster, with the sections in the following layout:

A   B

C   D (plus several other ideas included in DRAFT 1).

However, after consulting with my audience, I chose the following layout for various reasons:

A   C

B   D

Firstly, my audience remarked that generally people read in columns, rather than across a page. I agreed. We decided that the layout was much more balanced with the diagram at the centre of the poster, rather than to one side. It is the most effective position because the audience can refer quickly to the diagram when reading each section. Also, the language is less cluttered than if it was all at one side of the poster. Therefore, I used a similar layout on both sides of the poster.

11 Rewriting Texts

New texts for old

One of the practical skills that courses and examinations in English Language enable you to develop is that of producing texts that are based on what other people have written (and spoken). Indeed, this is what you are specifically required to do in the examinations set by a number of Boards. The work you have undertaken so far on **genre** will have helped prepare you for this. Such skills, of course, are useful not only in helping you succeed in examinations, but can also be very necessary during your own working life. For example, you might be asked to write a short leaflet that will be included in a tube of pain-relieving ointment. The leaflet, you are told, is to explain clearly and unambiguously to the patient what the ointment can do, when and how it should be applied and, perhaps most importantly of all, what the patient must *not* do with it. The manufacturer has given you a number of documents about the ointment, but these are obviously too technical for the patients to understand, as they have been produced by medical scientists. It becomes your job to adapt these texts for a different audience and purpose. Or, take a second illustration. You are a journalist on a local paper and your editor has asked you to write an article for the travel page comparing three holiday resorts and recommend which is the most suitable for families with young children. The deadline is next Friday. You haven't time to visit the resorts before you write the article, so the best you can do is to base it on various publications the resorts have supplied you with and to do some research in the paper's own library.

The next exercise will give you initial practice in rewriting a text for a different audience. To complete it successfully, you will have to study the conventions of the genre carefully and focus closely on the language choices and changes that you, the writer, have to make.

ACTIVITY

In order to introduce children to the classics of English literature, many publishers have issued adapted versions of such books. Here, together with the corresponding passage from the original, is an excerpt from a 1994 children's version of Mary Shelley's classic horror story *Frankenstein*, first published in 1818. It is the famous moment, so beloved of film makers, when the creature built by the scientist Victor Frankenstein comes to life.

Read the two passages very carefully and then complete the tasks that follow.

Mary Shelley's Frankenstein
It was on a dreary night of November that I beheld the accomplishment of my toils. With an anxiety that almost amounted to agony, I collected the instruments of life around me, that I might infuse a spark of being into the lifeless thing that lay at my feet. It was already one in the morning; the rain pattered dismally against the panes, and my candle was nearly burnt out, when, by the glimmer of the half-extinguished light, I saw the dull yellow eye of the creature open; it breathed hard, and a convulsive motion agitated its limbs.

How can I describe my emotions at this catastrophe, or how delineate the wretch whom with such infinite pains and care I had endeavoured to form? His limbs were in proportion, and I had selected his features as beautiful. Beautiful! Great God! His yellow skin scarcely covered the work of muscles and arteries beneath; his hair was of a lustrous black, and flowing; his teeth of pearly whiteness; but these luxuriances only formed a more horrid contrast with his watery eyes, that seemed almost of the same colour as the dun-white sockets in which they were set, his shrivelled complexion and straight black lips.

The different accidents of life are not so changeable as the feelings of human nature. I had worked hard for nearly two years, for the sole purpose of infusing life into an inanimate body. For this I had deprived myself of rest and health. I had desired it with an ardour that far exceeded moderation; but now that I had finished, the beauty of the dream vanished, and breathless horror and disgust filled my heart. Unable to endure the aspect of the being I had created, I rushed out of the room and continued a long time traversing my bedchamber, unable to compose my mind to sleep. At length lassitude succeeded to the tumult I had before endured, and I threw myself on the bed in my clothes, endeavouring to seek a few moments of forgetfulness. But it was in vain: I slept, indeed, but I was disturbed by the wildest dreams.

The children's version
It was on a dreary night in November that I finished my work. As I collected the instruments with which I might breathe a spark of being into the lifeless thing lying at my feet, I was so tense that I was almost in pain. It was already one in the morning; the rain fell dismally against the windows. My candle was nearly burnt out, when I saw the dull yellow eye of the creature open. It took a deep breath, and a sudden motion shook his limbs.

How can I describe my feelings at this sight? How can I describe the creature I had taken such pains to create? His body was well formed, and I had tried to make him handsome too. Handsome! Good God! The stirrings of life only made him horribly ugly. The muscles and veins were showing through his yellow skin. His hair was shiny black and his teeth were perfectly white, in horrid contrast to his dull eyes, which seemed to be almost the same yellow-grey colour as the rest of his face, apart from his thin black lips.

I had worked hard for nearly two years to reach this point. I had gone without rest and made myself ill. I had desired this moment more than a man should desire anything, but now that I had finished, the beauty of the dream vanished and disgust filled my heart. The thing I had created was so ugly that I could not look at it. I rushed out of the laboratory and for a long time paced up and down in my bedroom, trying to calm down. I did at last fall asleep, but it was a restless sleep, full of the wildest dreams.

1 a Identify the parts of the original that have been omitted from the children's version. As an example, you will notice that the adapter has removed 'by the glimmer of the half-extinguished light' from the first paragraph.

   b Decide if the omitted passages have any features in common. For instance, 'complicated' grammatical constructions will have been simplified, but there are some other features for you to consider.

2 **a** Select a number of sentences from the original which have amended equivalents in the children's edition. Here are two short examples, but you should be able to find longer sentences from Mary Shelley that have equivalents in the adapted version:

His limbs were in proportion, and I had selected his features as beautiful.
His body was well formed, and I had tried to make him handsome too.

For this I had deprived myself of rest and health.
I had gone without rest and made myself ill.

   b How do the sentences differ? You should examine carefully both the vocabulary and the **syntax** (word order and construction of phrases and clauses).

   c Select some sentences that illustrate the following methods that the adapter has used in his rewriting:
     (i)   summarising
     (ii)   paraphrasing
     (iii) shortening.

3 In completing this task, you will have to examine the passage as a whole.

   a Is the sequence of events in both versions the same?

   b Is the content of each paragraph approximately the same?

   c How much of the original has been removed?

   d Compare the average length of sentences in each version.

Now that you have completed your close analysis of the two passages, you should be in a position to tackle these individual assignments.

Assignment 1

Imagine that you are the editor of the series of books in which the adapted *Frankenstein* appears. You wish to issue more books in the series and want them to follow the **style** established in *Frankenstein*. Write a short sheet of instructions (between 150 and 200 words) that explains clearly to adapters what kinds of changes you wish to make to the novels they will be working on.

Assignment 2

Using the sheet of instructions as a guide, write your own version of this passage from *Frankenstein*, in which Victor Frankenstein encounters the creature he has made whilst walking in the Swiss mountains.

It was nearly noon when I arrived at the top of the ascent. For some time I sat upon the rock that overlooks the sea of ice. A mist covered both that and the surrounding mountains. Presently a breeze dissipated the cloud, and I descended upon the glacier. The surface is very uneven, rising like the waves of a troubled sea, descending low, and interspersed by rifts that sink deep. The field of ice is almost a league in width, but I spent nearly two hours in crossing it. The opposite mountain is a bare perpendicular rock. From the side where I now stood Montanvert was exactly opposite, at the distance of a league; and above it rose Mont Blanc, in awful majesty. I remained in a recess of the rock, gazing on this wonderful and stupendous scene. The sea, or rather the vast river of ice, wound among its dependent mountains, whose aerial summits hung over its recesses. Their icy and glittering peaks shone in the sunlight over the clouds. My heart, which was before sorrowful, now swelled with something like joy: I exclaimed – 'Wandering spirits, if indeed ye wander, and do not rest in your narrow beds, allow me this faint happiness, or take me, as your companion, away from the joys of life.'

As I said this I suddenly beheld the figure of a man, at some distance, advancing towards me with superhuman speed. He bounded over the crevices in the ice, among which I had walked with caution; his stature, also, as he approached, seemed to exceed that of man. I was troubled; a mist came over my eyes, and I felt a faintness seize me: but I was quickly restored by the cold gale of the mountains. I perceived, as the shape came nearer (sight tremendous and abhorred!) that it was the wretch whom I had created. I trembled with rage and horror, resolving to wait his approach and then close with him in mortal combat. He approached; his countenance bespoke bitter anguish, combined with disdain and malignity, while its unearthly ugliness rendered it almost too horrible for human eyes. But I scarcely observed this; rage and hatred had at first deprived me of utterance, and I recovered only to overwhelm him with words expressive of furious detestation and contempt.

The skills for rewriting

The skills of close reading and rewriting of texts are tested in all A-level English Language syllabuses. Indeed, some examination boards devote a whole paper to such skills. In these papers, you are given a file of material to read and are allowed a number of days in which to do this. The file will contain an assortment of extracts from a variety of sources – newspaper articles, interviews, encyclopaedias, leaflets, books and letters, for example. All the extracts are concerned with one subject, which may be anything from football to fashion, pollution to politics. From this variety of material you are to create a new text. To illustrate: based on a file of material about birds, you may be required to write the text of a wall poster for young children which is to be published by the Royal Society for the Protection of Birds and whose intention is to help the children recognise and care for the wild birds that visit their gardens. Another example: you may be asked to write the introduction to a glossy illustrated book on volcanoes for a non-specialist audience and must base your text on a number of quite technical texts that you have been given.

What then must you learn to do when composing one of these new texts? What skills are involved? You have to learn:

- to *select* material that is appropriate for the audience and purpose of your text
- to *edit* the selected material
- to *adapt* the language of the texts you are working with so that its style and **register** are appropriate
- to *organise* your material so that the **structure** and sequence is clear throughout your new text
- to *write* new text such as an introduction, links, captions and a conclusion
- to *rewrite, paraphrase* and *summarise* where necessary
- to *present* your material using charts, tables, diagrams, etc, where this would be suitable
- to *guide* the reader through the text
- to *conform* to the requirements of the specified genre.

That's quite a daunting list! So where do you start? Remember that you've got time to familiarise yourself with the texts before you actually have to start writing. This can be as much as three days in the case of some examinations.

❶ *Establish provenance*

The first stage is to interrogate each text you are dealing with to establish its provenance. This isn't as fearsome as it might seem! Establishing the provenance means finding out:

- who wrote the text
- when the text was written
- its intended audience
- its genre and purpose.

You need to have as much of this information about the text as possible before you start to adapt it. This will save you making silly mistakes when you come to compose your new text.

Suppose you had been asked to write the text for the wall poster about birds mentioned earlier, and that one of the pieces in the file of material you had been given had originally been written for university students of ornithology. It is most unlikely that this material would be suitable for your audience of primary-school children. This is an extreme example, of course, but there are others that are less extreme. For instance, if you had been asked to write a magazine article about the best new French wines, you would have to ensure that you knew the dates of your source material. It wouldn't be very helpful for your audience if you recommended a 'new' wine whose production had been discontinued in 1990! So you can see from these two illustrations how important it is to establish a text's provenance. How do you do this?

On most occasions you should find it quite easy to discover both the author and the date of publication, as this information is usually given to you, along with the original title. If it is provided, then the important task of deciding both its audience and purpose is made considerably simpler. If you are working, for example, with a text called *PCs for Dummies* by Dan Gookin and Andy Rathbone (1992) then you should have a fair idea that a computer novice would find the book useful and that a fully qualified programmer would be wasting his or her time even opening the book. However, the novice might be a little at sea with *Modifying Your AUTOEXEC.BAT File for Multiple Configurations* published by Microsoft (1993).

ACTIVITY

Here are a number of text titles. See if you can identify both the audience and the purpose of the text. An approach to the first one has been suggested below.

1 *A First Course in Linguistics* by J M Y Simpson (1979).
   Audience: students at the beginning of an academic course.
   Purpose: clearly the purpose is to instruct. 'Courses' may be entertaining or they may be persuasive, but their primary purpose is to teach or instruct.

A few hints:

- look for any clues in the title as to the purpose of the writing – words like 'Guide', 'a personal experience' or 'a study' should help you decide
- look for any direct indications of the intended audience – words like 'members' or 'readers', for example

- look for how formal or informal some of the words are – a word like 'kids', for instance, should give some clue.

2 *Rediscover Grammar* by David Crystal (1988).
3 *Multiple Sclerosis: A Personal Experience* by Alexander Burnfield (1986).
4 *From Birth to Five: A Study of the Health and Behaviour of Britain's Five-Year-Olds* by N R Butler and Jean Goldey (eds) (1986).
5 *The Right Food for Your Kids* by Louise Templeton (1984).
6 *Twelve Years a Slave: Narrative of Solomon Northup, A Citizen of New York* (1853).
7 *The Shell Book of Offa's Dyke Path* by Frank Noble (1969).
8 *The American Past: A Survey of American History* by Joseph R Conlin (1990).

Most of the authors were probably unknown to you, but this shouldn't have been a problem in reaching your decisions.

A brief word about purpose: there are many effects that an author might want his or her text to have. She or he might, for example, want to incite the audience, to defend a point of view, to allay fears or merely to establish friendly relations. The range of purposes texts might have could be vast. However, it will be easier for you in the initial stages of your work if you limit purpose to four broad categories:

- to entertain
- to instruct or advise
- to inform
- to persuade.

Some pieces you are working with will have clearly defined purposes. A car maintenance manual is designed to instruct, an election leaflet to persuade. Other texts may be more problematical in that they may tend to do two things at once. Many advertisements, for example, will both entertain and inform you, though their primary purpose is to persuade you to buy a product or service. Many newspaper reports will inform you, but hope to convey this information in an entertaining way. Of course, they may also be seeking to persuade.

❷ *Read and understand the material*

The next stage involves identifying the provenance and primary purpose of texts not merely from their titles alone. You have already had plenty of practice in this, when you were working on genre. In the following activity, however, you will find four short pieces all on the same subject, the Jewish festival of Passover (or *Pesach* in Hebrew).

ACTIVITY

1 Read the following texts carefully and for each identify:
   a the intended audience
   b what the text tells us about the author
   c the purpose of the text.
An approach to Text A has been suggested below.
2 The texts are followed by a list of titles, authors and sources. Try to link them with the appropriate text.

Text A

This evening, Jews throughout the world will welcome in Passover the oldest, and the most symbolically potent, of all the Jewish festivals. At the Passover meal – the Seder – we will recount from an ancient liturgical text known as the Haggadah the story of the Exodus from Egypt more than 3000 years ago. Led by Moses, the children of Israel made their escape from slavery to freedom. In every generation, the Haggadah enjoins us, it is our duty to instruct our children in the details of the Exodus story as if we have been personally redeemed from Egyptian slavery.

Because of its theme and associations, Passover is every Jew's favourite festival. In the words of the great German-Jewish poet Heinrich Heine, 'since the Exodus, Freedom has always spoken with a Hebrew accent.'

Audience: a non-Jewish one as most Jews are likely to know when Passover is celebrated; neither will they need 'Seder' and 'Haggadah' glossing, as these will be familiar terms, nor will they need 'Exodus' clarified as being 'from Egypt'.

Author: a knowledgeable Jew as we can see from his use of inclusive language – '*we* will recount and *our* duty to instruct *our* children'.

Purpose: to inform the audience about an important religious festival in the Jewish year.

Text B

The festival is celebrated for eight days (seven in Eretz Yisrael), from the 15th to the 22nd of Nisan. The Hebrew word *Pesach*, meaning 'passing over', refers to the smiting of the first-born in Egypt when God 'passed over' the houses of the Children of Israel (Ex. xii 27), the lintels and door-posts of which had been sprinkled with the blood of the Paschal lamb.

The Fast of the First-Born. As a token of gratitude for this miraculous deliverance, a fast is observed on Erev Pesach by every male first-born. If he participates in the last part of the Talmudic Tractate, it is unnecessary for the first-born to fast. The conclusion, as it is called, is celebrated as a festive occasion accompanied by a meal in honour of a religious act, which exempts those taking part from fasting. The Siyyum is held in the Synagogue just after the Shacharith service.

Text C

Passover is as old and as enduring as the Jewish people itself. It commemorates the great event when God redeemed the Israelites from slavery in Egypt and made them a free people. It is therefore a national feast celebrating the liberation and birth of a people but it is also a religious festival, for the event is remembered as the act of God who is man's redeemer. Its consequence was the Covenant at Sinai, when the Israelites pledged themselves to live according to the divine law, the *Torah*, and God promised that they would be his special people, a kingdom of priests, a holy nation (Exodus 19). Passover is a festival of freedom, of brotherhood, of faith and of hope.

Text D

The story of the Exodus, the consequent theophany on Mt Sinai, and the wanderings of the Children of Israel in the wilderness prior to their entry to the Promised Land, are primary themes of Jewish religious consciousness. All exile is seen, typologically, as an extension of the Egyptian experience, and all liberation and redemption as an extension of the Exodus. The Passover festival is the festival of the Exodus *par excellence*, although it is also an agricultural festival associated with the barley harvest.

Titles

The Passover, the Last Supper and the Eucharist by The Study Centre for Christian–Jewish Relations (1975).
Jews: Their Religious Beliefs and Practices by Alan Unterman (1981).
When Freedom Speaks with a Hebrew Accent by

Rabbi David J Goldberg (the *Independent,* 26 March 1994).
Introduction to Judaism by Isidore Fishman (1958).

To give yourselves more practice in identifying provenance and purpose, each member of the class or group should bring in a variety of texts on one particular subject and give them to the other members to work on.

Having established the purpose and provenance of the texts and ensured that you fully understand the material by checking the meaning of any words or expressions you are uncertain about, you should then move on to the next stage of your preparation – making an inventory.

❸ *Categorise the material*

Remember that the material you will have been given is all concerned with the same subject, each piece usually dealing with a different aspect. You should now try to produce a series of headings or categories which describe the content of the material. Don't go into too much detail; five or six main areas are as much as you will be able to work with easily.

Firstly, make a list of these main areas and then mark each page or extract with the heading showing the area(s) with which that page or extract is mainly concerned. Don't worry if you find that some of the material is labelled more than once. This is only to be expected.

For example, you could be dealing with a mass of information about the dropping of the first atomic bombs on Hiroshima and Nagasaki in 1945. You might have four pieces that you could label 'Immediate Effects' and each piece could be further categorised so that one piece might be labelled 'Immediate Effects – survivor's account'; a second 'Immediate Effects – 1980s history book'; a third 'Immediate Effects – view from American observer plane' and a fourth 'Immediate Effects – 1945 British newspaper account'. This system of multiple heading or labelling makes it much easier for you to have different perspectives on the material and to think about the different approaches you could take when constructing your new text. Don't worry if all the material doesn't fit neatly into the various areas you have chosen. There may be overlap between areas; you may feel that certain pieces (or sections of pieces) could fit into more than one of your categories. You may even find that certain sections seem to have little connection with the rest of the material.

By now, you should have a clear view of:

- the date and author of each text
- the primary purpose of each text

- the genre of each text
- an inventory of the texts.

④ *Make connections*

You are now ready to move on to the next stage, where you begin to make connections between the texts. You should be looking for any links that you can forge between the texts, as you seek to impose some order or structure on what you have read. This will help you when you come to write your own piece by suggesting some approaches you could take.

Of course, there can be no hard-and-fast rules here, as the order or sequence that you impose on the material will to some extent depend on its nature and content and your own personal preferences. Remember, you have already made a start by assigning the pieces to different categories. The following pointers are only suggestions, and examiners are more than happy to recognise and reward approaches that they themselves may not have thought of.

- If the material was produced at different times, it may be appropriate to sequence it according to the dates of composition.
- If the material refers to historical events, you could sequence it chronologically.
- If the material presents differing facets of an argument or differing points of view, you could choose to group together those on one side of the argument before grouping those on the other; or you might choose to present one piece from one side and then one from the other and so on.
- You could sequence the material according to the contrasting tones of voice adopted by the writers.
- It might be appropriate to group together all the pieces that were written for a particular audience. For example, pieces that were written for experts in a subject could contrast with those written for beginners.

These are just some of the ways in which you could begin to impose an order or sequence on the texts you are working with, but you will undoubtedly discover many others for yourself. Different topics suggest different approaches.

One very useful hint to bear in mind: if you take your booklet of material apart, you will find it much easier to see potential groupings, because you will be no longer influenced by the order in which the texts have been presented to you.

❺ *Summarise the material*

The next stage of your preparation is to summarise the contents of each piece in no more than two or three short sentences. This is an invaluable way for you to become even more familiar with the material and therefore better able to collect your thoughts in an examination. Some pieces are easier to summarise than others, of course. Factual material, for instance, is much simpler to deal with than material in which conflicting viewpoints and theories are presented.

❻ *Annotate the material*

The final stage involves annotating the texts in more detail. If you do this, it will be easier for you to find what you want during the exam. You won't then have the time to flick through all the texts to find exactly what you want. Facts and figures have an annoying habit of hiding themselves just when you need to refer to them! So you should develop your own system of annotation to avoid such problems when under examination stress. Obviously, you'll need most of the time in the exam to reflect on, plan and actually write your own text.

Here are a few suggestions that seem to work well.

■ Make cross-references. This will help you to identify those pieces of information (or ideas, opinions and theories) which should be considered together. You should devise a system of margin notes. For example: 'see page 13 lines 35–58'.
■ Underline or highlight key phrases, names or dates, though you should do this sparingly. If you underline too much in a text, then the exercise becomes self-defeating as the purpose is to highlight only the most important material. A passage that has almost everything underlined tells you almost nothing. Avoid your texts becoming a kaleidoscope of colour. It may be pretty, but it's pretty useless!
■ You could use colour coding to give a quick visual marker or indication of the contents of each page. As an example, imagine you have been given a set of texts about a famous film star who had moved into directing. You might devise a colour code like this:

blue: early life
red: career as an actor
green: career as a director
pink: adult and private life.

Again the same warning applies: use the colour sparingly. Overuse of colour will confuse rather than clarify.

Summary

1 Establish the date, audience and purpose of each text.
2 Ensure that you understand everything in the text, by use of a dictionary, if necessary.
3 Make an inventory and categorise each piece.
4 Identify ways in which the pieces could be linked.
5 Summarise the pieces.
6 Annotate the pieces.

Inside the examiner's head

The previous section has shown you some of the methods you can use to prepare for the task of creating a new text. In this section, you will be looking at three short texts that were produced by students under examination conditions and seeing how examiners would have assessed them.

You need, first of all, to consider how an examiner reads a text. Remember that there are many ways or strategies for reading (see page 105). But, just as there are many strategies for reading texts, so some texts might have many readers: newspapers, novels and travel brochures, for instance. Other texts have just one reader: a love letter, an income-tax demand and a geography essay, for instance.

So much is fairly obvious. But though some texts might be read by just one person, that one person might be reading it in a number of different roles. Two examples should make this clearer.

(i) Imagine a six-year-old child proudly bringing home a story he had written at school for his mother to read. Imagine also that his mother is a teacher. She could read his story both as proud mother and also as teacher. In her role as teacher, she might well look more critically at it than in her role as mother.

(ii) Imagine a reporter on a national paper reading an article in his local free weekly paper. He also could be reading it in two different roles. Firstly as a local resident keen to keep himself informed about developments in the area and secondly, as a fellow professional keen to judge the headline, structure and organisation of the article.

Similarly, an examiner, when faced with a text that a candidate has produced, also has a number of reader-roles. There are usually three of these.

The first role an examiner takes is that of prospective reader or listener. Exactly what this means depends, of course, on the nature of the text a candidate has been asked to produce. If, for instance, the text were a script for a radio programme for secondary-school pupils about the 1991 Gulf War, then the examiner would attempt to 'hear' the script as would a school pupil. If the task, however, were to write a guide book to Grasmere and its literary associations, then the examiner would have to adopt the reader-role of prospective purchaser and user of the guide.

The second role an examiner adopts is that of the editor or publisher who originally commissioned the piece. Editors have to decide whether the piece is good enough to be published or broadcast in its submitted form or whether alterations, major or minor, are required.

The third role is the most traditional. The examiner *is* an examiner and *will* be assessing scripts in the light of the criteria for a particular task. These criteria, however, are very firmly based on the first two reader-roles described above.

The examiners' criteria

So what *are* the criteria by which an examiner judges a text? In essence, there are three of these, and examiners will be asking three questions based on these criteria about each script they are reading.

Question 1: Has the candidate constructed a new text?

Remember that you have been asked to produce a piece of writing for a specific purpose, a specific audience and of a specific type. You haven't been asked to produce a hotch-potch of other people's writing. In other words, you have been asked to weave together separate elements into a cohesive whole. This weaving **metaphor** is a very apt one. For just as a piece of cloth is woven from different strands of material with the result that we are usually unaware of the separate pieces that go to make the finished article, so the text you create is one that is also constructed from a number of separate elements. Your reader ought to be unaware of this as he or she reads what you have constructed.

So the examiner, when considering your piece, will be looking to see whether you have:

- an effective title, introduction and conclusion
- used editorial features such as headings and subheadings, captions, 'text-boxes' for key information, highlighted quotations and summaries (remember that these are only examples of editorial features – there are many others you could use)
- provided a context for any of the extracts from the source material you have incorporated into your text
- avoided any stylistic or grammatical clashes between any extracts you have used and your own writing.

Question 2: How does the argument, theme or narrative run through the text?

The examiner will look at the overall structure or organisation of your text. The sequence in which you have placed the various components that go to make up your text can be crucial, because, if you fail to give it a clear structure, then a reader is very likely to get lost and confused and thus cease reading. In which case, it was pointless writing the text in the first place! Questions that an examiner might ask about your text are:

- What is this piece of writing saying?
- Does it follow a logical and interesting line of thought?
- Does it have a clear structure – a beginning, a middle and an end?

Question 3: Has the text found the right voice?

This is quite straightforward. What an examiner will be looking at, or more accurately, listening to here, is the tone of voice that you have adopted to address your readers or listeners. Tone of voice is the way you signal that you know there is an audience out there worth addressing. Think about what would happen if you got the tone wrong. Your readers or listeners could feel, for example: angry, insulted, puzzled, patronised, worried and so on. The one person you are not addressing is, of course, yourself. So, above all, don't talk to yourself when you write your text. The examiner will be looking to see whether:

- you have chosen the appropriate level of formality (or informality)
- you have glossed, simplified or paraphrased the source material, where necessary
- you are addressing the reader in the right register.

You can see then how the three reader-roles that an examiner has to take when he or she is assessing a script are inextricably intertwined. For example, if the examiner is looking at a text as a prospective reader or listener (or more practically as a prospective purchaser of, say, the newspaper or magazine in which the text was to appear) then he or she will also be making judgements about it on the basis of the three questions discussed above.

The examiners' comments

Now that you have looked at how examiners read and assess texts, it is time to move on and look at how some students answered one rewriting assignment. Neither the source material nor the assignment itself are as long as those you might be faced with in some examinations, but the reading and rewriting skills remain the same.

You have already looked at four texts about the Jewish festival of Passover; here are two further ones about another Jewish festival – Hanukkah.

Text A

Hanukkah or Chanukah (Hebrew, 'dedication'), annual festival of the Jews celebrated on eight successive days. It begins on the 25th day of Kislev, the third month of the Jewish calendar, corresponding, approximately, to December in the Gregorian calendar. Also known as the Festival of Lights, Feast of Dedication, and Feast of the Maccabees, Hanukkah commemorates the rededication of the Temple of Jerusalem by Judas Maccabee in 165 BC after the Temple had been profaned by Antiochus IV Epiphanes, king of Syria and overlord of Palestine.

In 168 BC, on a date corresponding approximately to December 25 in the Gregorian calendar, the Temple was dedicated to the worship of Zeus Olympius by order of Antiochus. An altar to Zeus was set up on the high altar. When Judas Maccabee recaptured Jerusalem three years later, he had the Temple purged and a new altar put up in place of the desecrated one. The Temple was then rededicated to God with festivities that lasted eight days. According to talmudic tradition, only one cruse of pure olive oil, sealed by the high priest and necessary for the rededicatory ritual, could be found, but that small quantity burned miraculously for eight days. A principal feature of the present-day celebration, commemorating this miracle, is the lighting of candles, one the first night, two the second, and so on until a special eight-branched candelabrum is completely filled.

Text B

In terms of Jewish ritual it is not the military victory of the Maccabees nor even the rededication of the Temple which is celebrated. Rather it is the miracle wrought by God which enabled a small jar of oil to burn for such a long period which is emphasised as having religious worth. The outstanding ritual feature of Chanukah is the kindling of lights, one on the first day, two on the second, etc, and eight on the last night followed by the singing of a hymn, *Maoz Tzur.* This has given rise to a whole ritual art form, the eight-branched candelabrum known as a menorah or in modern Israel as a *chanukiyah.* Although specially coloured candles are normally used for these lights, pious Jews endeavour to use olive oil with wicks, since the miracle involved a jar of olive oil. The Chanukah lights have to be kindled in a doorway or a window, so that they may be seen by passers-by, in order to publicise the miracle. Chanukah is not a festival in the true sense, for there is no prohibition on profane work and no kiddush or sanctification to introduce it. There are, in fact, no festive meals prescribed although various food customs, such as eating cheese pancakes and doughnuts, have developed in the course of time. Children are given presents of money and encouraged to play with a small spinning-top on the sides of which are Hebrew letters, whilst adults, somewhat to the dismay of the halakhic authorities, have adopted the habit of playing cards during the festival.

Students were given an additional two texts to read about Hanukkah, which are not reproduced here. This was the assignment they were given:

A primary school is keen to promote the understanding of the major world religions and, as part of its programme, it has invited a local representative of each faith to address the pupils for five minutes at morning assembly. The speakers have been asked to explain the importance of *one* festival of their religion and to talk about how it is celebrated. They can use the school's audio-visual aids, if they wish, but do not need to do so. You have been asked to speak to the children (aged seven to eleven) at Thursday's assembly about Hanukkah. Using the texts provided, write your script for this talk.

This is the *opening* part of one student's script, followed by the examiner's brief assessment comments. Read them both carefully and see if you agree with the examiner.

Student's script

During the middle of winter, the Jewish religion celebrates Hanukkah. The Hanukkah festival lasts for eight days. It is the Jewish festival of light. We, the Jews, remember a miracle story to do with the Maccabean victory over the rulers of Palestine over 2000 years ago. A temple was destroyed in the battle and after the victory had to be rebuilt. The builders could only find a small amount of oil to burn to give light, about this much oil (LIGHTS SMALL AMOUNT OF OIL). This oil should have only lasted one day, and it was going to take much longer to find any more oil. Amazingly, the oil burned for eight days, which was more than enough time for them to get some more.

Don't think that Hanukkah is a festival that celebrates the battle with the Palestinians. The Hanukkah festival is a celebration of the miracle that God provided to make this little jar of oil burn for so long. (BLOWS OIL OUT)

Examiner's comments
Sounds like an essay/too much information packed in, difficult for audience to follow/what is a 'Maccabean victory'?/no friendly opening or address to children/who *is* the speaker?/significance of oil not explained/attempts some use of visual aid, but why blow out the oil?/

ACTIVITY

1 Assume the role of examiner and write your brief comments on each of the following. Remember that they are only the *opening* part of the students' answers.

Answer A
Good morning. Thank you for inviting me to your school this morning to talk to you. I'm Rebecca and I've come to tell you about one of the most enjoyable and exciting festivals in our Jewish religion. It's one that children particularly like, so I'm sure that you'll enjoy hearing about it. The festival is called Chanukah, which means 'dedication' and we celebrate it round about the same time as Christians celebrate Christmas.

There's a very interesting story that explains how Chanukah began and I'd like to tell it to you. A long time ago, about 200 years before Jesus was born, a miracle occurred in Palestine, which is right here (POINTS TO MAP). It was in the year 165 BC and the overlord of the country said that everyone had to worship the Greek gods and that no one could be Jewish anymore. A small band of brave warriors, led by Judas the Maccabee, decided to fight against this, because they wanted to be able to worship their own

God. After a great battle, they beat the enemy and went to the sacred Temple to repair it and make it holy again, because it has been smashed up by the Syrians.

Answer B
Hello, boys and girls. Christmas may have come and gone, but for some boys and girls it doesn't come at all. They don't believe that Jesus has arrived yet. One festival Jewish people celebrate is Chanukah, a festival of light. This celebrates a victory over the rulers of Palestine by a people called the Maccabees. The Maccabees could only find one small jar of pure oil to burn in their temple, and, although it should have only lasted for one day, it lasted for eight. By this time the Maccabees had prepared more pure oil and Chanukah celebrates this miracle – not the victory over their enemy or going back to their temple, but the miracle God gave to them to keep the oil burning for such a long time.

2 Having read and assessed what other students have written in answer to this assignment, you should now attempt it yourself. Pass your completed scripts around the class for other people to comment on.

Do-it-yourself

One very good way of improving your performance in any examination is to have a go at setting some questions yourself. It can give you a clear insight into what an examiner is looking for in the real examination. This is particularly true of the type of question you have been working on in this chapter, where you have to create a new text from a set of material an examiner has provided for you. You can compile a set of materials yourself or with a group of fellow students. If you work through the activity below, you will gain a valuable understanding both of the types of material that examiners can use and of the different tasks that can be based on it.

ACTIVITY

1 Choose a subject that interests you and which you know something about, but don't forget that it should be one for which there is a lot of material available.

2 Decide what different types of material you will need to use for a complete understanding of your chosen subject. Think about articles from magazines and newspapers, pamphlets and leaflets, textbooks, reports, extracts from novels, short stories or poems, statistics, autobiographies, diaries.

3 Collect the material together. You might have some of it already, but don't forget to ask the school or college librarian for help. Many libraries have files of current material on important topics. You will also be able to find lots of material on the Internet and on CD-ROM.

4 Put the material together. Don't just use complete pieces, but use extracts from longer ones.

5 Look over the package you have compiled and ensure that it contains a varied and wide-ranging set of extracts. If it doesn't, then you will have to find some more and exclude some you have already chosen.

6 Now write three *different* tasks that could be based on the material. Remember that the tasks should have different purposes, genres or audiences in order to provide different writing challenges for your candidates.

7 You are now in a position to ask someone to complete your task! If you have been working in a group, your group could swap its material with that from another. Complete the task as if you were working under examination conditions.

8 The difficult part – you will have to mark the work! Of course, this means that you must know what constitutes a good answer and a poor one. You will have to write a mark scheme as well.

12 Language Change

Caterpillars change into butterflies, tadpoles into frogs and winter into spring. Change is an essential part of life; without change, life ceases. Language, too, must change, if it is to remain alive. A language that does not change is a dead language. Who today speaks Ugaritic or Etruscan? In general, language changes because society changes and though some people regard any change in language as regrettable, they are powerless, thank goodness, to prevent it. There have been such people in every age:

The Society aims to encourage high standards of written and spoken English, and in so doing defend … the language against debasement and changes.

(The Queen's English Society, founded 1972)

if [English] were once refined to a certain Standard, perhaps there might be Ways found out to fix it for ever.

(Jonathan Swift, 1712)

But a glance at almost any sample of English from the past will demonstrate change and may well seem strange to us today. Look at this piece written in 1440 in which, yet again, a writer, Osbern Bokenham, is complaining about the corrupting changes wrought on English – this time by invasions from Scandinavia and by William the Conqueror. You will probably have a little difficulty in following it but, be fair, Osbern Bokenham wouldn't find it all that easy to read either this book or the *Daily Mirror*!

And þis corrupcioun of Englysshe men yn þer modre-tounge, begunne as I seyde with famylyar commixtion of Danys firste and of Normannys aftir, toke grete augmentacoiun and encrees aftir þe commyng of William conquerour by two thyngis.

But you don't have to look back 600 years to see how English has changed. Changes occur over very much shorter periods of time. These two advertisements for make-up appeared in *Good Housekeeping* with only 60 years between them.

Bare just became more beautiful.

Estée Lauder invents

Enlighten

Skin-Enhancing Makeup

Discover a new kind of make-up. So weightless and flexible it floats on the skin's surface – never drying or settling into pores or fine lines. So sheer it gives you the look of impeccable skin, invisibly. Feels comfortable hour after hour. So innovative it compensates for oiliness or dryness. Enlighten is *oil-free*, soothes even sensitive skin, protects with a non-chemical SPF 10.

(1996)

So unnecessary!

A shiny nose is so unnecessary! End that powder-puff habit once and for all with Elizabeth Arden's No-Shine. Just a touch of it on your nose in the morning, fluff on your powder and you're safe all day. And our fashion scout tells us that a bit on the forehead has helped more than one bright young girl to present a smooth unshining brow to the world beneath her new Autumn hat. Elizabeth Arden's No-Shine 4/6, 10/6.

Face Powder must be used and not seen.

It must give a soft, lovely finish and not a coated look. It must blend imperceptibly with your skin. It must be pure and fine. In other words ... it must be Elizabeth Arden's powder. One of the nicest things about Miss Arden's powder is that it comes in a big box ... which lasts and lasts and lasts, because you need so little ... and it stays on so long. Flower Powder 6/6 Ardena Powder 12/6

(1935)

1 Read the advertisements carefully, either on your own, or in pairs and write down any changes in the language that you notice.

Then compare your notes with the ones below.

Words and phrases

from 1935 that sound slightly dated:
'powder puff'; 'fashion scout'; 'fluff on'; 'bright young girl'; 'Miss Arden's powder'; 'one of the nicest things'

technical-sounding lexis probably not used in 1935:
'non-chemical SPF 10'

much is quite similar, many words and phrases haven't changed in meaning:

1935	1996
'smooth'	'sheer'
'pure and fine'	'impeccable'
'imperceptibly'	'invisibly'
'soft and lovely'	'soothes even sensitive skin'

Name of product is more punning in 1996:
'Enlighten' *v.* 'No-Shine'

1996 stresses newness:
'new kind'; 'innovative'

1935 stresses economy:
'it comes in a big box'; 'need so little'

1996 is sexier:
'Bare just became more beautiful' *v.* 'smooth unshining brow'

Phonology
more alliteration in 1996:
'Bare just became more beautiful'; 'skin's surface'; 'soothes even sensitive skin'
repetition of name in 1935:
'Elizabeth Arden'; 'Elizabeth Arden's No-Shine'; 'Miss Arden's powder'

Grammar
Both use repeated structures:
1935 'It must ...'; 1996 'so' + adjective + 'it' + verb *eg*, 'so sheer it gives ...'
1996 uses more ellipses with subject of sentences frequently omitted:
(It is) 'so weightless ...'; (It) 'feels'

The result is that the 1996 advertisement seems more casual than the 1935 one.

---

2 Now investigate how language has changed in the following two advertisements. This time there are no answer notes, though you might find it helpful to follow the structure suggested for the advertisements for make-up above.

Look the bee's knees without being stung

Ignore the fact it's a Volkswagen. You know, durability, solidity, reliability, incidentals like that. With our new 1.4 Golf SE, you have full permission to be seduced by looks. Those Gti wheel-arch extensions, for example, smartly rounding off the Sport Räder alloy wheels. Those front white indicator covers complementing the white instrument dials within. Other stylish touches range from twin headlamps and roof aerial to colour-coded bumpers and tinted glass. All this over and above standard fare like power steering, driver's airbag, immobiliser and Sony radio/cassette. Here's the real beauty of it, though. The SE's price. As little as £10,801 on the road. Can't you just see yourself buzzing round in one? **The Golf SE.**

(1996)

POPULAR FORD
(£6 Tax)

For years past, August and September have been among the best of months, throughout the British Isles, more dependable than May and June, less scorchingly hot than July.

Why not a Popular FORD (£6 Tax) for your August and September journeyings?

Amply powered for four and holiday baggage, picnic impedimenta and the like, surprisingly roomy, yet very compact in overall measurements, for ease of parking and garage away from home, the essence of simplicity to handle over strange roads, smart but not ostentatious, with its famous weatherproof finish, and aboundingly economical to run and maintain, the Popular Ford will pay handsome dividends of service and pleasure.

Its gear change, steering, brakes and suspension confound the sceptical, while delighting the expert. And the Popular Ford Double-Entrance Saloon is still Britain's lowest-priced saloon with four doors. Remember!

The local Ford Dealer will be glad to furnish an exhaustive demonstration, and explain Ford facilities, everywhere, Britain's least costly service-organisation.

(1937)

ACTIVITY

This exercise will give you more practice in identifying language change. For each of the following newspaper reports of cricket matches, you should identify:
1 *where* the language has changed;
2 *how* it has changed, by referring to the appropriate language level (eg lexical, semantic, grammatical, orthographic, etc);
3 *why* it has changed. You may need to make some educated guesses here!

Remember that you can't answer question 3 until you've answered questions 1 and 2.

Each group should choose one report and note down their observations on the three questions on a piece of paper. When the group has finished, the piece of paper should be passed on to another group for further observations to be recorded, until all groups have commented on the document. There is no need, of course, to duplicate observations. Only add new ones to the piece of paper! When the process has been completed, the class should discuss its findings.

Report A

CRICKET

MATCH BETWEEN THE OFFICERS, &C., OF THE 1ST LIFE GUARDS AND ELEVEN GENTLEMEN OF THE NEIGHBOURHOOD OF WINDSOR. – A very excellent match was played on Monday, between the officers, &c., of the 1st regiment of life guards, in garrison at Windsor, and a party of friends, chosen by Mr. Nash from the neighbourhood of Langley and Colbrook, upon the lawn of the cavalry barracks at Spital. The lawn and several spacious marquees were crowded during the afternoon by most of the principal families residing in the vicinities of Windsor and Eton to witness the play. The excellent band of the regiment was also stationed upon the lawn, and performed until the conclusion of the game, which was not, however played out, in consequence of the rain, which commenced shortly before five o'clock. The following was the score when the wickets were struck – The 1st Life Guards. – 1st innings, 103; 2d innings, 67: Total, 170. Mr. Nash's Eleven. – 1st innings, 26; 2d innings, 61: Total, 87. – A splendid entertainment was given in the evening, at the barracks, by the officers of the 1st life guards, to Mr. Nash and his friends.

(News of the World, 1 October 1843)

Report B

WEST INDIES AT LORD'S

A Century by Hammond

An England XI beat the West Indies at Lord's by 166 runs in a match for the benefit of the Colonial Comforts Fund. The crowd of 12,000 had the pleasure of seeing in action two of the world's greatest cricketers, W. R. Hammond and L. N. Constantine. The former scored a century, and the latter, in his second innings, hit 42 in only ten minutes. Constantine, having sent England in to bat, set the attack going on a slowish pitch with Christian, fast medium, and himself at the Pavilion end, buttoned as to the sleeves, various in scheme and pace. Barnett, attended by Simpson had three 4's and a 6 in his first 19 runs. At 34 Achong, left hand slow, relieved Constantine, and for the rest of the innings gave a fine exhibition of his craft. At 56, Simpson squeezed a ball from Clarke under the end of the bat and was neatly run out by Messado at wicket. Four runs later, Barnett, who had waxed gaily impudent, was caught at close cover by Constantine at the second juggle. And so to Hammond.

(The Observer, 11 June 1944)

Report C

Essex riding high

ENTERTAINING batting by Essex yesterday overcame time lost to the weather on Friday. By building a first-innings lead of 252, and then claiming four Gloucestershire wickets, they left themselves well placed to force their fifth successive win tomorrow, a victory which, depending on what happens at Leicester, could take them to the top of the Championship table. I rather like Essex. There's a feel of heartland about it. If this was America, Essex would take their cricket around county fairs. There'd be the pick-up truck with exhaust extensions in the car park instead of Cavaliers and Escorts, and country music in the intervals. Good ol' boys like Waylon and Willie and Goochie.

Sadly we had to settle for Graham Gooch as the warm-up yesterday. He had been batting since Thursday, of course, and from the way he began yesterday he looked in the mood to improve on his overnight 105. It wasn't to be. Courtney Walsh, digging the ball in short and getting lift, kept pushing Gooch so far on to his back foot that the Essex old-timer eventually trod on his stumps.

(The Independent, 25 August 1996)

ACTIVITY

Here are two versions of the opening paragraph of Thomas Hardy's *The Mayor of Casterbridge*. The first is what Hardy wrote in 1886 whilst the second is an attempt at a modern 'translation' of the paragraph.

Hardy's version

One evening of late summer, before the nineteenth century had reached one third of its span, a young man and woman, the latter carrying a child, were approaching the large village of Weydon-Priors, in Upper Wessex, on foot. They were plainly but not ill-clad, though the thick hoar of dust which had accumulated on their shoes and garments from an obviously long journey lent a disadvantageous shabbiness to their appearance just now.

A modern 'translation'

One evening in late summer, about the year 1830, a young man and woman were approaching the large village of Weydon-Priors, in Upper Wessex, on foot. The woman was carrying a child. They were plainly but not badly dressed, although the thick coating of dust on their shoes and clothes from an obviously long journey made them look unfortunately shabby just now.

1 Make a list of the changes the 'translator' has made. You will notice a few, though not many changes of vocabulary; some changes of phrasing. The main effect of the changes is to make the passage 'lighter'. Look, for instance, at the effect of the change from 'lent a disadvantageous shabbiness to their appearance' to 'made them look unfortunately shabby'. What grammatical changes has the 'translator' made here? This is not to suggest that the modern version is better, but what it does highlight is the difference between the English Thomas Hardy used in novels in 1886 and that used today.

2 Now, here are three short passages for you to

'translate'. The first is the opening of another well-known Hardy novel. Your 'translations' should enable present-day readers to accept them as being contemporary texts.

Text A

The rambler who, for old association's sake, should trace the forsaken coach-road running almost in a meridional line from Bristol to the south shore of England, would find himself during the latter part of his journey in the vicinity of some extensive woodlands, interspersed with apple-orchards. Here the trees, timber or fruit-bearing as the case may be, make the wayside hedges ragged by their drip and shade, their lower limbs stretching in level repose over the road, as though reclining on the insubstantial air.

(Thomas Hardy, The Woodlanders, *1887)*

Text B

So I down to the waterside and there got a boat and through bridge, and there saw a lamentable fire. Poor Michells house, as far as the Old Swan, already burned that way and the fire running further, that in a very little time it got as far as the Stillyard while I was there. Everybody endeavouring to remove their goods, and flinging them into the river or bringing them into lighters that lay off.

(Samuel Pepys, Diary, *1666)*

Text C

There dwelled in the Citie of *Metelyne*, a certain Duke called *Clerophontes*, who through his prowesse in all martiall exploites waxed so proude and tyrannous, using such mercilesse crueltie to his forraine enimies, and such modelesse rigour to his native citizens, that it was doubtfull whether he was more feared of his foes for his crueltie, or hated of his friends for his tyrannie.

(Robert Greene, Carde of Fancie, *1587)*

3 When you have completed your versions, comment on the changes you made and on any difficulties that you encountered.

Your work so far in this chapter will have shown you that the evidence for language change can be examined in a number of different ways. You can look for changes in:

- vocabulary and meaning (**lexis** and **semantics**)
- spelling and punctuation (orthography)
- morphology and **syntax** (**grammar**)
- sounds and pronunciation (phonology).

However, if you want to learn more about the *history* of the English language and gain a chronological view of the changes that have occurred from the very earliest days to the present, then there are a number of very good and readable books that you could consult. The classic one of these is A C Baugh and T Cable's *A History of the English Language* (Routledge), which contains lots of detailed examples, particularly of lexical developments, together with a section on American English. *The Story of English* by R McCrum, W Cran and R MacNeil (Faber/BBC Books) accompanies the BBC TV series of the same name and is particularly good on developments in later English. Martin Wakelin's *The Archaeology of English* is also good. If you become very interested in the history of English and wish to research further, then there are many books more technical and detailed than these, and your teachers and librarians would be able to advise you.

Lexis and semantics

Whilst it might seem to a casual observer that phonological, grammatical and orthographic changes have all but ceased in contemporary English (though, as you shall see, this is certainly not the case), even a casual observer would be in no doubt that lexical change is continuing apace. Many **words** cease to be used, as this advertisement demonstrates.

FAMILY LINEN and SHAWL ESTABLISHMENT,

21, Piccadilly, Manchester

R. HOSKIN begs to apprise the Ladies of Manchester and Neighbourhood, that, according to his usual custom at this season of the year, he will submit to their inspection the whole of his Stock of FURS, consisting of Pelerines, Mantillas, Boas, and Muffs, of every description at *Cost Price*. R.H. has just received some very elegant designs in SHAWLS, a great variety of very choice colours, in Gros-de-Naples, Gauze Scarfs and Handkerchiefs, Tissues and Ærophanes. A choice assortment of FRENCH MERINOS and FLOWERS; several Bales of REAL WITNEY BLANKETS; a few boxes of very prime Irish Linens. Also, very Rich Black Veils, Thread and Gymp Laces, all of which R.H. flatters himself (from having selected them with the most scrupulous care) will give the most decided satisfaction to purchasers, and secure to him a continuance of that patronage he has so liberally experienced.

(The Courier, 1 January 1831)

But the English lexicon (or word-stock) has vastly expanded in the last 200 years and continues rapidly to do so. Recent influences have been the rise of feminism, the electronic revolution and the immigration into Britain of settlers whose first language is not English. You will certainly be able to think of others. Words are being added to the language all the time.

ACTIVITY

In this piece of fiction, the writer comments on the changing and expanding English lexicon.

Some other unfamiliar expressions I've come across: threever, pingle, he-male, to widge off, palacize, cobnoddling, synthy. The newspapers advertise such products as tishets, vanilliums, nurches, autofrotts (manual). The title of a column in the city edition of the *Herald*: 'I Was a Demimother.' Something about an eggman who was yoked on the way to the eggplant. The big Webster isn't too helpful: *Demimother* – like demigran, demijohn. One of two women jointly bringing up a child into the world. See Polyanna, Polyandrew.' '*Eggman* from mailman (*Archaic*). A euplannner who delivers licensed human gametes (female) to the home.' I don't pretend to understand that. This crazy dictionary also gives synonyms that are equally incomprehensible. '*Threever* – trimorph . . .' '*Palacize, bepalacize, empalacize* – to castellate, as on a quiz show.' '*Paladyne* – a chivalric assuagement.' '*Vanillium* – extract emphorium, portable.' The worst are words which look the same but have acquired entirely different meanings. '*Expectorant* – a conception aid.' '*Pederast* – artificial foot faddist.' '*Compensation* – mind fusion.' '*Simulant* – something that doesn't exist but pretends to.' Not to be confused with '*simulator*, a robot simulacrum.' '*Revivalist* – a corpse, such as a murder victim, brought back to life. See also *exhumant, disintermagent, jack-in-the-grave*.'

(Stanislaw Lem, *The Futurological Congress*, 1974)

1 What two lexical processes does the author draw attention to?
2 Attempt definitions of words that Lem claims not to understand.
3 The following new words appeared, not in a science-fiction novel, but in British quality newspapers in 1996.
   a What do you think they mean?
   b What word-formation processes do they illustrate?

   alcopop   booosterism
   communacopia   frontlash   gabfest
   gastroporn   miserabilism   netiquette
   opinionista   webvertising
   quangocracy   upskill   sociobabble

   c How many of them do you think will stand the test of time?

ACTIVITY

This next activity will provide you with a fascinating glimpse, decko, shufty or butcher's into the way meanings have changed over the years. Here are definitions of three words from three different dates: 1951, 1996 and 2015. The 2015 definitions were all invented by English teachers.

Bell	**Grief**	**Window**
1951 n. A metal device designed to give a ringing tone when struck.	1951 n. A feeling of woe and bereavement.	1951 n. A rectangular opening in a wall for admitting light and air.
1996 vb. To call someone by using a telephone.	1996 n. Excessive authoritarian aggravation as in 'You're giving me grief'.	1996 n. A space in one's programme, an opportunity.
2015 vb. To attach an electronic device to a convict licensed to be outside prison.	2015 n. An indoor sport based on fighting to the death with bare hands.	2015 vb. To perceive hidden meaning or implications in an apparently innocuous statement.

Research the words on the right and provide similarly accurate definitions of them for the three years in question. You will need, of course, a 1951 edition of a suitable dictionary, but, if one is not available, choose one from around the same time.

bad	bonk	ace	house	gay
grass	wasted	queen	sky	
thatcher	monkey	awesome		

Why do words change?

You will have obviously noticed that words *do* change meaning over time. There are four main reasons for this:

(i) Words simply die or are abandoned, because they are no longer needed. 'stomacher', 'bassinet' and 'galantine' are examples of this.

(ii) Words are replaced because of fashion or other cultural influences. 'Teacher' may be in the process of being replaced by 'learning facilitator' or 'library' by 'learning resources centre'.

(iii) New words enter the lexicon. These may be borrowed from other languages ('risotto', 'curry') or newly coined by the word-formation processes available to English. For example, 'affixing': *unfriendly = un + friend + ly*; *wanderer = wander + er*. 'Compounding': *teapot = tea + pot*; *runway = run + way*. 'Abbreviating': *phone* from *telephone*; *flu* from *influenza*. 'Back-formation': *edit* from *editor*; *intuit* from *intuition*.

(iv) Existing words alter their meaning to take account of changes in society. There are two important processes that can occur when words change their meaning over time. These processes work in opposite ways: sometimes the meaning of a word broadens and sometimes it narrows. An example of the former process is 'butcher' which meant originally only 'killer of goats', whilst 'doctor' is an example of the latter. This used to mean 'teacher' or 'learned man', not solely, as today, 'learned in medical matters'. There is a remnant of the original meaning in the university degree of Doctor of Philosophy (PhD).

This brief explanation will suggest to you the questions you need to ask of a document or passage when looking at lexical or semantic change.

■ Are there any words or expressions no longer in use? What reasons can you suggest for their disappearance?

■ Are there any words or expressions still in use today, but which clearly had a different meaning when the passage was written? What did they mean then? What reasons can you suggest for this change?

To give you an indication of how alert you have to be when looking at this aspect of language change, look at these examples of Jane Austen's English, quoted in David Crystal's indispensable *Cambridge Encyclopaedia of The English Language*:

The supposed inmate of Mansfield Parsonage
'inmate' had not yet developed its sense of someone occupying a prison.

Her regard had all the warmth of first attachment
'regard' had a much stronger sense of 'affection'.

She was now in an irritation as violent from delight as . . .
'irritation' could be caused by a pleasurable emotion.

A good etymological dictionary will always show you how words have
changed their meaning over time.

Here are two short passages, both from the same period. In the first, the words and expressions that have either died out or changed their meaning are highlighted, whilst the second has been left for you to investigate. For both of them, you should indicate the meanings of the words as used in the passages.

Text A

(*The writer is requesting his readers to praise and support his work.*)

Every one of you after the perusing of this pamphlet is to provide him a case of **poniards** that, if you **come in company with** any man which shall **dispraise** it or speak against it, you may straight cry **Sic respondeo**, and give him the **stoccado**. It **stands not** with your honours, I assure ye, to have a gentleman and a page abused in his absence. Secondly, whereas you were **wont** to **swear** men on a **pantofle** to be true to your **puissant** order, you shall swear them on nothing but this chronicle of the King of Pages henceforward. Thirdly, it shall be lawful for **any whatsoever** to play with false dice in a corner on the cover of this **foresaid Acts and Monuments**. None of the fraternity of the **minorites** shall **refuse it for a pawn** in the times of famine and necessity. Every **stationer's stall** they pass by (whether by day or by night) they shall **put off**

their hats to and **make a low leg**, **in regard** their grand printed **capitano** is there entombed. It shall be **flat** treason for any of this fore-mentioned catalogue of the **point-trussers** once to **name** him within forty foot of an alehouse; **marry**, the tavern is honourable.

(*Thomas Nashe,* The Unfortunate Traveller, *1594*)

Text B

(*Benedick is complaining about Beatrice's treatment of him.*)

O, she misused me past the endurance of a block! An oak but with one green leaf on it would have answered her. My very visor began to assume life and scold with her. She told me, not thinking I had been myself, that I was the Prince's jester, that I was duller than a great thaw; huddling jest upon jest with such impossible conveyance upon me that I stood like a man at a mark, with a whole army shooting at me. She speaks poniards, and every word stabs. If her breath were as terrible as her terminations; there were no living near her; she would infect to the north star. I would not marry her, though she were endowed with all that Adam had left him before he transgressed. She would have made Hercules have turned spit, yea, and have cleft his club to make the fire too. Come, talk not of her.

(*William Shakespeare,* Much Ado about Nothing, *1599*)

Spelling

English spelling as we know it is relatively unchanging; by the eighteenth century, in fact, it had reached more or less the state in which we find it today and there have been only minor alterations since then. This has not stopped those in favour of spelling reform, of course. There is a long history of attempts to 'reform' the spelling system of English and make it more 'logical' from John Hart in 1569 to the Simplified Spelling Society of today. Sir Isaac Pitman in the late nineteenth century founded a journal devoted to spelling reform called *The Speler* which gave a religious dimension to the cause. It was 'Devoated (1) tu the Wurship and Luv ov the Lord God and Saivier Jesus Christ . . . (3) The Investigashon ov Spiritiual Tru'th; (4) Speling Reform; (5) Shorthand; (6) Pees on Er'th'. By the mid-twentieth century, many people began to make fun of the reformers, as you can see from the following extract.

In 1951 we would urg a greit step forward. Sins bai this taim it would have ben four years sins anywun had used the leter 'c', we would sugest that 'National Easy Languag Wek' for 1951 be devoted to substitution of 'c' for 'th'. To be sur it would be som taim befor peopl would bekom akustomd to reading ceir newspapers and buks wic sutsh sentenses in cem as 'Ceodor cought he had cre cousand cistles crust crough ce cik of his cumb.'

In ce saim maner, bai maiking eatsh leter hav its own sound and cat sound only, we kould shorten ce language still mor. In 1952 we would elimineit ce 'y'; cen in 1953 we kould us ce leter to indikeit ce 'sh' sound, cerbai klarifaiing words laik yugar and yur, as wel as redusing bai wun mor leter al words laik 'yut', 'yore', and so fore. Cink, cen, of al ce benefits to be geind bai ce distinktion whitsh wil cen be meid between words leik:

ocean now writen oyean
machine now writen mayin
racial now writen reiyial

Al sutsh divers weis of wraiting wun sound would no longer exist, and whenever wun kaim akros a 'y' sound he would know exaktli what to wrait.

Kontinuing cis proses, year after year, we would eventuali hav a reali sensibl writen langug. By 1975, wi ventyur to sei, cer wud bi no mor uv ces teribl trublsm difikultis, wic no tu leters usd to indikeit ce seim nois, and laikwais no tu noises riten wic ce seim leter. Even Mr. Yaw, wi beliv, wud be hapi in ce noleg his drims fainali keim tru.
(*Dolton Edwards*, Meihem in ce Klasrum, *1946*)

The main variation in contemporary English spelling is between British English and American English and we can all recognise differences between the two varieties. Can't we? Decide whether the words in the following list are:

- spelt in the British way
- spelt in the American way
- spelt this way in both varieties

color	torpor	ax	acknowledgment	recognize	honour
honorary	center	diarrhoea	appall	encyclopaedia	
civilise	catalog	monologue	jewelry	tyre	ameba
skillful	massacre	somber			

It was the arrival of printing in England in the late fifteenth century that helped to establish the fixed patterns of English spelling, which over the next 300 years or so became regularised into the system as we know it today. The consequence of this is, of course, that the conventions of English spelling reflect how the language was pronounced several centuries ago rather than how it is pronounced today.

In this activity, you will learn how to investigate spelling changes.

William Caxton (the man who brought printing to England from Europe) is writing in 1490 about a group of merchants who were trying to sail from the Thames ('tamyse') to Zealand in the Netherlands, but were becalmed and so went ashore to try to buy some eggs. They had considerable difficulty in making themselves understood, as the housewife thought they were speaking French, not merely a different dialect of English!

It happened that certayn merchauntes were in a shippe in tamyse, for to have sayled over the see into zelande, and for lacke of wynde, thei taryed atte forlond, and went to lande for to refreshe them. And one of theym named Sheffelde, a mercer, cam in-to an hows and axed for mete; and specyally he axed after eggys. And the goode wyf answerde, that she coude speke no frenshe. And the marchaunt was angry, for he also coude speke no frenshe, but wolde have hadde egges, and she understode hym not. And thenne at laste a nother sayd that he wolde have eyren. Then the goode wyf sayd that she understode hym wel. Loo, what sholde a man in these dayes now wryte, egges or eyren?

forland = headland
mercer = textile dealer
axed = asked

1 Make a list of the words that Caxton spells differently from modern English. You should end up with about 45 words.
2 Can you identify any patterns in the spelling? Here are just two of the categories that you can use to sort out the patterns of late fifteenth-century spelling:

- words that have an 'e' ending
- words that have a double consonant ('shippe').

You should be able to find other categories as well.

3 Do the spellings tell us anything about the way some words might have been pronounced?
4 When words are used more than once, are they always spelt in the same way? Is there any consistency in the spelling? For instance, what class of words have 'e' at the end?

Grammar

You are not going to look at the history of English grammar in this section; there are many books you can consult on this subject, as mentioned on page 198. Remember, though, that the most dramatic changes in English grammar occurred before the end of the Middle Ages. However, there are two dates of particular interest:

1542 Publication of *A Short Introduction of Grammar* by William Lily. 'This remained the national grammar for several centuries and versions of it were used in English schools down to the nineteenth century. Although written in English, it was essentially a grammar of Latin, but it provided the basic introduction to grammar that ... Shakespeare was brought up on.' (Dick Leith)

1762 Publication of *A Short Introduction to English Grammar* by Robert Lowth. This book, which had an enormous influence on the teaching of grammar almost to the present day, stressed the notion that there was only one correct grammar for English. It was almost as if for Bishop Lowth, grammar was next to godliness. Lowth laid down rules (such as never put a preposition at the end of a sentence) and illustrated them by examples.

You will know, of course, from your studies, that it is impossible to 'fix' a language. It is constantly in a state of flux. You will also know that different dialects of English have different grammars, as do different national Englishes. For example, look at these differences in the grammar of American and of British Standard English:

American	I've just gotten these new jeans.
British	I've just got these new jeans.

American	It's ten after six.
British	It's ten past six.

American	He dove into the sea.
British	He dived into the sea.

How to recognise grammatical change

One of the difficulties you might face when asked to identify changes in grammar in a passage or a document is to know exactly what you should be looking for. Here then are some of the more important questions, together with some very brief examples, that you can use to examine any passages you may encounter.

Ask yourself whether there are any differences between the passage and modern English in:

- verb inflections (eg pleaseth/pleases; gotten/got; think'st/thinks)
- formation of the past tense (eg My life is run its course/My life has run its course; I am come/I came)
- use of modal and auxiliary verbs (especially 'do')
- the personal pronoun system (eg thou/thee/ye)
- the relative pronoun system (eg Our Father which art in heaven/Our Father who art in heaven)
- formation of negatives (eg I see not/I do not see; I cannot see no longer/I cannot see any longer)
- formation of questions (eg seest thou?/do you see?)
- noun and adjective endings or inflections (eg mankinde/mankind)
- formation of plurals (eg shoon/shoes)
- sentence **structure** (eg **co-ordination** or subordination?)
- the use of prepositions.

This is not, of course, an exhaustive list, but it does cover the main areas of grammatical change you are likely to encounter.

ACTIVITY

The following short quotations and extracts illustrate grammatical **forms** and constructions that are no longer found in modern English. Turn them into acceptable contemporary English and comment on the grammatical changes that you have had to make to do this. The spelling has already been modernised for you.

Seventeenth century

1 Do thou meet me presently at the harbour. (presently = immediately)
2 If thou be'st valiant.
3 No, I hear not your honest friend.
4 If she will return me the jewel, I will give over my suit. (suit = courtship)
5 What are you here that cry so grievously?

(all from Shakespeare, Othello)

Eighteenth century

6 There lived a good substantial family in the town.
(Daniel Defoe)
7 Even the streets round the Pump room are pulling down for new Edifices.
(Fanny Burney)
8 A gentleman sat smoking a pipe at the door, of whom Adams inquired the road.
(Fielding)

9 The principal design of a Grammar of any Language is to teach us to express ourselves with propriety in that Language, and to be able to judge of every phrase and form of construction, whether it be right or not...
(Lowth)
10 Would it not be hard that a man who hath as ancestors should therefore be rendered incapable of acquiring honour?
(Fielding)
11 And finally, a longer extract that has been left unaltered, so you may need to comment on changes in lexis and spelling as well as in grammar.

But after a speach is fully fashioned to the common vnderstanding, and accepted by consent of a whole countrey and natiõ, it is called a language, and receaueth none allowed alteration, but by extraordinary occasions by little and little, as it were insensibly bringing in of many corruptiõs that creepe along with the time; of all which matters, we haue more largely spoken in our bookes of the originals and pedigree of the English tong.
(George Puttenham, The Arte of English Poesie, 1589)

Phonological change

The main change in the way that English was pronounced took place gradually in the fifteenth century and was known as The Great Vowel Shift. No one is quite sure why this shift took place, but the effects are fairly clear.

Here is an example of how a sentence was probably pronounced before this change took place:

And saw it is team noo to say hose narma is on the show and if the sarma fate can doe the daunce toneet that hath such farma aroond the toon.

Here's what it sounds like in modern English:

And so it is time now to see whose name is on the shoe and if the same feet can do the dance tonight that has such fame around the town.

Pronunciation change, however, has been a feature of English throughout its history. This is due, in part, to population shifts and migration, and it is still going on today. Recent research by Paul Kerswill and Ann Williams has shown that children in the new town of Milton Keynes pronounce words differently not only from their parents, many of whom are not native to the town, but they also speak differently from the original inhabitants of this area of Buckinghamshire. Their speech more closely resembles that of children 50 miles away in London and of children throughout the south-east of England.

Word	Buckinghamshire 1950	Milton Keynes parents	Milton Keynes children
arm	arrm	arrm	ahm
fill	fill	fill	fiw
three	three	three	free
feather	feather	feather	fevver
night	noit	noit	naa-it
round	raind	raind	round
woman	umman	woman	woman
letter	le'er	le'er	le'er

Migration of peoples can also account for the differences in the American and British pronunciations of English. Try reading aloud the following passage. There are at least sixteen words in it that Americans pronounce differently from Standard English speakers. Do you know how Americans pronounce the words in italics?

Can't you give me the *address* of the *leisure* centre in *Derby*? The hotel *clerk* couldn't answer my *inquiry* and I've got to get there by the fastest *route* if I'm to keep to *schedule* to see the *ballet* at *half* eight. And another thing! All I've had to eat today has been a *tomato* and *herb* omelette made with *margarine* not *butter* and a *banana* fritter with *yoghurt*.

ACTIVITY

Here are a number of words whose pronunciation in British English is still a matter of dispute. (Dis*pute* or *dis*pute?) Investigate the most common pronunciation in your area for each word. Does it vary according to the age/gender/ethnic origin/educational level of the speaker? This investigation could form the basis of a language project.

economics	controversy	homosexual
dilemma	privacy	status
scone	apparatus	migraine
ate	often	forehead
archipelago	schedule	lieutenant
evolution	(n)either	gooseberry
wrath	medicine	envelope

Can you think of any other words to add to this list?

It is difficult to be certain how English was pronounced before the age of tape and video recording, and much of the evidence comes from literature and poetry. Here are just two examples of how literature can help us. In the first, the schoolmaster, Holophernes, is complaining about someone's pronunciation, and in the second, note how the poet uses rhymes that are not possible today.

I abhor such fanatical phantasimes, such insociable and point-devise companions; such rackers of orthography, as to speak 'dout' fine, when he should say 'doubt'; 'det' when he should pronounce 'debt' – d-e-b-t, not d-e-t. He clepeth a calf 'cauf', half 'hauf'; neighbour vocatur [is called] 'nebour'; 'neigh' abbreviated 'ne'. This is abhominable – which he would call 'abbominable'.

(Shakespeare, Love's Labour's Lost, *1594*)

Here Thou, Great Anna! whom three Realms obey,
Dost sometimes Counsel take – and sometimes Tea.

(Pope, The Rape of the Lock, *1714)*

ACTIVITY

Sometimes writers use **accents** and dialects to indicate either the social class of a speaker and the area he or she comes from. It is difficult to convey exactly what the speaker's accent sounds like using only the 26 letters of the alphabet. Read this example of traditional nineteenth-century Lancashire dialect in which a Standard English speaker encounters a local man. Convert the dialect speech into modern Standard English.

'Do you think Dr James will be at home?' inquired the rider.

'Sure to be,' replied Ben. 'He's seldom off, except when he's oather huntin' or shootin'; an' then he doesn't go far fro' whoam. Well, yigh; he gwos into th' Red Lion a bit of a neet, after he's done.'

'What kind of a place is the Red Lion?' inquired the horseman.

'Oh, the best shop i' Whit'orth, if yo wanten to put up. I know th' folk 'at keeps it, very weel. Th' landlady's an owd friend o' my wife's. I left my wife theer this forenoon. They'n a rare good stable, too.'

'Thank you!' said the rider, and flinging a shilling towards Ben, he galloped off.

'Yon's moor money nor wit, I deawt,' said Ben, looking after the disappearing horseman. Then, walking up to where the shilling lay, he looked down at it, and said,

'Well, I never expected that, as heaw … He met ha' gan it one decently, beawt flingin' it o'th floor … But it's no use lettin' it lie theer. It'll come in for summat better nor mendin' th' hee-road wi'.'

(Edwin Waugh, Lancashire Sketches, *1855)*

Examination practice

The passage below was set for comment in an examination. Beneath it are suggestions for *some* of the points that you could make to impress the examiner. The text is an edited letter written by Queen Elizabeth I to her cousin, King James VI of Scotland in 1587. Elizabeth is trying to justify her decision to have James's mother, Mary, Queen of Scots, executed. Perhaps because of the subject matter of the letter, Elizabeth is writing in quite a tortuous **style**.

To my deare brother and cousin, the kinge of Skotz.

Be not caried away, my deare brother, with the lewd perswations of suche, as insteade of infowrming you of my to nideful and helples cause of defending the brethe that God hath given me, to be better spent than spilt by the bloudy invention of traitors handz, may perhaps make you belive, that ether the offense was not so great, or if that cannot serue them, for the over-manifest triall wiche in publik and by the greatest and most in this land hathe bine manifestly proved, yet the wyl make that her life may be saved and myne safe.

Your commissionars telz me, that I may trust her in the hande of some indifferent prince, and have all her cousins and allies promis she wil no more seake my ruine. Deare brother and cousin, way in true and equal balance wither the lak not muche good ground when suche stuf serves for ther bilding. Suppose you I am so mad to truste my life in anothers hand and sent hit out of my owne?

Make account, I pray you, of my firme frindship loue and care, from wiche, my deare brother, let no sinistar whisperars, nor busy troblars of princis states, persuade to leave your surest, and stike to vnstable staies. And so, God hold you ever in his blessed kiping, and make you see your tru frinds. Excuse my not writing sonar, for paine in one of my yees was only the cause.

Your most assured lovinge sistar and cousin,
ELIZABETH R.

Spelling
- patterns of words ending in 'e' ('deare', 'suche', 'brethe')
- the use of 'u' and 'v' as both vowel and consonant ('serue'/'serves', 'loue', 'vnstable')
- representation of vowels and dipthongs ('bine'/'nideful', 'traitors'/'way', 'sinistar'/'whisperar')
- individual variation within passage ('perswations'/'persuade')
- s/z variation ('Skotz'/'handz'/'telz', 'perswations'/'commissionars').

Lexical items
Changes in usage and meaning of:

- words ('lewd', 'invention', 'staies')
- idioms and phrases ('better spent than spilt', 'make account', 'greatest and most', 'your most assured')
- metaphors ('good ground ... for their bilding', 'stike to vnstable staies').

Grammar
- word-order changes ('wither the lak or not', 'pain in one of my yees was only the cause', 'suppose you')
- use of prepositions ('trust my life in anothers hand')
- verb inflections ('God hath given', 'your commissionars telz me')
- formation of plurals ('handz', 'troblars', 'yees').

ACTIVITY

To close this chapter, here is a complete examination question for you to attempt. The following passage is from a book called *The History of Myddle* which chronicles the life of a small English town. The book was written over a period of years after 1700, but was not published until over a century afterwards. The events described in this passage took place around 1701.

By referring in detail to the passage, describe and comment on some of the changes which have taken place in English spelling, vocabulary and grammar since it was written.

One William Cleaton marryed a daughter of this Reynolds, and soe beecame tenant of this farme, and had a lease for the lives of himseife, his wife, and Francis, his eldest son. Her lived in good repute, and served severall offices in this parish. Hee had 4 sons. 1. Francis, who displeased his father in marrying with Margaret Vaughan, a Welsh woman. 2. Isaac who married a daughter of one White, of Meriton, and had a good portion with her. 3. Samuell, who marryed Susan, the daughter of Thomas Jukes, of Newton on the Hill. 4. Richard, an untowardly person. He married Annie, the daughter of William Tyller, a woman as infamous as himselfe. Richard Cleaton soone out run his wife, and left his wife bigge with child.

Richard Cleaton went into the further part of this County; and below Bridgnorth hee gott another wife, and had severall children by her. At last, Anne Tyler, his first wife, caused him to bee apprehended, and indicted him att an Assizes at Bridgnorth upon the statute of Poligami. Shee proved that shee was marryed to him, but could not prove that hee was married to the other woman, but only that he lived with her, and had children by her. The other woman denied that shee was marryed to him; and thereupon the Judge sayd 'Then thou art a whore.' To which shee answered 'the worse luck mine my lord.' Cleaton was acquitted, and went out of the country with the other woman, and I never heard more of him.

13 Language Diversity

In 1832 a young Englishman, Charles Darwin, twenty-four years old and a naturalist on *HMS Beagle*, a brig sent by the Admiralty in London on a surveying voyage round the world, came to a forest outside Rio de Janeiro. In one day, in one small area, he collected sixty-eight different species of small beetle. That there should be such a variety of species of one kind of creature astounded him.

During the next three years, the *Beagle* sailed down the east coast of South America, rounded Cape Horn and came north again up the coast of Chile. The expedition then sailed out into the Pacific until, 600 miles from the mainland, they came to the lonely archipelago of the Galapagos. Here Darwin's questions about the creation of species recurred, for in these islands he found fresh variety. He was fascinated to discover that the Galapagos animals bore a general resemblance to those he had seen on the mainland, but differed from them in detail. There were cormorants, black, long-necked diving birds like those that fly low along Brazilian rivers, but here in the Galapagos, their wings were so small and with such stunted feathers that they had lost the power of flight. There were iguanas, large lizards with a crest of scales along their backs. Those on the continent climbed trees and ate leaves. Here on the islands, where there was little vegetation, one species fed on seaweed and clung to rocks among the surging waves with unusually long and powerful claws. There were tortoises, very similar to the mainland forms except that these were many times bigger, giants that a man could ride. The English Vice-Governor of the Galapagos told Darwin that even within the archipelago, there was variety: the tortoises on each island were slightly different, so that it was possible to tell which island they came from.

(David Attenborough, *Life on Earth*, 1979)

Charles Darwin was astounded that he found 68 different species of beetle outside Rio and was fascinated to discover that the tortoises on each island in the Galapagos archipelago were slightly different, so that it was possible to tell which island they came from. Darwin also had an interest in language and, had he pursued this interest whilst on his voyage rather than concentrating on natural history, he would have been similarly astonished at its infinite variety. The **analogy** can be taken a little further. Instead of observing that there were 68 species of beetle outside Rio, Darwin *might* have found that there were at least 68 varieties of native languages spoken in the area. Instead of discovering that the tortoises of the Galapagos differed slightly from each other depending on which island they came from, he *might* have found that the languages spoken by the inhabitants, though bearing a general resemblance to each other, differed in detail. Of course, had he been an observer of language, he need not have ventured as far afield as the middle of the Pacific Ocean to make these discoveries. Darwin would have found a great diversity of language in mid-nineteenth-century Britain. Most of the varieties would have been

'English', but they would have differed from each other, just as did the Galapagos tortoises. The natives of Thomas Hardy's Wessex spoke English, but it was not the English of Charlotte Brontë's West Yorkshire, as you saw on page 136. Had Darwin been observing language, and specifically the English language, then he might have had to describe and explain, for example, the differences between American and English English, between women's English and men's English and between legal English and religious English. This short list of examples could easily be extended for there is, indeed, an 'infinite variety' of Englishes.

From his observations in the Galapagos, Darwin wrote his Theory of Evolution – that species are constantly adapting in response to the changing circumstances in which they find themselves. Those creatures that cannot change and adapt will die. In *Life on Earth*, David Attenborough makes very explicit the connection between human language and survival. As language evolved, and with it man's capacity for recording and storing knowledge,

then a new and immensely important threshold had been crossed. His pictographs and his writings, his books, micro-film and computer tapes can be seen as extra-corporeal DNA, adjuncts to our genetical inheritance as important and influential in determining the way we behave as the chromosomes in our tissues are in determining the physical shape of our bodies. It was this accumulated wisdom that eventually enabled us to devise ways of escaping the dictates of the environment. Our knowledge of agricultural techniques and mechanical devices, of medicine and engineering, of mathematics and space travel, all depend on stored experience. Cut off from our libraries and all they represent and marooned on a desert island, any one of us would be quickly reduced to the life of a hunter gatherer.

History is, unfortunately, littered with examples of individual languages that have become as extinct as the dodo because of their inability to adapt. English seems, however, to be one of the more flexible of languages, thus ensuring (so far!) its survival, though not, of course, in an unaltered form. In the chapter on language change you saw that English can alter over a relatively short period. Darwin himself would not be entirely comfortable with the English that we speak and write today.

However, according to some communications experts, writers themselves are faced with extinction. They suggest that a major change is about to take place as 'the printed book seems destined to move to the margin of our literate culture. Print will no longer define the organisation and presentation of knowledge, as it has for the past five centuries.' What you are reading, then, may well become a dinosaur, on the verge of disappearing for ever! Treasure it!

The replacement for the printed word on the page will, it is suggested, be the multimedia text, in which the relationship between writer and reader will be changed forever. This evolution will result in an even greater diversity of English. This is what one writer who is involved in creating multimedia texts has to say:

The fact is, multimedia can do things the printed page never even dreamt about. It's digital, which means that obscene amounts of data can be stored on a four-inch, wafer-thin laser disc. It's also interactive, which means that all those digitised artefacts – hundreds of photos and graphics, video clips, my wee texts – can be linked in a kind of electronic-semantic web. You can access my 'essay' on Mozart, for example, from any number of other texts on the disc, simply by finding the word 'Mozart' in highlighted, or 'hot', text and clicking on it with your mouse. You could be reading something on eighteenth-century music, say, or Viennese opera, and – click – up pops my terse little bio. But there's more. Once inside my text, you might click on *Don Giovanni* and get yet another text, or a few seconds of music from the opera, or a video clip from *Amadeus*. And once in *Don Giovanni*, you might encounter the word 'Italy' and click up a nice little geopolitical summary. And so on. Each text – and, theoretically, each word in each text – can be an electronic portal to an infinite number of other digital locations. You can hop from one object of fascination to any number of others, branching this way and that along various semantic trails, creating your own, custom-built, non-linear narrative from a vast reservoir of recombinant texts. Non-linearity might seem like little more than channel surfing, but its proponents – ranging from wealthy software gurus to tenured English professors – champion it as an authentic yet functional postmodern form, a critical break from the age-old, rigidly linear format of the printed page. Non-linearity, we're told, re-distributes narrative power to readers. It undermines the tyranny of the Author. Its branching 'intertextuality' is a much closer match to the brain's own networks. Indeed, advocates believe that with non-linear text, or hypertext, literature can at last give full expression to the kinds of unconventional discursive impulses that folks like Joyce and Barthes were forced to convey via the grotesquely obsolete linear format. For that matter, non-linearity provides a kind of running critique of the linear format, laying open the myth that 'stories' can be told only one way, in only one direction, and towards only one conclusion; towards 'closure'. With non-linearity, as with thought itself, there is no closure, only additional links. Thus non-linearity, to its proponents, is the beginning of a new, more honest and complex literature – and, perhaps, the beginning of pthe end of an old one.

From a distance, a multimedia text looks exactly like a paragraph plucked from a standard linear narrative. But closer inspection reveals important differences. In 'normal' writing, the writer uses the Paragraph as a bridge between specific points. Not so with the multimedia text block. Each must, almost by definition carry out its minimal literary function in virtual independence from the rest of the story. If I'm writing multimedia Text A, for example, I can assume no specific prior knowledge on the part of the reader, because he or she may be arriving at Text A from any of a number of previous texts. Similarly, I can't use Text A to set up Text B, because the reader may be bouncing to any number of Text Bs. For that matter, I can't even infuse Text A with a meaning or sentiment that is essential to the reader's understanding of, or pleasure in, the larger narrative, because the reader, as narrative boss, may skip Text A entirely. The style of the multimedia text, if you want to call it a style, is one of expendability.

I realise that even with a conventional article, I can't make my 'linear' readers read what I write in the order that I write it. Linear readers skim. They jump ahead, looking for interesting parts, then refer back for context – behaving, in some respects, like the multimedia user. But the non-linear interactive process undeniably accelerates this haphazardness. The nexus of creativity is shifted from the writer to the producers, who lay out the textlinks, or the readers, who make use of those links. To be fair, if a multimedia writer has the technical expertise and the financial resources to control the entire story-line process, some interesting literary and journalistic forms are possible. Allowing readers to choose their own research paths, or in the case of non-linear fiction, to choose among multiple outcomes, probably qualifies as a genuine step forward in literary evolution.

This article gives rise to a number of activities, in addition to your being able to subject it to stylistic analysis!

ACTIVITY

The writer, in the same article, said that the task of the multimedia writer is 'to absorb and compress great gobs of information into small, easily digestible on-screen chunks. Brevity and blandness are the elements of the next literary style. Of the roughly 7000 "essays" I've written for the CD-ROM companies . . . fewer than 40 ran longer than 200 words.'

1 Collect some of these multimedia texts – there are many possible sources: encyclopaedias or other reference books like *Chronicle of the 20th Century*, for example.
2 Study their style and structure carefully and write a text of your own, either on subjects with which you are familiar or on subjects that are completely new to you. The second of these tasks reproduces more faithfully the role of writers of multimedia texts in that they may find that they are composing a text on a subject about which they know little or nothing. This is why many regard such writing as hack work. Remember not to exceed 200 **words**, even if you are writing on such huge subjects as 'The Operas of Mozart' or 'Adolf Hitler'.
3 Compare a text on the same subject that has been published both in multimedia and in printed form.

This chapter is concerned with diversity in more mainstream English, but because of its infiniteness only a limited number of instances will be examined. You have, of course, already explored in depth the major variations in English language in the section on spoken and written language.

It would be as well, perhaps, before venturing any further, to define a 'variety' of English. All texts, whether spoken or written, arise from particular situations and, as you know, all texts have distinctive linguistic features. If these distinctive features appear in a number of texts because of a similar situation giving rise to them, then we can say that this set of features is a variety of English. So, for example, if the situation is that all speakers of English who were born within the sound of Bow Bells in London use a distinctive set of linguistic features, such as their pronunciation and their use of rhyming **slang**, then it is permissible to say that there is a variety of English known as Cockney. Or, to give another illustration, if all TV weather forecasters use a distinct set of features (a very restricted **lexis** being, perhaps, the main one), then we can speak of this as a variety. You can see, then, why there is an 'infinite variety' of Englishes and why it is not possible to examine them all in this chapter.

In general, there are two types of feature that identify a variety: the sociolinguistic and the stylistic. David Crystal in his invaluable *Cambridge Encyclopaedia of the English Language* defines them thus:

Sociolinguistic features relate to very broad situational constraints on language use and chiefly identify the regional and social varieties of the language (eg Canadian, Cockney, upper-class, educated). They are relatively permanent, background features of the spoken or written language, over which we have relatively little conscious control. We tend not to change our regional or class way of speaking as we go about our daily business, and usually do not even realise that it is there.

Stylistic features refer to constraints on language that are much more narrowly constrained, and identify personal preferences in usage (poetry, humour) or the varieties associated with occupational groups (lecturers, lawyers, journalists). They are relatively temporary features of our spoken or written language over which we do have some conscious degree of control. We often adopt different group uses of language as we go through our day (eg family, job, religion, sports) and frequently change our speaking or writing style to make a particular effect.

Varieties of discourse

People are remarkably good at identifying a particular variety of **discourse**. Often it only takes a very few words for us to realise that we are encountering legal or religious discourse, for example. We are very sensitive to the codes and conventions that writers (and speakers) use in particular discourse.

ACTIVITY

1 Here are fragments from fifteen different discourses. For each one, list as many clues as you can that enable you confidently to identify the variety the fragment comes from.
  a Babies in Drug Test Overdose
  b Dear Sir or Madam
  c Sirloin steak pan-fried in a classic sauce flamed with brandy presented on a bed of crushed herb potatoes
  d non-payment will result in prosecution
  e Almighty God, our heavenly Father, who of thy great mercy hast promised forgiveness of sins to all them that with hearty repentance and true faith turn unto thee
  f There was an Englishman, an Irishman
  g Does the Right Honourable gentleman agree that the report of the Select Committee
  h These varicosities, whilst containing synaptic vesicles and granules
  i The responsibility for the initial

communication of the company's corporate culture lies with the local company training centre
  j When did anyone ever tell you you had beautiful specs?
  k Weather lovely. Wish you were here.
  l 2 hours allowed
  m 'big, hilarious, intricate, furious, moving' – *Guardian*
  n During the day our light comes from the sun. The sun is brightest in the middle of the day.
  o and they're off

2 Now imagine that you are responsible for writing the entry in a language encyclopaedia on 'Types of Discourse' in which you briefly have to describe and illustrate three or four different types. Base your entries on the work you have just been doing, though you will need to find more extended examples than those given above.

Here, for example, is the beginning of an entry on religious discourse, based on extract (e) above:

Religious discourse is marked by relatively archaic language. This can be seen in its pronoun (thee and thou) and possessive adjective (thy, thine) systems and in its retention of archaic tenses (hast, hath). Much religious language begins with a direct invocation (Almighty God)...

Complete this entry and then write some entries of your own.

Interestingly, even when religious language is modernised, the variety is not radically changed. It still remains recognisably religious language. Look, for example, at these three versions of 'The Lord's Prayer'. What is it about the language of the modern versions that enables you to identify it as religious? Perhaps it would be more accurate then to refer to there being a **genre** of religious writing that uses a particular **style** of language.

Version A
Our Father which art in Heaven, Hallowed be thy name.
Thy Kingdom come. Thy will be done in earth, as it is in heaven.
Give us this day our daily bread,
And forgive us our debts, as we forgive our debtors.
And lead us not into temptation, but deliver us from evil:
For thine is the kingdom, and the power, and the glory, for ever. Amen.

(Authorised Version, 1610)

Version B
Our Father in heaven,
thy name be hallowed;
thy kingdom come,
thy will be done,
on earth as in heaven.
Give us today our daily bread.
Forgive us the wrong we have done,
as we have forgiven those who have wronged us.
And do not bring us to the test,
But save us from the evil one.

(New English Bible, 1961)

Version C
Our Father in Heaven:
May your holy name be honoured;
may your Kingdom come;
may your will be done on earth as it is in heaven.
Give us today the food we need.
Forgive us the wrongs we have done,
as we forgive the wrongs that others have done to us.
Do not bring us to the hard testing,
but keep us safe from the Evil One.

(Good News Bible, 1976)

It has been suggested that there is an infinite variety of 'Englishes' and that therefore to cover all the 'dialects' and 'idiolects' would be an impossible task. However, it can be argued, as a generalisation, that all human beings are represented by one from each of the following oppositions:

■ male/female

- old/young
- black/white.

For instance, you may well be a young, black female, whereas we, the writers are young (!), white males.

Depending on the situations we find ourselves in, our language use can be determined by cultural factors such as

- our gender role (whether we are male or female)
- our role as an adult or as a child (whether we are young or old)
- our role as a member of a majority or a minority (for example, in Britain, whether we are black or brown or white).

You are now going to look at some of the diversity of language that is involved when people are forced to adopt these culturally defined roles.

Black English

The English that is spoken (and sometimes written) by the Afro-Caribbean or West-Indian community in Britain is sometimes stigmatised as being an inferior variety, because it differs from Standard English. It is nothing of the sort. Rather it is an English that has distinctive grammatical, lexical, phonological and *prosodic* features (eg rhythm, stress, pitch, intonation and loudness in speech) and is thus no more an inferior English than is any other regional variety, such as Irish, American or Australian. Try telling an Aussie that his English is inferior to a Pom's!

Two conversations in 'Black English'

The first extract is from a longer conversation which took place in London between four members of a British-Jamaican family. R and F are brothers, aged about 50; B and L are F's children and are about eighteen. R, F and L were born in Jamaica and speak with more or less strong Jamaican **accents**. B was born in Britain.

B is also speaking in the second extract. It is part of a conversation recorded between her and a friend in their school in London. Both girls were seventeen.

Conversation A
Key: (.) = pause; % = glottal stop

B   it's only because there's halfcastes in it now, right
               | why(.)there's a mixup
F | no no no I'm not talkin' I'm not | sayin'
L | no no
    me a show you we as a race Brenda
    is a example me a show you right ...   all the
    races should come together right
B   if there wasn't no
    | halfcastes then you could distinguish, right
F | distinguish
B   cause some of them you see,(.) outside the street (.)

```
       right     | and you say da% is a halfcaste
L                | an' you don' know you can't
B      | an im stone black he he you know what I mean?
F      | yeah yeah
B      stone black
       (.)
L      cause I  | know true
F                | no sir no sir
B      yes daddy oh come off it there's Holly
R      generation it's a whole generation
       you no  | see it
F               | yes a can't be full black
L      it's a way it's a way      | (.)how do you t'ink seh
B                                 | whe you mean?
L      how do you know what you is, dat's what me
       was comin' to (.) seh (.) you know wha' I mean?
       when you say he's a
B      well I mean by stone black I mean their
       parents  | is
L                | how do you know what you is
```

Conversation B

```
B      anyway Amy(.)              | choh (.) Karen tol' me (.) yes
A                                 | Karen
B      this is Karen to me now (.) she goes to me (.) well (.)
       about I mus' come to 'er par%y right
A      | 'cause she told you init?
B      | yeah mhm 'course 'n' that (.) yeah
       right well anyway I went down there (.) me bring my
       sister-dem all me sister-dem come wid me y'know (.)
       come all the way down the (.) ah (.) party there
       she goes to me abou% i% now when we ge% there (.)
       we walk pas' the door to number fifty-nine – no lights
A      mhm
B      righ% (.) so w' walk up the top of the road (.) couldn't
       'ear no music at all so my sister-dem start cussin' me like any-
       thing you know (.) 'bout me bomboklaat    | an' all dis business
A                                                | mhhhm
B      dere (.) well anyway (.) go back down dere right (.)
       an' we look 'pon now we see Jerry but dem come
       tell us  | 'bout um aks us where de    | party de (.) right?
A                | mhm                          | party is
B      so we say well definitely we come up 'ere 'cause
       Karen say it was 'ere right?
A      yeah
B      couldn' fin' not'in' so (.) we went back down dere
       lookin' at de gates (.) we find a letter there so
       f' say 'bout (.) party cancel
A      mhm
```

ACTIVITY

Study these two conversations carefully and list any features, together with examples, which seem to differ from Standard English. You might find it helpful to list them under the separate headings of **grammar**, lexis and accent.

Literary 'Black English'

The next two examples of Black English are taken from literary sources. The first is an extract from *The Lonely Londoners* by Samuel Selvon in which Galahad, a West Indian living in London, has been unable to get employment and resorts to unusual methods to provide a meal for himself.

Galahad used to go walking in Kensington Gardens, the fog never clear enough for him to see down to High Street Ken. That particular winter, things was so bad with him that he had was to try and catch a pigeon in the park to eat. It does have a lot of them flying about, and the people does feed them with bits of bread. Sometimes they get so much bread that they pick and choosing, and Galahad watching them with envy. In this country, people prefer to see man starve than a cat or dog want something to eat.

   Watching these fat pigeons strut about the park, the idea come to Galahad to snatch one and take it home and roast it. When he was a little fellar his father had a work in High Street in San Fernando, a town about forty miles from Port of Spain. It used to have pigeons like stupidness all about the street I nobody know where they come from, and Galahad father used to snatch and send them home to cook.

The second piece is a poem by James Berry. He was born in Jamaica in 1924, and has lived in Britain since 1948.

Words of a Jamaican Laas Moment Them

When I dead
mek rain fall.
Mek the air wash.
Mek the lan wash good-good.
Mek dry course them run, and run.

As laas breath gone
mek rain burst –
hilltop them work
waterfall, and all
the gully them gargle fresh.

Mek breadfruit limb them drip,
mango limb them drip. Cow, hog, fowl
stan still, in the burst of clouds.
Poinciana bloom them soak off, clean-clean.
Grass go unda water.

Instant I gone
mek all the Island wash – wash away
the mess of my shortcomings –
all the brok-up things I did start.
Mi doings did fall short too much.
Mi ways did hurt mi wife too oftn.

You now have a considerable amount of data available in British Black English: two conversations and two literary pieces.

ACTIVITY

Working in pairs, one of you should be responsible for each of the following language areas: grammar (morphology and syntax) and lexis. Your task is to produce a wall chart for display in secondary-school classrooms that illustrates the differences between Standard English and British Black English. Make sure that you present the results of your investigation into this data in as lively and interesting a way as possible. If you can find other examples of British Black English to aid your investigation, so much the better. There are, for instance, many collections of poetry available or you may have recordings of some raps. Of course, you may use Black English yourself, in which case you'll have a plethora of material available!

If you can make recordings of speech then you will be able to investigate pronunciation and prosody which are only hinted at in the four examples here. You will probably find that the main contrast between Black English accents and British Afro-Caribbean accents is that syllables in Black English are usually equally stressed. This gives the speech its distinctive rhythm.

If you can research something of the history of Black English, this will add an extra dimension to your wall chart.

Pidgins and Creoles

A 'pidgin' language is one that grew up amongst people who needed to communicate with each other, but had no common language. This made communication difficult, though not impossible. What tended to happen was that a language grew up with a very restricted range of vocabulary, grammatical **structures** and **functions** that was derived from a language such as English, French or Dutch. For instance, it is thought that the first African slaves in the USA and the Caribbean, who shared no language with each other or with the slave-owners, developed an English-based pidgin, because English was the language of the owners. A pidgin language then is the native language of no one.

As more and more contact with the dominant community became inevitable, these pidgin languages developed and became drawn towards the European language, though never becoming identical with it because of the influence of the original African languages and dialects. This process of development is known as creolisation and the languages which develop into the mother-tongues of a community are known as Creoles. The Creole languages spoken by Afro-Caribbeans are sometimes called patwas (or patois) even when they are spoken by people who were born in Britain and whose parents were born in Britain. Many Creole-speaking people in Britain today can switch readily between patwa and other varieties of English.

Krio is an example of a Creole that is spoken and written in Sierra Leone. Here is a list of sentences that will give you an idea of the differences in **syntax**, tense and spelling between Krio and Standard English.

Krio	Standard English
i bay binc	He bought beans
a bay res	I bought rice
i go it banana	He will eat bananas
a go bay tamatis na di makit	I will buy tomatoes at the market

i go it rrs na di kicin	He will eat rice in the kitchen
i bay tamatis na salon	He bought tomatoes in Sierra Leone
na banana i bay	He bought bananas
na binc a go it	I will eat beans
na tamatis i go bay na friton	He will buy tomatoes in Freetown
na di kicin i it binc	He ate beans in the kitchen
na di makit a go it banana	I will eat bananas at the market
na di makit a bay tamatis	I bought tomatoes at the market
na salon i go it res	He will eat rice in Sierra Leone
na I go it rrs	He will eat rice
na mi bay binc na frit	I bought beans in Freetown
na I it binc na di kicin	He ate beans in the kitchen
na mi go it tamatis	I will eat tomatoes

ACTIVITY

1 Compare the Krio and Standard English sentences, noting down any similarities and differences.

2 What grammatical rules of Krio is it possible to deduce from these sentences?

3 Below is a folk tale in Jamaican Creole about Babiabuo the little boy who avenged his mother: Gyashaani Bull. It is followed by a partial translation by M Heslop. Can you complete it?

'nou, 'das a 'neks 'tuori, 'nou, a'bout Ba'bia'buo, an a 'bwai, an di 'bwai 'step'mada. Nou 'dis babia'buo waz a 'wandaful 'uol 'insek ... wel wi 'kalim insekt ... 'wandaful 'tig! yu 'kudn 'kal im 'niem a'tal, 'non 'taim, 'nou'badi. we'yer yu 'kal im 'niem, im 'kil yu 'ded. yu 'kyaan 'kal im 'niem, dis 'bia'buo. 'suo de waz a 'likl 'bwai 'huu babia'buo 'kil im 'mada. 'afta Babia'buo 'kil im 'mada wen im waz a 'biebi ... di 'mada 'went 'wan 'maanig fi 'guo 'tek 'wata, an 'wen im 'guo, im 'sii ba'bia'buo 'roun di 'sek'shan wer di 'wata 'lie fi 'tek. 'so 'shi an babia'buo 'kom tu ka'nekted an babia'buo 'kil ar. at 'dis 'taim shi 'had di 'yog 'biebi 'lef a 'yaad.

Now the next story is about ... and a boy and the boy's stepmother. Now this ... was a wonderful ... insect ... well, we call him insect ... wonderful thing! You could not call him ... at all, not name, nobody. Whenever you call him ... you dead. You cannot call him ... So there was a little boy ... kill his mother. After ... kill his mother when he was ... the mother went ... to take water and when he went ...

Women's language: capitulation or co-operation?

Man Talk (Rap)
Woman
Rabbit rabbit rabbit women
Tattle and titter
Women prattle
Women waffle and witter

Men Talk. Men Talk.

Woman into Girl Talk
About Women's trouble
Trivia 'n' Small Talk
They yap and they babble

Men Talk. Men Talk.

Women yatter
Women chatter
Women show the fat, women spill the beans
Women aint been takin'
The oh-so Good Advice in them
Women's Magazines.

A Man likes A Good Listener.

Oh yeah
I like a Woman
Who likes me Enough
Not to nitpick
Not to nag and Not to interrupt 'cause I call that treason
A woman with the Good Grace
To be struck dumb
By my Sweet Reason. Yes –

A Man likes A Good Listener.

A Real
Man
Likes A Real Good Listener

Oh
Bossy Women Gossip
Girlish Women Giggle
Women natter, women nag
Women niggle niggle niggle

Men Talk.

Men
Think First, Speak Later
Men Talk.

Half of you reading this poem will probably disagree strongly with its sentiments, though the authors can't be sure what male readers will think! It does, however, reinforce the view that women's spoken language differs from men's. The expressions used by the male speaker in this poem to describe women's talk all have negative connotations:

rabbit   tattle   prattle   waffle   witter   yap   babble   yatter
chatter   show the fat   spill the beans   nitpick   nag   gossip
natter   niggle

Is the speaker right to assign these words solely to women's talk? Can you add to the list? What words are used to describe men's talk? What does the imbalance between the lists imply?

Communicative competence

Communicative competence is a way of analysing and assessing language in use, that takes into account not only what is said but also the social and cultural factors that influence the way we use language. People can demonstrate that they are competent in this respect by using language that is appropriate to the situation, to what is said and to the speaker. You would therefore be deemed communicatively incompetent if you addressed the Queen in the same way as you addressed your friends at school or college. This, of course, is a somewhat extreme illustration, but it does indicate that there are rules of language behaviour that have to be learnt by everyone. The language behaviour expected in a courtroom is rather different than the language behaviour expected at a party. It is part of every child's acquisition of language skills that she or he learns what is and what isn't appropriate to say in particular situations. You don't swear forcefully when the vicar comes to tea!

Here are some less extreme examples of language use that demonstrate both appropriate and inappropriate behaviour. A competent communicator will know when to speak, when to stay silent, what to talk about and how to talk about things, whereas an incompetent communicator will speak at the same time as someone else, fail to answer questions put to him, change the subject constantly and/or fail to laugh at jokes or laugh at the wrong time.

Of course, there are many other ways in which a person can demonstrate his or her (in)competence. Many studies have implied that men and women differ in terms of their communicative competence and that there is such a thing as 'women's language'. For instance, it has been suggested that women:

- talk more than men
- talk too much
- are more polite
- are indecisive
- complain and nag
- are hesitant
- ask more questions
- support each other
- are more co-operative

whereas men

- swear more
- don't talk about emotions
- talk about sport more
- talk about women and machines in the same way
- insult each other frequently
- are very competitive and try to outdo each other in conversation
- dominate conversations
- speak with more authority
- give more commands
- interrupt more.

In a much-challenged American study, Robin Lakoff identified these ten features of women's language:

1 hedges eg 'sort of', 'kind of', 'I guess'
2 (super) polite **forms**, eg 'would you please...', 'I'd really appreciate it if...'

3 tag questions, eg 'don't you?', 'isn't it?', 'shouldn't we?'
4 speaking in italics, eg emphatic *so* and *very*, intonational emphasis equivalent to underlining words in written language
5 empty adjectives, eg 'divine', 'charming', 'sweet', 'adorable'
6 hypercorrect grammar and pronunciation
7 lack of a sense of humour, eg poor at telling jokes
8 direct quotations
9 special vocabulary, eg specialised colour terms
10 question intonation in declarative contexts.

ACTIVITY

1 Record a conversation between male and female speakers. This could be from television, video or the radio or from real life. If you are using TV, radio or video as a source, you must make sure that what you record is a real conversation and not a scripted one, as the conversation would not then be spontaneous.
2 Transcribe a short section of the conversation as accurately as you can, identifying pauses, breaks, interruptions and overlaps.
3 Investigate the linguistic features of the conversation to see (i) whether the suggestions made above about 'women's language' and 'men's language' are accurate and (ii) whether Robin Lakoff's hypotheses are correct.
4 Write up your findings as a research report.

Youth and age

This final section of the chapter suggests a number of investigations you could undertake that focus on the language people use when they are in roles that are age related. Some of the investigations will involve you in recording and transcribing spoken English.

Investigation 1: Adult–baby talk

It has been suggested that when adults (and even other young children) speak to very young children and babies they adopt a form of language sometimes known as 'caretaker' talk which has a number of particular restricted features. These include simplified grammar, special vocabulary and exaggerated intonation. It is interesting to note that such talk can also be used in very intimate situations (such as between husband and wife) and also when talking to pets! Put a tape recorder beneath a budgerigar's cage and you'd be surprised what sort of language you'd hear from people talking to the bird: 'Who's a pretty boy, then?'

ACTIVITY

Record and transcribe a 'conversation' between an older person and a young baby. Describe and comment on what seem to be its distinctive features.

Investigation 2: Slang

Nothing dates more quickly than slang and very little can mark the age of a speaker more clearly than the slang she or he uses. It can be embarrassing when an adult, in a vain attempt to be trendy, uses the slang of contemporary youth. Slang, of course, has always been around. Its characteristics – linguistic playfulness and inventiveness and its use as 'secret' group speech – suggest that for as long as there have been spoken formal standard languages, so there have been informal alternatives. For instance, here are a number of slang words for 'excellent', taken from Jonathan Green's entertaining book *Slang Down the Ages*:

rum/bene (sixteenth century)
bully/crack (seventeenth century)
bobbish/rich (eighteenth century)
brahma/plummy (nineteenth century)

You will easily be able to supply late 20th-century examples of your own.

ACTIVITY

Investigate the use of slang in different generations by designing a questionnaire that you give to both males and females of widely differing ages in which you ask them to tell you the slang terms they use (or used in their youth). You will find it more manageable if you concentrate on a few, restricted areas. For example, productive ones would be terms for money, the police, fools and insanity, drunkenness, clothing, excellence and, of course, sexual habits and racial terms. You will have to be very sensitive when dealing with these last two!

Investigation 3: Narrative

ACTIVITY

In this investigation, you will be looking to see if there are any differences between the way that adults and children narrate. You will need to design a simple story board and then ask both children and adults to tell you the story that is depicted on the board. You should choose whether to investigate spoken or written narrative.

Variations on this type of investigation would be to provide a photograph or painting that you ask your respondents to describe or to provide a comic strip with speech bubbles from which the speech has been removed and which you ask them to fill in.

Investigation 4: Classroom language

There are many possible ways in which classroom language can be studied. The language used in classrooms reflects very clearly the role that the participants adopt, of course, and this may be constantly changing. The language used is also very dependent on the age of the children in the class.

ACTIVITY

Investigate one or more of the following topics (you may wish to add others to this list):

- the language teachers use to maintain order
- the role of questions
- address terms: teacher to pupil/pupil to teacher/teacher to teacher/pupil to pupil
- how language is used in problem-solving discussions between pupils
- a day in the language life of one pupil
- language differences between subjects
- the use of standard and non-standard language
- the language performance of ESL pupils.

14 Language and Society

The title of this, the final chapter of this book, could equally well have been the title of the first chapter. Indeed, language and society are so interchangeable that the whole book could be called 'Language and Society' as could all A-level English Language syllabuses. However, a language isn't a kit for labelling a society's thoughts, moral beliefs, political attitudes, cultural practices and everyday living; the connection between the two is far more complex and much more interesting. Whatever variations there are in national languages and national characteristics, the inevitable force of language to shape, as well as reflect any human social group, large or small, is universally demonstrated.

The concepts of 'language' and 'society' are huge in scope; they are yet further examples of the way in which **abstract** nouns can mean anything and everything. Some clarity and precision of thought in these areas are nevertheless essential to any kind of success in getting to grips with the study of English language (or any other language, for that matter). Unjustifiable or unquestioned assumptions about the relationship between the two lead to projects and examination answers getting off on the wrong foot and ultimately to wrongheaded conclusions. The aim of this chapter is to engage you in activities that will help you sort out in your own mind just what *you* mean by language and society.

Making some connections

Notice how the word 'and' is frequently used to join 'language' and 'society'. It connects two abstract nouns that can mean all sorts of different things to different people. Notice too that whilst 'and' joins them together, it also implies that they are two different things.

ACTIVITY

1 What differences in meaning are there between the following: 'language *is* society' and 'language *in* society'?

2 Draw a large circle on a sheet of A4 and label it 'Social Functions'. Now write in as many things as you can think of that go on in a society. You may find it helpful to use present-participle verb **forms** such as 'working', 'marrying', 'policing', 'legislating', 'schooling', 'governing' and so on.

3 Next, draw a similar circle labelled 'Language Functions'. Write in as many **functions** as you can think of, such as writing records and reports; addressing

people formally; seeking answers to questions; informing people.

4 Now put the two circles side by side and look for connections between social functions and language functions. There will be many; concentrate on the connections that interest you. You will find it helpful to focus first on one social function and to find a number of language connections with that function, before looking at others.

As you will have discovered in the activity above, there is a web or network of causes and effects, influences and consequences which binds together the ways in which we live our social lives and use language. Here are two examples:

(i) Defending the innocent, prosecuting the guilty and protecting property rights are major social functions of lawyers. They achieve these ends by a variety of means but notice the crucial role of language in these functions and even in the terminology: pleading cases in court; cross-examining witnesses under oath; pronouncing sentence; a new law is not effective until written in the statute book; summing up; a deed is not just a written document, it is a legal action. There are also forms of **words** such as 'Have you anything to say before sentence (!) is passed', 'objection sustained' and 'evidence in writing', as well as popular sayings such as 'throw the book at him', 'condemned by her own words' and 'smart-talking lawyer' that remind us of the close connection.

(ii) Three important functions of modern business management are administering, marketing and employing staff. These involve a network of complex language functions such as running difficult meetings, writing effective memos, interviewing job applicants, advertising and issuing public statements. An important aspect of business management training at any level is personal competence and **style** in uses of language.

The connections between social **structures** and language *structures* are equally as important as functional connections but not quite as easy to identify and describe. The term 'social structures' means the groups into which people are organised, or organise themselves, and the relationships within these groups. Families, schools, colleges and places of employment are the most familiar social structures, but most people are also aware of larger structures such as socio-economic classes, ethnic communities, and religious groups. The term 'language structures' means the overall forms into which words are constructed, such as novels, essays, poems, business letters, diary entries, shopping lists, reports, and smaller forms such as paragraphs and grammatical constructions in written sentences and spoken utterances.

ACTIVITY

Draw another pair of circles labelled 'Social Structures' and 'Language Structures' and see what connections you can find. A-level examinations, for example, are a social structure; quotations and answers are corresponding language structures as are the written certificates awarded at the end of it all.

The following examples, again from law and business management, illustrate some of the connections between the two.

(i) The forms of both spoken and written language in legal contexts tend toward extreme formality matching the tightly regulated procedures by which legal matters are normally conducted. In court, for example, there are very distinct forms of language which can intimidate some witnesses. This is partly a matter of legal vocabulary and partly a matter of sentence construction, especially of questions by lawyers. When it comes to written language, the Plain English Society has, over the past 20 years, contributed to making legal language more accessible to non-specialist readers.

(ii) One very observable feature of modern business management is the language it has acquired. A chief function of management training is to teach a new vocabulary. An important aspect of social structure is power and control, and one effective strategy for acquiring and exercising control is to introduce new forms of language for a new order of management. George Orwell, in *Animal Farm* and *1984*, satirised very well attempts to influence the way people think by changing the words they use to think with. See also David Edgar's article on page 20.

Constructing a view of society

Generally speaking, people fluctuate between feeling at one with society and feeling outside it or at odds with it. But however much society may seem 'out there', the truth is that language actually puts society inside our heads. The vastness of what society contains is encoded by language into mind-sized units. This is not just a matter of knowing the names of all the people, places and things but of being able to think and talk about things virtually created by language. This is what is meant by the idea that language does not just name reality; it actively constructs it. For example, the **compound** noun 'greenpeace' hardly existed 20 years ago, yet in constructing that word, one section of society has constructed an idea of caring for both the natural environment and the human race which has entered everybody's mind/vocabulary whether they believe in it or not.

'Binary opposition' is the tendency to divide people and things into two contrasted or opposing groups. You will have noticed already some binary oppositions that are very common in the English language: us and them; right and wrong; mine and yours. Many English idioms (everyday sayings) consist of similarly paired words: black and white; ins and outs; the long and the short of it; give and take; more or less; on and off; his and hers; haves and have-nots. There are in fact hundreds in everyday use.

A term given to these paired words is binomials. There are also many trinomial constructions in idiomatic English, such as the popular expression 'left, right and centre'. Notice the customary word order; it would cause a slight surprise if anyone said 'left, centre and right', yet there is a certain logic to it.

ACTIVITY

1 Collect as many binomial and trinomial expressions in idiomatic English as you can.
2 a How helpful are binomial and trinomial constructions to the way you look at life?
  b Is there any significance in the fact that they sound very odd when reversed (eg 'forget and forgive' or 'the ugly, the bad and the good')?

  c Why do you think trinomial phrases and slogans are so popular with advertisers and politicians? Why are these expressions satisfying and powerful, even when, in the back of your mind, you don't believe a word of them?

Much of the data you have just been considering works in metaphorical ways (as in 'hook, line and sinker'). **Metaphor** is another way in which our perceptions of society are constructed. It is fascinating, for example, to observe how metaphors are used in newspapers and political argument. Expressions such as 'a fair slice of the cake' and 'getting your act together' are examples of meanings taken from familiar and specific social experiences and then fed back again via language into a much wider range of social activities. There seems to be a tendency for metaphors to catch on quite quickly in both the media and everyday talk, and to resist popular metaphors takes considerable strength and presence of mind. The use of popular metaphors or figures of speech appeals to popular opinion; if you wish to resist, you have to refuse to see the economy in terms of a big cake, or to see running a school or a college as a kind of playacting.

ACTIVITY

Collect four different newspapers: two tabloid and two broadsheet. Look through them, noting metaphors used to influence the way in which readers will interpret items of news or comment. List your data and ask yourself what the metaphor contributes. Some of them may have been taken for granted for years.

Before turning to some longer texts for evidence of interactions and connections between language and society, it would be helpful to look in some detail at ways in which language creates social ideas.

ACTIVITY

Look at the following recruitment advertisement for the newly formed Bath and North-East Somerset District Council:

The new authority will be: Member led, Officer driven, Customer focused; a team environment where the whole is greater than the sum of the parts; a flat management structure where employees and managers are fully empowered and decisions are devolved close to the customer; a culture of learning rather than blame; a clear sense of direction and purpose. A firm commitment to delivering high-quality public service through a combination of direct provision and effective partnerships.

Read this advert three or four times. Don't be put off if you find it difficult to understand. It is, in modern terms, a mission statement (there's an interesting metaphor, by the way) seriously attempting to do something worthwhile for the society it is intended to serve. It is written in the language of management theory. Rewrite it so it makes some sense to Aunty Flo and Uncle Jack, or whoever are your favourite, down-to-earth members of the family (note again, how unavoidable metaphors are: why, 'down-to-earth?').

What comes through very clearly in the recruitment advertisement is a vision of modern social management expressed in abstract language. It is interesting to replace abstract noun phrases by a mixture of **concrete** nouns and verbs just to explore what they could mean. Does 'A culture of learning' mean that the councillors will learn from their mistakes, or that customers must not blame them for mistakes? A 'flat management structure' could mean more equality among Council staff but it could also mean sacking middle managers, reducing promotion incentive and making the managers more powerful than ever over the employees.

Society is not just people living together in physical, economic circumstances; it also consists of ideas that are no less powerful and significant for being abstract. Language generates ideas and puts people's minds in tune with these ideas, for good or ill, by providing the means for talking, thinking and believing in them. Those who have lived under the Nazi and Stalinist regimes bear witness to how new words, phrases and ideas took over even critical minds. Terms frequently used to describe these processes are 'propaganda' and 'ideology'.

This aspect of the relationship between language and society is not however always, or even mostly, sinister. It just is. Idioms, metaphors, proverbs, sayings, folklore, all become part of our language common sense without our even noticing. Changing attitudes toward aspects of society frequently show in a change of language, which is why language change is so much more important as a linguistic study than just a historical study. The feminist movement, the new confidence in black consciousness, the multicultural nature of the English vocabulary and its spellings and cultural changes in sexual behaviour have all brought about changes in the language through changed perceptions of social reality.

Investigating language and society

You can investigate language and society in two ways. You can systematically collect data relevant to a question you have asked or an issue you have raised. Sometimes this will take the form of a hypothesis but not always. You could, for example, investigate possible differences between women's and men's speech; you could observe ways in which power shows itself in interviews; you could explore the jargon of different occupational groups to understand the role of jargon in defining expertise and authority.

Another way is to search texts for the clues they contain about the society that produced them, and it is this approach you are now going to practise. First consider the following repertoire of systematic ways in which you can investigate a text, then examine the worked example, and finally work through some other texts for yourself.

It is always a good idea to scan the text fairly quickly as a first read to get a general impression. You will need to do this to get an idea of why the text was written, by whom and for whom. You may modify your initial ideas as you read more closely but your first impressions will be useful.

The questions you should ask yourself and the repertoire of strategies you should use have been set out in the following framework:

(i) immediate social context of reader, writer and purpose

(ii) detailed exploration of phonological, lexical, grammatical, semantic, pragmatic and **discourse** features of the text

(iii) observations, based on (ii), and conclusions about functional and structural features of the particular variety of text you have investigated. This will lead appropriately back to (i).

ACTIVITY

The text 'My Visit to Drages' is a full-page advertisement that appeared in a 1930s edition of *Good Housekeeping* magazine.

1 Read the text for yourself, then read the annotation which accompanies it, based on the framework suggested previously.

2 Write a mini-project report on what investigation of this text reveals. Use the annotated information provided beside the article, plus any thoughts of your own.

"MY VISIT TO DRAGES"
by
the Countess of Oxford & Asquith

I KNEW very little about hire purchase till I visited Drages. I had imagined that under the hire purchase system very expensive or rather inferior furniture would be sold, but I was wrong. At Drages, I saw in their great store really excellent furniture at most moderate prices, but nothing of mediocre or inferior quality. Every taste and income will be met there with alacrity, understanding, and efficiency , and it is amazing to think that a man of moderate means can furnish for £100 on a payment of only £2.

Naturally, when people furnish on credit they run a certain amount of risk, so I enquired, "What happens if some misfortune comes to these nice folk I see buying furniture to-day?" Then I was told and understood the new developments of hire purchase. If the customer should die, all the furniture immediately becomes the property of his wife or children, and nothing more need be paid. If he should be ill or unemployed, then another protection comes into force. The customer keeps what he has paid for - less an allowance for the use of the furniture. I think this is a kindly and wise provision, and that Drages are to be congratulated for having originated it. As I surveyed all the great floors of furniture I could not help thinking what a help this must be to the average man who wishes to have a home of real comfort and beauty.

When I was first invited to see the great Drages store I wondered whether I would find anything different from the many fine stores I have seen here and in other countries. I do not wish to claim for myself exceptional qualities, but I am a woman of taste, and could never live in ugly surrounding or with ugly things. I dislike the bungalow buildings which deform the outskirts of beautiful towns. Not having a "Box-office" mind, I would not care to make a profit out of Aunt Sally petrol pumps, vulgar hotels, or shoddy furniture. It is one thing to please, and another to pander to the public taste, and when I was taken round every department of this store I was amazed at the variety, craftsmanship, and beauty of most of the furniture I saw there. Our modern craftsmen are equal in every respect to the old masters of the furniture craft. Even more surprising was the silver department, where perfect reproductions of old plate and charming canteens could be bought at most moderate prices.

I think all those who need furniture will be well advised if they visit this great store, with its fine choice of furniture and its courteous, kindly treatment if its customer.

In case you think I am exaggerating or inaccurate you should go to Drages and find out for yourself.

Margt Oxford

DRAGES LTD. 73-77 OXFORD ST., LONDON, W.1

OPEN DAILY FROM 9-6.30 P.M.
CLOSED ON SATURDAYS AT 1 P.M.

OPEN THURSDAYS TILL 8

BIRMINGHAM SHOWROOMS: 101 BULL STREET
OPEN ALL DAY ON SATURDAYS

COUPON Please send me free the Drage Book and particulars of your 50 Pay Way terms for approved accounts.

NAME ....

ADDRESS ....

Cut out and post in stamped addressed envelope to Drages Ltd., 73-77 Oxford Street, London W1

IMMEDIATE SOCIAL CONTEXT OF READER, WRITER AND PURPOSE

Purports to be written by Countess but did she really write it? It sounds almost like a school essay to judge from the title. Why the inverted commas?

Purpose of the text is to persuade readers about the advantages and respectability of hire purchase offered by Drages.

'Writer' of the text is placed, as it were, in a neutral position between the reader and the store. You could call it an honest broker text.

Defines the reader (audience) quite specifically.

Also defines target audience.

Drages Ltd, a furniture store. They are the author of the text when it comes down to it - whoever actually wrote the words. Note the amount of factual information included here.

'Writer' assumes role of congratulator which possibly reinforces idea of impartial judgement.

An advertisement from Good Housekeeping, 1936. Date means that immediate context is now historical. Watch out for evidence of social and language change. But there are similarities with today's adverts - nostalgia is bringing back older styles.

Expects readers to be willing to read quite a lot of words for an advert.

Partly explains the origin of the text.

The text is actually signed. Why? Is it an endorsement, a guarantee?

A direct invitation to the reader to visit the store.

Invitation to reader to send for more texts, and indirectly, to embark on hire purchase.

The advert is targeted in the first instance at Good Housekeeping readers about whom some assumptions may be made as to their level of income, social class and aspirations. Be careful though about social class and don't forget the historical context.

"MY VISIT TO DRAGES"
by
the Countess of Oxford & Asquith

I KNEW very little about hire purchase till I visited Drages. I had imagined that under the hire purchase system very expensive or rather inferior furniture would be sold, but I was wrong. At Drages, I saw in their great store really excellent furniture at most moderate prices, but nothing of mediocre or inferior quality. Every taste and income will be met there with alacrity, understanding, and efficiency, and it is amazing to think that a man of moderate means can furnish for £100 on a payment of only £2. Naturally, when people furnish on credit they run a certain amount of risk, so I enquired, "What happens if some misfortune comes to these nice folk I see buying furniture to-day?" Then I was told and understood the new developments of hire purchase. If the customer should die, all the furniture immediately becomes the property of his wife or children, and nothing more need be paid. If he should be ill or unemployed, then another protection comes into force. The customer keeps what he has paid for - less an allowance for the use of the furniture. I think this is a kindly and wise provision, and that Drages are to be congratulated for having originated it. As I surveyed all the great floors of furniture I could not help thinking what a help this must be to the average man who wishes to have a home of real comfort and beauty.

When I was first invited to see the great Drages store I wondered whether I would find anything different from the many fine stores I have seen here and in other countries. I do not wish to claim for myself exceptional qualities, but I am a woman of taste, and could never live in ugly surroundings or with ugly things. I dislike the bungalow buildings which deform the outskirts of beautiful towns. Not having a "Box-office" mind, I would not care to make a profit out of Aunt Sally petrol pumps, vulgar hotels, or shoddy furniture. It is one thing to please, and another to pander to the public taste, and when I was taken round every department of this store I was amazed at the variety, craftsmanship, and beauty of most of the furniture I saw there. Our modern craftsmen are equal in every respect to the old masters of the furniture craft. Even more surprising was the silver department, where perfect reproductions of old plate and charming canteens could be bought at most moderate prices.

I think all those who need furniture will be well advised if they visit this great store, with its fine choice of furniture and its courteous, kindly treatment if its customers.

In case you think I am exaggerating or inaccurate you should go to Drages and find out for yourself.

Margot Oxford

DRAGES LTD, 73-77 OXFORD ST., LONDON, W.1

OPEN DAILY FROM 9-6.30 P.M.
CLOSED ON SATURDAYS AT 1 P.M.

OPEN THURSDAYS TILL 8

BIRMINGHAM SHOWROOMS: 101 BULL STREET
OPEN ALL DAY ON SATURDAYS

COUPON Please send me free the Drage Book and particulars of your 50 Pay Way terms for approved accounts.
NAME
ADDRESS

Cut out and post in stamped addressed envelope to Drages Ltd., 73-77 Oxford Street, London W1

DESCRIBING WHAT VARIETY OF ENGLISH THIS IS: DISCOURSE AND BROADER ASPECTS OF SEMANTICS

The register is fairly formal: no colloquialisms or minor sentences.

Begins by anticipating an objection.

Despite its first person pronouns the discourse is very much a business organisation addressing a potentially large market.

Putting "Box-office" in inverted commas expresses a reservation, an apology. There is tension here, often expressed in writing by the use of inverted commas.

This is a slightly awkward sentence because it contains a passive verb immediately followed by a verb in the active form: 'was told' and 'understood'.
The text has an educative function within its intention to persuade - education towards attitude change.

This paragraph addresses the main objection - the risk factor. Note the disarming adverb 'naturally' that governs how you read the whole paragraph.

No female customers for hire purchase?

Is the congratulation for the benefit of Drages, or to persuade the reader to trust them?

Though their name appears prominently in the graphology, Drages Ltd. remain 'silent' in the background.

The one feature in the whole text that is close to everyday speech.

Type of discourse – the text has been disguised to look like an article yet it is an advertisement. It speaks as though it is reporting but it is in fact the discourse of selling. What is said is important but the status of the speaker gives the message a high status; it legitimises, endorses, makes its topic respectable.

Drages have chosen a woman to speak on their behalf. Is this then a text targeted mainly at women? Most references are to the male breadwinner, the principal reference to women being understood.

Mode of writing is undoubtedly persuasive. Explicit, literal meaning is that you should buy furniture from Drages by means of their hire purchase scheme. Implied meaning is that likely readers will have taste beyond income. Could also mean that the furniture is not selling very well and the price can't be lowered. Hire purchase is described as new.

A risky remark. It excludes people who live in bungalows!

A person of distinction, chosen to speak to a wide public. Snob appeal!? What is today's equivalent? You do not need to know that she was the wife of a prime minister.

Direct speech introduced here. Has the effect of drawing the reader into a real situation. The remark may well strike modern readers as patronising or hilariously funny.

The identification created by 'our' makes buying good furniture an act of national pride. She is almost addressing the nation.

Concludes by acknowledging possibility of disbelief. Strong use of modal verb form 'should'.

It is not difficult to detect in this text, once the linguistic details have been investigated, significant socio-economic change, class distinctions, gender bias, and the fact that, as always, advertisers sell a way of life, a set of ideas and images, as much as they sell a product. Don't assume amateurs wrote this; it is a very professional job.

"MY VISIT TO DRAGES"
by
the Countess of Oxford & Asquith

I KNEW very little about hire purchase till I visited Drages. I had imagined that under the hire purchase system very expensive or rather inferior furniture would be sold, but I was wrong. At Drages, I saw in their great store really excellent furniture at most moderate prices, but nothing of mediocre or inferior quality. Every taste and income will be met there with alacrity, understanding and efficiency, and it is amazing to think that a man of moderate means can furnish for £100 on a payment of only £2. Naturally, when people furnish on credit they run a certain amount of risk, so I enquired, "What happens if some misfortune comes to these nice folk I see buying furniture to-day?" Then I was told and understood the new developments of hire purchase. If the customer should die, all the furniture immediately becomes the property of his wife or children, and nothing more need be paid. If he should be ill or unemployed, then another protection comes into force. The customer keeps what he has paid for - less an allowance for the use of the furniture. I think this is a kindly and wise provision, and that Drages are to be congratulated for having originated it. And I recall that the great floors of furniture I could not help thinking what a help this must be to the average man who wishes to have a home of real comfort and beauty.

When I was first invited to see the great Drages store I wondered whether I would find anything different from the many fine stores I have seen here and in other countries. I do not wish to claim for myself exceptional qualities, but I am a woman of taste, and could never live in ugly surroundings or with ugly things. I dislike the bungalow buildings which deform our outskirts of beautiful towns. Not having a "Box-office" mind, I would not care to make a profit out of Aunt Sally petrol pumps, vulgar hotels, or shoddy furniture. It is one thing to please, and another to pander to the public taste, and when I was taken round every department of this store I was amazed at the variety, craftsmanship, and beauty of most of the furniture I saw there. Our modern craftsmen are equal in every respect to the old masters of the furniture craft. Even more surprising was the silver department, where perfect reproductions of old plate and charming canteens could be bought at most moderate prices.
I think all those who need furniture will be well advised if they visit this great store, with its fine choice of furniture and its courteous, kindly treatment of its customers.
In case you think I am exaggerating or inaccurate you should go to Drages and find out for yourself.

Margt of Oxford

DRAGES LTD. 73-77 OXFORD ST., LONDON, W.1

OPEN DAILY FROM 9-6.30 P.M.
CLOSED ON SATURDAYS AT 1 P.M.

OPEN THURSDAYS TILL 8

BIRMINGHAM SHOWROOMS: 101 BULL STREET
OPEN ALL DAY ON SATURDAYS

COUPON Please send me free the Drage Book and particulars of your 50 Pay Way terms for approved accounts
NAME
ADDRESS
Cut out and post in stamped addressed envelope to Drages Ltd., 73-77 Oxford Street, London W1

You don't need much pragmatic awareness to detect tensions within this text. These tensions express social realities: e.g. the potential customers, and their rate of income (wages) cannot afford Drages furniture but their predictable aspirations make them want it. That's one tension. Another is that it is highly unlikely that the Countess furnished her house from Drages Ltd. There is also a tension between traditional values and modern urban development (see the semantic fields). The 'Box-office' and 'profit' also contain tension: they are the motive behind this advertisement but they have to be made as respectable as the craft of the furniture maker. Embedded in the text is a socio-economic class system. Detecting these tensions, contradictions, implications by attending to the details in the text and its interweaving with the context is called deconstruction.

Phonology - don't underestimate this! It's a written text but there is a voice coming through - a cross between Lady Bracknell and Mr Kipling of the exceedingly good cakes!

DETAILED EXPLORATION OF LINGUISTIC FEATURES OF THE TEXT

Graphology (don't overdo this!) – immediate prominence given to Countess linking her name with the store s. Formal camera portrait. Handwritten signature. Double column format – still a common layout.

Grammar – immediate use in title and opening sentence of first person pronoun. Direct address to the reader.

Grammar – adverb used to intensify adjective. This feature occurs seven times in the advert.

Lexis – this introduces the real topic of the advert straightaway.

Lexis – synonym for 'hire purchase'. Is there a different nuance – then or now?

Grammar– 3rd person reference to Drages.

Lexis – a triple noun phrase, beloved of advertising copy writers.

Grammar – reassuring adverb – why 'naturally'?

Grammar – there are 21 uses of 'I' altogether.

Lexis – not a very acceptable adjective for people nowadays.

Grammar - passive voice - makes her a receiver of information on our behalf.

Pragmatics – is there an implied meaning here? Is she being paid to endorse Drages and the HP scheme?

Lexis – 'most' but not all!

Pragmatics – a modern reader may detect snobbery here but would a 1930s reader? Or would they be expected to share the attitudes?

Grammar – note the negative statement here,

Punctuation – more inverted commas, why? What do they mean?

Lexis – is this a bit of language change I don't know about?

Grammar – concludes with direct address to second person reader.

Lexis – imitations, not the real thing.

Lexis – another triple noun phrase

Grammar – sudden appearance of 1st person plural possessive pronoun. Implies that we all share ownership of the craftsmen. Is there more to it?

Grammar – coupon is in effect a second person reply in directive form.

Grammar – a favourite adjective which is applied to the store four times. (Call this a lexical point if you prefer.)

"MY VISIT TO DRAGES"
by
the Countess of Oxford & Asquith

I KNOW very little about hire purchase till I visited Drages. I had imagined that under the hire purchase system very expensive or rather inferior furniture would be sold, but I was wrong. At Drages, I saw in their great store really excellent furniture at most moderate prices, but nothing of mediocre or inferior quality. Every taste and income will be met there with alacrity, understanding, and efficiency, and it is amazing to think that a man of moderate means can furnish for £100 or a payment of only £2. Naturally, when people furnish on credit they run a certain amount of risk, so I enquired "What happens if some misfortune comes to these nice folk I see buying furniture to-day?" Then I was told and understood the new developments of hire purchase. If the customer should die, all the furniture immediately becomes the property of his wife or children, and nothing more need be paid. If he should be ill or unemployed, then another projection comes into force. The customer keeps what he has paid for - less an allowance for the use of the furniture. I think this is a kindly and wise provision, and that Drages are to be congratulated for having originated it. As I surveyed all the great floors of furniture I could not help thinking what a help this must be to the average man who wishes to have a home of real comfort and beauty.

When I was first invited to see the great Drages store I wondered whether I would find anything different from the many fine stores I have seen here and in other countries. I do not wish to claim for myself exceptional qualities, but I am a woman of taste, and could never live in ugly surroundings or with ugly things. I dislike the bungalow buildings which deform the outskirts of beautiful towns. Not having a "Box-office" mind, I would not care to make a profit out of Aunt Sally petrol pumps, vulgar hotels, or shoddy furniture. It is one thing to please, and another to pander to the public taste, and when I was taken round every department of this store I was amazed at the variety, craftsmanship, and beauty of most of the furniture I saw there. Our modern craftsmen are equal in every respect to the old masters of the furniture craft. Even more surprising was the silver department, where perfect reproductions of old plate and charming canteens could be bought at most moderate prices. I think all those who need furniture will be well advised if they visit this great store, with its fine choice of furniture and its courteous, kindly treatment if its customer. In case you think I am exaggerating or inaccurate you should go to Drages and find out for yourself.

Margot Oxford

DRAGES LTD. 73-77 OXFORD ST., LONDON, W.1

OPEN DAILY FROM 9-6.30 P.M.
CLOSED ON SATURDAYS AT 1 P.M.

OPEN THURSDAYS TILL 8

BIRMINGHAM SHOWROOMS: 101 BULL STREET
OPEN ALL DAY ON SATURDAYS

COUPON Please send me free the Drages book and particulars of your 50 Pay Way terms for approved accounts.
NAME
ADDRESS
Cut out and post in stamped addressed envelope to Drages Ltd., 73-77 Oxford Street, London W.1

Semantics
–Two distinct semantic fields contrasted:

beautiful/good taste *and* **ugly/vulgar**

excellent furniture   *rather inferior*
mediocre or inferior   *ugly things*
comfort and beauty   *bungalow buildings*
    etc.

Lexis - what does this mean? Was it a new expression? Has it died the death?

Pragmatics – Countess is speaking on behalf of Drages furniture store but impression is that she is looking after readers' interests. Notice pronoun shift between penultimate and final paragraph from 3rd person to 2nd person. The 'those' and 'they' change to 'you' and 'yourself'.

Lexis – what is an 'approved' account?

Lexis - this word seems to exclude by implication the countess and her readers. Who then are the public of 'public taste'?

The following text illustrates very well a recurring language and society topic, namely attitudes toward uses of language. Disapproval can often be ferocious, as is evident in this *Sunday Express* article. Unlike the *Good Housekeeping* advertisement, this text is specifically about language. You should, however, overlook the content to begin with and do a stylistic analysis along the lines demonstrated in the previous activity. When you have done this, identify in clear statements of your own the language and society issues raised from this news item.

FIGHT TO SAVE THE QUEEN'S ENGLISH

EXCLUSIVE

TEENAGERS who cannot speak or write English properly are to be targeted in a major "get the grunt" campaign.

Education Secretary Gillian Shephard has warned senior civil servants that Britain cannot afford to carry on producing inarticulate school leavers who rely on "communication by grunt".

Standards of spoken English have plummeted in the last two decades. Many youngsters are simply unable to express themselves clearly, concisely and courteously.

Dismayed employers have warned that our status as a major trading nation could be seriously affected unless future generations are taught basic communication skills.

Now Mrs Shephard is planning a new initiative, expected to be unveiled at next month's Tory party conference, to revive the use of the English language – which is one of her personal crusades.

School pupils will be graded to show potential employers how well they express themselves when dealing with colleagues or future customers.

The scheme, which has taken more than 12 months to formulate, is aimed at eradicating sloppy use of language by emphasising the need for clear expression.

Ministers believe this will be complemented by changes already made to the national curriculum, stressing the basics of grammar, spelling and punctuation. But a new system of assessing how articulate youngsters are is seen as vital.

Details are still being discussed by a special working party at the Department for Education and Employment.

The problem was highlighted last week when the National Association of Head Teachers wrote to Mrs Shephard listing concerns about pupil discipline and parental responsibility.

Among major worries it raised were the increased use of foul language by children as young as five and the problem of pupils starting school with few or no social skills.

Academics are concerned at the way British pupils lag behind youngsters from competitor countries, such as America, in communication skills. The problem is even apparent among brighter pupils who go on to university.

Two-thirds of firms and public bodies quizzed by the Association of Graduate Recruiters claim that graduates lack communication skills.

The Confederation of British Industry has been campaigning for five years for good communication skills to be developed in schools.

Mrs Margaret Murray, CBI head of training policy, said: "Communication skills are essential for all jobs.

"Employers need people who are articulate and good at listening, as well as good at reading and writing.

"Jobs now involve so much time on the phone and working in teams that good oral and listening skills are incredibly important."

Mrs Shephard told last year's Tory party conference: "Why should anyone expect to get a job if he or she can't speak or write clearly in our marvellous language?

"For too long we have been slack in our treatment of English. And we have impoverished our children in the process."
(*Sunday Express*, 24 September 1995)

Sometimes the leap from the individual to Society with a capital 'S' is too great and as a consequence leads to generalisations on a large scale and/or very subjective conclusions. Good meeting places between the two are areas of social psychology, a discipline in its own right that makes connections between individuals and groups of all kinds. Job interviews, for example, are ideal events for social psychological investigation and in such investigations, language is key data.

ACTIVITY

The following text, from a pamphlet in a Citizens' Advice office, gives advice on job interviews. Do a thorough stylistic analysis first (context, writer/reader, purpose; linguistic details; what variety of discourse) and then write some statements of your own about the role of language in a vital area of social success, job hunting.

"How can I come across better in interviews and what are the secrets of finding a new job?"

Creating the right impression is vital in a job interview and it's not just what you say that matters, but how you say it. Just as important, is ensuring you have the right skills to get an interview in the first place.

Both the interview skills and the job-search courses are designed to offer you a package of information which will help you impress your interviewer and hopefully get you that job. The courses include:

- important information on how to prepare for an interview
- specialist advice and support to develop your interview skills
- help with steps you can take towards: promotion; employment; training or further study via the use of tried and tested interview techniques

- an interview rehearsal so you can make your mistakes here and not in the real thing!
- feedback on your "mock" interview
- an opportunity to discuss with others who are in the same situation as you
- advice on planning, organising and developing your own job-search activities.

Peter, in his early 40s, from Cleckheaton, feels he benefited from the interview-skills course.

"It really did work for me, as a direct result of the information I received, the rate of interviews I was offered increased dramatically. I found employment along with five other job offers – all within four weeks of attending the course! Together with

help in producing a CV the course gave me that extra push to get me the job."

Many people have combined the interview-skills course with a job-search course (and CV workshops available in a separate leaflet called 'How do I produce a good quality CV?'). Job Search will help you find the right job in the shortest possible time. The course includes:

- advice on planning, organising and developing your own job-search schedule
- how you can develop a "market" approach to finding a job
- practical guidelines on completing application forms
- the latest "inside" information on what employers look for when recruiting.

Sally, a former sales executive in her mid-30s, who lives in Dewsbury, lost her job when the company was taken over. In addition to receiving some redundancy counselling, she completed a job-search course.

"I didn't realise just how organised and structured you have to be in order to get a job. It's a bit like planning a military campaign. The course gave me the skills to plan what I should be doing, the section on what employers are looking for was very useful. At first I thought I didn't need help in 'just' looking for a job, but I did and it worked. I'm now working for a telesales company in Huddersfield."

Both courses are delivered by qualified and experienced trainers with specialist knowledge of current job hunting and interview techniques.

The length of the courses will vary depending on the organisation planning the training.

The cost for employed people is £9 for a full day or £4.50 for a half-day.

ACTIVITY

As a final, field activity, visit a Citizens' Advice information section for yourself to see an example of a sociolinguistic network in action. Ask them about language and the part it plays in their work. Does it cause problems?

Afterword

You will remember that we suggested in our introduction that the purpose of this book was to help you develop expertise in applying knowledge about language to your own and other people's uses of the spoken and written word. We certainly hope that this has been the case and that you now feel very confident in applying such knowledge.

We began and continued by showing you how many perspectives there were that could be taken on language. We hope that you now may want to pursue some of these approaches further.

Obviously we hope that this book leads to your eventual success in any public examinations that you will be sitting, but we hope too that you will feel better equipped to use and reflect on our living language throughout your life. Remember: language *is* for life!

George Keith
John Shuttleworth

A Selective Glossary for Examination Candidates

The words in the following glossary are linguistic terminology signifying some central linguistic concepts. In examinations it is understanding and applying the concepts behind the terminology that earns marks. Frequently the terminology is used or rather misused which is unfortunate in an otherwise good answer. Definitions of terminology can be helpful but knowing why a term is useful is more important. Throughout the book, linguistic terms are explained in context and the index will help you locate those explanations. Look on the following as a mini-revision course of terms most frequently misused. Further discussion of terminology may be found in:

The Longman Reference Guide To A and AS Level English, by G R Keith and B Keith (1991), ISBN 0 582 06396 5. This is alphabetically arranged for students of A-level English Language and English Literature.

More detailed description and explanation will be found in the following major works of reference:

The Oxford Companion to the English Language, edited by Tom McArthur (1992).

The Cambridge Encyclopaedia of the English Language, by David Crystal (1995).

Glossary

ABSTRACT   This is a term usually applied to nouns and noun phrases to distinguish them from the concrete. Texts containing lots of abstract words are very different in their effect on the reader from text full of concrete words. Abstraction however is not just about nouns; it is a power of the mind made possible by language. There are many other words that have no concrete characteristics but which we cannot manage without. Conjunctions such as 'although', 'because', 'if' and adverbs like 'moreover' and 'therefore', have no concrete existence, they are very much creations of language, but we could not manage without them. So, abstractness is both a necessary part of everyday language as well as a stylistic feature of certain kinds of discourse eg science, mathematics, religion, psychology, sociology, philosophy.

ACCENT   Usually the term refers to characteristic features of regional pronunciation or of social class. It also refers to deviations from Received Pronunciation in the speech of people whose first language is not English. The term can also be used to denote emphasis on a particular word or syllable. In written French, for example, the word refers to signs added to individual letters to indicate their pronunciation.

ADVERBIALS   This refers to words and phrases that tell how, why, where and when the action of a verb occurred. The main verb of any clause or sentence is the main point of what is being said, so anything 'added' to it is an important modification of what is being said. Adverbials add modifications, qualifications, additional information to the verb.

AFFIX   Affixes are an important feature of English words. They are the 'bits' that can be added to the beginning (prefixes) or ends (suffixes) of words to change their meanings. Many are Anglo-Saxon in origin, others come from Greek and Latin.

ALOPHONE   An allophone is the distinctive way in which an individual pronounces any one of the forty four phonemes that make up the sound system of the English language. Allophonic variations can sometimes be extreme, sometimes very slight. Extreme allophonic variations can make a regional or foreign accent very difficult to understand, especially if there are a number of them close together. Usually our knowledge of the forty four phonemes (norms of pronunciation) help listeners to guess what is intended.

ANALOGY   This is a term frequently used in linguistics, especially in the areas of language acquisition and language change. It refers to expectations and predictability. Young children, for example, learn irregular verb forms alongside regular ones, but it is clear that when faced with a new verb they tend to use the '-ed' form when they want to express the past tense eg wented, buyed, goed, gived. Having noticed how frequently the '-ed' form occurs, they apply it, by analogy, until they learn to use the irregular form. The same process occurs with regular and irregular plurals. Features of a language that are exceptions to the 'rules', ie not analogous, are sometimes referred to as anomalies.

ANAPHORIC REFERENCE   This occurs, usually by means of pronouns, when a reference is made back to something mentioned earlier in a text eg The woman entered the room with a grand flourish. She immediately became the focus of everybody's attention. 'She' refers back to 'The woman'. Cataphoric reference anticipates something later in the text eg This is what we did ...

ANTONYM   The English language is full of words that are opposites in meaning or which contrast very strongly. Some antonyms are universally accepted eg heavy/light but each language user has a personal store of antonyms which may not seem immediately obvious to others eg independent/weak; truthful/diplomatic; optimist/realist. All kinds of moral, political, psychological assumptions underlie antonyms eg left/right; tough/tender; winners and losers.

AUXILIARIES   Auxiliary verbs are drawn from 'to be', 'to have' and 'to do'. They help other verbs to change their tenses and to express the passive voice eg 'I have opened it' and 'I was being brainwashed'.

CLAUSE   A clause is a group of words that contains a finite verb. It may be independent as in, 'The cat sat on the mat', in which case it is the same as a simple sentence if it is concluded with a full stop. If a clause begins with a word such as 'if', 'although' or 'when' it is called a dependent clause because it cannot function on its own as a sentence; it is dependent upon an independent clause.

CODE   This is a word that has many meanings ranging from the fairly straightforward activity of decoding literal meanings from a set of alphabetic symbols to the less obvious, implicit rules and conventions that govern the way people use language in particular circumstances. Just as there are unwritten codes of behaviour that define sportsmanship, good manners, fair play, sexual relations, courteous driving, so there are language codes that govern ways in which we talk and write to each other. There are many such codes in all walks of life and the terms 'register', 'style', 'dialect' are often more appropriate for linguistic investigations.

COLLOCATION   Words that occur together so frequently that they are more or less predictable are said to be collocations ie they are often located together, 'Blue skies', 'Fish and chips', 'Night and day', 'Boys and girls' are obvious examples.

COMMAND   Commands, sometimes called **imperatives** or **directives**, are a distinctive class of sentences. Their function is to tell somebody to do something, though sometimes they may take the form of questions or statements for the sake of politeness. 'Will you try again please' and 'I think we should go in now', for example, leave little doubt about what the speaker wants the listeners to do.

COMMON NOUN   There are thousands of these in the English vocabulary and probably form the largest single class of words. They are the general names of things, and can be either concrete (chair, pen, sausage, computer) or abstract (love, rationality, benefits, patriotism).

COMPLEX   This word has an exact use in linguistics, and doesn't just mean complicated or 'more difficult'. Complex structures, whether words or sentences, contain at least two elements one of which is dependent upon another. When there are several dependencies in a word or sentence, meaning can become rather complicated, but it is the number of complex elements, not complexity itself that demands careful attention. A word like 'antidisestablishmentarianism' contains five dependent elements, while a sentence such as the following also contains five dependent elements: The driver who was forced to retire from the race that was held in Monaco, decided that he would need a faster car if he were ever going to turn in a performance of which he could be proud.

COMPOUND   Compound words and sentences consist of two or more independent elements: eg headrest, input, offbeat and 'I came, I saw, I conquered', 'She laughed, she cried, she nearly died'.

CONCRETE   Language symbolises both ideas and objects. Ideas tend toward the abstract, whereas words that refer to physical objects create a more concrete impression in the mind (see also **abstract**)

CONNOTATION Words do not often work alone nor do they occur in alphabetical order in real life as they do in dictionaries. Centuries of familiar, everyday and literary use, create networks of words that trigger each other off without any intention on the user's part. Poets, advertisers, politicians and propagandists of all kinds can rely on networks of connotations to generate added meanings to the words they use. Equally, they try to avoid words that will trigger off connotations they do not want. Sometimes the term 'associations' is used though some writers maintain a distinction between connotations as socially shared networks and associations as more personal strings of words.

CO-ORDINATION This describes the connection between the elements of compound words and sentences. Elements of equal or independent rank are said to be co-ordinated. Thus, words such as 'and' 'but' 'or' 'then' are frequently used as co-ordinating conjunctions because they connect elements of equal grammatical status.

DECLARATIVES This is another name for statements. It means that the function of an utterance or statement is to declare that something is so.

DEIXIS (DEICTIC) This refers to the necessity in linguistic communication for speakers/listeners and writers/readers to know exactly who is who and where is where. Deictic references are made by the use of pronouns (you, me and them), by the use of adverbs (here and there) and by the use of demonstratives (this and that). The impersonal pronoun, 'it', however ordinary it may seem, is a key word for making deictic reference; we use it all the time and take it for granted but the moment a reader or listener becomes uncertain about what 'it' is referring to, effective communication falters.

DENOTATION This is not exactly the opposite of **connotation** but it is usually regarded as an **antonym**. Whereas connotation extends meaning into a wide variety of nuances and possibilities, denotation limits meaning to a specific instance and is concerned with the direct connection between a word and the thing or action or quality to which it refers. Dictionary definitions denote meanings whereas thesauruses extend words into groups or networks of meanings.

DIALECT This refers to the way in which different groups of people use the same language in different ways. The differences may lie in pronunciation, vocabulary and grammar, and they will be consistent and frequent enough to form a distinctive variation in the common language. Regional dialects are the most familiar, but there are also social, cultural and occupational dialects. The term 'standard English' refers to a variety of English which does not contain dialectal vocabulary and grammatical forms but which may be spoken with a regional accent.

Dialectal variation is the normal state of a healthy, living language, and standard English may be regarded as an additional, though prestigious, dialect used for education and many aspects of social, political and economic life. More especially, standard English is preferred for formal writing.

DISCOURSE   There are two uses for this word in language study. One use refers to the general ways in which people talk and write about particular subject areas or human concerns: eg law, medicine, science, religion, philosophy, music, literature, social services, business management, information technology, the pop scene, fashion, counselling. The other use refers to any stretch of language longer than a single utterance or sentence. Discourse analysis, for example, consists in investigating how language is used in a conversation or in a particular document. Discourse features that are especially significant are (in conversation) turn-taking, types of utterance, power and control, introductions, terms of address, leave takings, length of utterance. Features important in written discourse are text construction, the movement of ideas through the text, register or tone of voice, sentence construction, editorial presentation.

ELISION   This refers to the omission of a vowel or syllable in a written word eg didn't, won't, gonna, must've.

ELLIPSIS   This refers to the omission of whole words from an utterance or sentence because they are grammatically implied. For example, it is sufficient to reply 'Yes I can' to the question 'Can you cook?' The word 'cook' has become redundant. It is also likely in many conversations that even the word 'can' would be redundant, the answer 'Yes' being sufficient for meaning.

ETYMOLOGY   This is one of the oldest branches of language study and refers to the origins and development through time of individual words and phrases.

EXCLAMATION   A distinctive kind of sentence, occurring most often in everyday talk and literature. It conveys strong emotion and is typically non-interactive. Verbs are rarely used explicitly though the verb 'to be' is often implied: eg Rubbish! How stupid! Wonderful! Ouch! What a beauty!

FAMILY   Though a modest, commonplace word, and none the worse for that, 'family' is an important metaphor in linguistics. Languages are divided into families with ancestors, parents and offspring eg the Indo-European family; the Altaic family. Native languages are referred to as mother tongues, while individual words are formed naturally into family groups eg

> loyal, loyalty, loyalist, disloyal, loyally

> book, bookworm, overbooked, bookmaker, bookmark, booklet, bookish.

FINITE   This is a term applied to verbs and indicates definiteness in the sense that there is explicit information about who or what did the action and when. The use of a finite verb is the essential feature of a clause and of sentences. There can be no doubt about the following:

> The cat sat on the mat.

If, however, that were written:

The cat, sitting on the mat . . .

there is doubt. The addition of a finite verb such as 'is', 'was', 'will be' makes everything explicit:

The cat is sitting on the mat.
The cat was sitting on the mat.
The cat will be sitting on the mat.

'Sitting on the mat' is a phrase not a clause simply because, although it contains a form of a verb 'sitting', we do not know who or what or when.

FORM   This is another word frequently used in language study. It refers to the appearances and structures of language. Verbs have all kinds of forms: eg buy, bought, buying. Nouns may be formed into adjectives: eg play → playful. In standard English grammar formal agreements are expected between, for example, subject and verb eg 'We are' not 'we be'.

FUNCTION   This is a concept often contrasted with **form** or **structure**. It refers quite simply to the purpose any use of language can accomplish. The linguistic philosopher, Ludwig Wittgenstein, even went so far as to say that the meaning of a word is its function; in other words, what the user is trying to do with it. Sentences can be grouped into functions; language acquisition in young children can be effectively studied by asking the question at any stage, 'What is language being used for?'. Knowing the purpose of a piece of writing, whether from the point of view of a reader or a writer, is essential to communication.

Language study is frequently a matter of comparing and contrasting the structure any particular bit of language takes with the function it is performing.

GENRE   This is a French word meaning 'kind' and has traditionally referred to different kinds of literature eg poetry, prose, fiction, drama. Within these groups there are genres such as detective stories, spy stories, romances, science-fiction, fantasy sagas, comics, soap operas.

More recently the word has come to signify an area of socio-linguistic study in which close attention is paid to the conventions, codes and implicit understandings whereby writers construct texts and readers receive them. Genre studies are particularly interested in functional, non-fictional texts in which important issues of power, education and social status are apparent. Examples are medical records, local housing department documentation, legal form filling.

GRAMMAR   There is an important sense in which this whole book is about grammar. Do not restrict its use to the correctness or otherwise of the words being used in any given utterance or sentence. Do not restrict its use to assessing the correctness or otherwise of words when they finally arrive at the surface. Grammar is a generative process or, if you like, a meaning-making kit for keeping thoughts and communications tidy and comprehensible, that generates structures to fulfil whatever it is you want your language to do in a given psychological or social situation.

IDIOLECT   This is your own, personal language profile. Everybody has one. It will consist of elements from the local, regional dialect of your early years and elements from the sociolects you have been influenced by since childhood eg educational, socio-economic class and occupational variations in uses of language. The most obvious personal characteristics of your idiolect are voice features and style of delivery. Other features are distinctive choices of vocabulary and phraseology, favourite grammatical constructions and levels of humour, formality and confidence.

IDIOM   These are the richly varied and fascinating words and phrases in a language that are taken for granted by its native speakers but which do not literally mean what they say eg She's thrown a wobbler; he's kicked the bucket. Idioms in any language cause second language learners difficulties that can be comic, embarrassing and even painful.

LEXIS   This is a Greek word for 'word'. As a linguistic term, it refers to single words as units of meaning. Lexicology is the study of words; lexicography refers to the compiling of dictionaries. The word 'vocabulary' means the same as 'lexis'.

METAPHOR   Metaphor, or 'speaking metaphorically', is a process whereby speakers express meanings in non-literal ways. Most idioms are metaphorical in that they do not mean literally what they say.

Metaphors are not just the devices of poets, they occur constantly in everyday language. Some are very familiar, almost automatic (see **idiom**) others are carefully thought to communicate extra meanings that are difficult to express literally. Clearly they influence the way we think about something and if we wish to think about something differently, a change of metaphor sometimes achieves this. You could for example think of examinations as a battle ahead with unknown forces (how intimidating!). You could on the other hand, think of them as gateways to a new future. 'Battles' and 'gateways' are quite different metaphors but all an examination is literally, is sitting down on an appointed day and writing answers to some questions.

PASSIVISATION   Verbs are said to be in the active or passive voice. If active, it means that the action is performed by the actor; if passive it means that the action was done unto the actor. Most of the time we generate active voice constructions: eg The cat sat on the mat; I like fish and chips. Passivisation of these two sentences would lead to The mat was sat on by the cat and Fish and chips are liked by me. The first example does not sound too odd but the second makes you wonder what is the point of putting it this way. Look however at the following headlines:

> Rioting students set government offices alight.
> Government offices set alight by rioting students.
> Government offices set alight.

You can see that the active form of the first one puts the focus squarely on the action of the students; the second puts the focus on the government buildings as victims of violent action; the third is also in the passive form but with no mention of the rioting students. Passivisation of verbs creates subtle but important nuances of meaning.

PRAGMATICS   Pragmatics is about the implied meanings, the everyday codes and the taken-for-grantedness that are essential features of everyday communication. It is surprising, in fact, that more misunderstandings do not occur when you consider that most misunderstandings are a failure of implied meaning. If you laugh at the following cartoon, you have understood exactly what pragmatics is.

PRE-MODIFICATION and **POST-MODIFICATION**   Whenever adjectives (eg excellent) or adjectival phrases (eg a well-groomed and elegant . . .) are placed before a noun, the noun is said to be pre-modified. In other words judgements, opinions, points of view, attempts at precise description, have been made before you know what is being described. Post-modification does the opposite, often by use of a form of the verb 'to be' as in 'The garden was extraordinarily lush'.

The word 'modification' means the same as 'qualification'.

PSYCHOLINGUISTICS   The ways in which people use language are indicators of how people think. Language plays a big part in moulding thought processes, and the connections between thought and language define what is meant by psycholinguistics. Studies of language acquisition, reading processes, persuasion, second language learning all contribute to and draw upon ideas in this area of study.

REGISTER   See **style**.

SEMANTICS   Semantics is concerned with meaning: how meaning is constructed, interpreted, clarified, obscured, illustrated, simplified, negotiated, contradicted, paraphrased. The study of semantics includes ambiguity, denotation, connotation, metaphor, synonymy and antonymy, simile, analogy, semantic fields, etymology, lexicology, pragmatics, idioms, and so on. It is a big topic and best treated as one that includes almost everything eg grammar, phonology, discourse, lexis, because all these contribute to meaning. It is very rare that people intend to use language in meaningless ways; even babies under six months use what phonology they have to communicate meaningfully. Whilst it makes sense to conduct a stylistic analysis under the sub-headings of lexis, grammar, phonology, discourse, for example, it does not make sense to add semantics to that list because a good analysis adds up to a fuller understanding of a text's meaning. Remember too, that meanings depend on three factors: the writer's purposes, the text constructed and the reader's reception of and response to, the text.

SIMILE   Unlike metaphors, similes do not blend the meanings of different words. They make comparisons keeping the two things compared quite separate. As with metaphors, the language is full of common ones eg as happy as a lark; he ran up and down like a madman. The distinctive feature of similes is the use of words 'as' and 'like' which compare things but keep them separate.

SLANG   This is a term that almost always carries with it disapproval. It is not a linguistic term as such and is generally used to refer to informal expression used in both speech and writing. Slang consists chiefly in the use of words and phrases coined by particular groups: eg bomber crews; skate boarders; car enthusiasts; bikers; schoolchildren; petty criminals; gamblers. All these non-standard forms are of special interest to students of language because they signify identity and have interesting origins and histories. Mostly the term refers to spoken English across the country. Words and phrases used in regional dialects are not slang.

Another term carrying almost as much disapproval is 'jargon'. This refers to formal and specialist uses of language that have a higher social status than slang but which have similar functions.

STRUCTURE (also **form**)   This is a term frequently contrasted with **function**. The two work hand in hand in language use. Language fulfils functions by means of structures and, more specifically by structural variations and interconnections. Words are structured (eg morphemes); sentences are structured (phrases and clauses); the sounds of spoken English are structured (eg phonemes; intonation patterns). Similarly whole conversations, stories, essays, poems, plays, newspaper articles are all larger scale structures. Don't think of structure in language as something rigid, metallic, brittle, constricting, but as something flexible and remarkably ingenious.

STYLE   Style is a term that applies to almost anything in life. Usually it carries with it approval. In language study, style is essentially a descriptive term to describe the ways in which lexical and grammatical choices in speech and writing cumulatively create an overall effect. The analysis of these effects is called stylistics.

Closely related to the term style is **register** which describes overall features of style appropriate to particular purposes and contexts. You will find it helpful to think of register as the agreed conventions for particular language occasions, formal and informal and all stages in-between. Compare it with wearing appropriate clothes for different social events. Style is the room within register for personal touches which nevertheless do not flout register conventions. To use the clothing analogy again, a suit may be cut and worn with quite different individual styles.

SYNONYM   The English language has an extraordinary number of synonyms in its word hoard. It sometimes looks as though nothing borrowed or invented is ever discarded. Ignore definitions that tell you that a synonym is a word with the same meaning as another eg 'faith' and 'belief'. It is true that they look very close, but as with all synonyms, there is a nuance of difference and it is the nuance that matters, else why bother to keep them both in a language well known for its economies in other departments? You have only to look at the morphological variations of each and the grammatical functions fulfilled to see how differently they can be used. **Etymologically** speaking too, there are quite different stories behind these words, one originating in Latin and arriving in English via Old French, the other originating in Old English and continuing into Modern English via the English of Geoffrey Chaucer.

SYNTAX   This is a word that always seems to carry the echo 'structures' as in 'syntactic structures'. It refers to the grammatical units in which two or more words work together. Whenever you refer to phrases, clauses, sentences and punctuation, you are describing syntax. Words are bound together and their effective use is governed by syntactic rules and conventions. 'Elephant the' is not a syntactic unit; 'the elephant' is. This is a very simple instance but it exemplifies precisely a rule of syntax for nouns and the use of the definite article. In French, for example the syntactic ordering of nouns and adjectives is the reverse of English syntactic order: eg vin rouge; vin blanc; Le Moulin Rouge; haricot vert; la maison grise; café noir.

TRANSITIVITY   Transitivity and intransitivity are functions of verbs comparable to passivity and activity. The terms active and passive refer to the actor or agent of the verb and the action itself: was it done by someone (active), or was it done unto him (passive). The terms transitive and intransitive refer to whether or not the verb acts directly on a person or object. Some verbs are 'just done' without the action passing over to another person or object. Because the action is not transmitted across, such verbs are called intransitive: eg she slept; he choked; they cried; it stank; we laughed; you sing.

When verbs are used transitively, the action passes over quite clearly from actor (or the subject) to someone or something else (the direct object): eg they eat fish; she likes apples; he hit me; I train dogs.

The distinction is important because it has stylistic effects. A sequence of transitive verbs creates a dynamic, interactive effect, whereas a sequence of intransitive verbs creates a self contained effect. A few years ago, it was general practice in magazine stories and Mills and Boon novelettes to use (probably quite unconsciously) a combination of passive and intransitive verb forms to depict women, and a combination of active and transitive verb forms to depict men. It is not difficult to see the implications of this for gender bias in uses of language.

WORDS   It is appropriate to end a word list with a note on words. In dictionaries, words lie there inert but the moment they are put to use they take on new dimensions. There is always something to say about a word once it is in action: its precise, denotative meaning; its connotations; its grammatical use in a given instance; its collocations; its internal structure (morphology); its sound and rhythm; its appropriateness; its spelling. Even when it is not in use there are always its origins and subsequent history, its family connections, its spelling, its synonyms and antonyms, and statistical frequency to consider. Words are so multi-dimensional that more than one linguist has been driven to the simplest definition of all of words in writing ie the bits between the spaces. In *A Mouthful Of Air*, a very readable book about language, the novelist Anthony Burgess points out that it is only in the Western world that such a priority is given to grammar. In the East words are viewed as much more powerful and well able to take care of themselves.

Whichever way you look at it, the answer to the old question, 'What's in a word?' must be, 'Far more than the ear can hear and the eye can see'.